SOLIDARITY AND SALVATION IN CHRIST IN THE LIGHT OF *GAUDIUM ET SPES*

AN ANTHROPOLOGICO-THEOLOGICAL STUDY

Msgr. Albert Kuuire

En Route Books and Media, LLC
St. Louis, MO

⊕ENROUTE
Make the time

En Route Books and Media, LLC
5705 Rhodes Avenue
St. Louis, MO 63109

Cover credit: Dr. Sebastian Mahfood, OP
Dagara Cosmology sign, Tingan + Tenbalu, the elements of
Water, Earth, Mineral, Fire, and Nature

Library of Congress Control Number: 2020934503

ISBN-13: 978-1-950108-98-5

ACKNOWLEDGMENTS

This work owes its realization, in many ways to many people; relatives, friends, and benefactors, without whose very cherished help; financial and otherwise, it would never have been brought to completion. Among these, I would especially like to thank the late Peter Cardinal Porekuu Dery, who gave me the rare opportunity as a rather young priest to study both in Brussels and in Rome. His interest in my carrying out this piece of work was great and was a source of encouragement to carry it on to the end. His Eminence Cardinal Tomko, retired Prefect of Propagation of the Faith, provided the finances for the work, without which the research might never have taken off.

I am grateful to the late Professor Bernard Häring, C.Ss.R., who showed untiring interest; and as a "peritus" at the Council, particularly as one of the secretaries for the production of the Pastoral Constitution of the Church in the World, his assistance in helping me in the research was immeasurable.

Of the many benefactors, the late Pastor Joseph Bayer of Eilendorf, and Sister Julia McDonald of the St Joseph Sisters, Toronto, Canada, were of great help to me, both financially and morally. In this way, they sustained me and gave me much courage to go ahead in the achievement of this work.

My deep gratitude goes to my parents, Ignatius and Sylvia Kuuire, who gave me life and nourished it with love, thus giving me the opportunities to look further for its maturation and perfection, thereby preparing it for its ultimate salvation in Christ. And, finally, I cannot fail to acknowledge my family, especially my siblings, in the midst of whom I learnt to share my life and to enjoy their solidary feeling of brotherhood.

Msgr. Albert A. Kuuire, STD, PhD.
Palm Sunday, March 14, 2019

ABBREVIATIONS

AAS Act Apostolicae Sedis

ADCOVat. Acta et Documenta Concilio Oecumenico Vaticano II
Apparando.

AdGen Ad Gentes, "Decree on the Church's Missionary Activity"

ASSCO. Vat. II Act Synodalia Sacromencti Concilii Oecumenici Vaticani

Aux. Auxiliary Bishop

Card. Cardinal

Coadj. Coadjutor Bishop

DBS Dictionnaire de la Bible

DV Dei Verbum

GSp Gaudium et Spes

IFAN Institut Français d'Afrique Noire (Bulletin)

LGen Lumen Gentium

loc.cit. Loco citato (in the place cited)

LThK Lexicon fur Theologie und Kirche

Mgr. Monseigneur

Mons. Monsignor

MS Manuscript

OIC International Catholic Organisation

PCCMW Pastoral Constitution on the Church in the Modern World

SacMdi Sacramentum Mundi

SCD Schemata Constitutionum et Decretorum

ThWNT Theologisches Worterbuch zum Neuen Testament (Ed. Kittel)

Vat. II The Second Vatican Council

VThB Vocabulaire de Theologie Biblique (directed by X.L. Dufour)
WCC World Council of Churches

TABLE OF CONTENTS

PREFACE

That the 'maintenance' of life received and its gradual growth to maturity are at the core of every activity of man is a reality which cannot be disproved. For if man eats, he does so to nourish that life which he has received; if he sleeps, he does so in order to give rest to what conditions his life so that it may have the best condition for bringing the entire person to more fulfilling experiences, to more life. If he has to work, he does so that he may give opportunity to the life in him to grow to greater maturity. Every activity of man, therefore, refers in one way or another to that life which he has received and for which he has the obligation to care.

But deep within him, man longs for a better and more lasting life. He knows through the experience of generations that this bodily life, besides leaving something qualitative to be desired still, is also quantitatively limited and therefore does not measure up to what he feels and longs for so deeply in himself. This deep longing for a better and longer-lasting life is not only an empty, wishful speculation on the part of man, but a desire which is directed towards a reality, the existence and possibility of the attainment of which Jesus Christ has both confirmed and demonstrated. Such a life does truly exist, and he, Jesus, has the power to lead man to it. In fact, it is to it that he invites all of humanity, without distinction, without exception. He offers it to all human beings as SALVATION that comes through him, and, in virtue of which, all human beings become brothers and sisters to one another through him.

This book is an attempt to examine how essential the brotherhood of all humankind is to the achievement of the better life that Christ promises and actually demonstrates in himself. In researching this reality, the brotherhood of all human beings, which is the essential element for the salvation of all human beings, I believe that the best and authoritative means is The Pastoral Constitution of the Second Vatican Council, *"Gaudium et Spes."* This document is what I will use as a search-light. And to use this search light most effectively, I will use the Solidarity of brotherhood as it exists among the Dagara in West Africa, straddled adjacently in the North-West of Ghana, South-West of Burkina Faso, and North-East of Cote d'Ivoire. The reader will be the judge as to how far the objective of the paradigm has been realized.

INTRODUCTION

Statement of the question: Throughout human history and in all human societies, there are certain moral demands that have always been made on man in all areas of his life. These demands regulate the conduct of man in his economic activities, his social behaviour, his attitude towards other people, and his political engagements. They order the totality of man's life towards a certain harmony within the society and situations in which he finds himself; towards, that is, a particular destiny. As the religious aspirations and practice of man everywhere manifest themselves, these moral demands have their 'raison d'etre' in man's deep feeling for harmony in his existence; a feeling which leads him to a sometimes latently and other times overtly passionate quest for this harmony, an ever better situation in which he believes he will arrive at a maturity which will thus permit him to "exist" in peace and happiness; a destiny for which he believes himself to have been made.

This quest for such a better situation for man is universal and is the reason for the many religions that man has practiced in various societies under various circumstances and in the different epochs of human history. All have been preoccupied with this fundamental question that confronts all of humanity: the quest for and achievement of this better situation and mode of existence for man, THE SALVATION OF MAN.

One of the many answers to this search for the true destiny of man is what is at the core of the Christian venture which has its foundation in Christ and the "Christ Event." As Christianity has always asserted, the purpose of the coming of Jesus Christ into the world of man is to save man from the disastrous state of life within which the whole of humanity has been immersed since man first sinned. The sum-total of that which creates this situation of disaster is what constitutes man in the situation of "sin" and so puts him in danger of **perdition**. In this state of disaster, man feels himself unable to find any exit. He gropes round, trying in vain to extricate himself from the entanglements of such a situation of helplessness into which he seems to sink only deeper. This seems to be the predicament as if in view of making more conspicuous and outstanding the necessary role of a saviour who would come to liberate him, thus making evident the truth of what the Apostle Paul said: "Where sin was thus multiplied, grace immeasurably exceeded it, in order that, as sin established its reign by way of death, so God's grace might establish its reign in righteousness, and issue in eternal life through Jesus Christ our Lord" (Rom.5: 20-21).

With its doctrine of salvation of all men through Christ, Christianity therefore claims to be the answer to the fundamental and universal quest of all men throughout all periods of history. Jesus Christ becomes the unique Saviour of men irrespective of their race, time of existence, and culture. Though himself born in time and space, and therefore belonging to a given race and culture, his message of salvation, with the moral demands that it makes on men everywhere, transcends time and space, and supersedes the barriers and compartments into which men have been divided. He thus calls man from whatever situation it is in which he finds him to salvation – that state to which man has been destined from the dawn of creation.

If the Christian claim is indeed the true answer to the universal quest of man, as it is believed to be, then the message of salvation that Jesus Christ the Saviour has proclaimed and continues to this day to proclaim through the Church which he founded for this purpose must be able to enter into all the various situations, using whatever values may exist in these situations, to elevate man from his state of misery to a better state of peace and happiness, which is the aspiration of all men. The peculiarity of a given human situation may make the moral values that have been cultivated in it assume some pre-eminence that the message of Christian salvation cannot ignore without adverse repercussion on the practice of those moral demands which could themselves be the "pierres d'attente" that could lead man in the particular situation to the realisation of that state of existence, his destiny for which he is searching, which the Christian message claims to offer.

The Hypothesis: The theme of the salvation of man, and particularly salvation in Jesus Christ, has been the subject of many illustrious reflections and studies in theology. The research shows man's longing for, and so unending quest for salvation, and exploration of the avenues that would lead him to it. However, this does not deter the present research from making its own modest contribution in its own way. The aim of this research is to examine a given cultural and moral human value – the value of solidarity – in a well-determined cultural milieu in the light of the salvation proffered by Jesus Christ. The determined cultural milieu is that of the Dagara, a West-Sudanese people, sprawling around the north-western part of Ghana, the adjacent areas of the Republic of Burkina Faso, and some little part of Cote D'Ivoire. The Dagara first learned of the Christian message of salvation only some ninety years ago

The enthusiasm with which this people received the Christian salvation message is evidenced by the remarkable growth of the Church herself in its midst. Yet the question still remains open as to the extent their traditional cultural values have been truly an asset to the Christian salvation message proclaimed to them. In the examination of the value of solidarity in this given milieu in the light of the Christian salvation, the thesis further limits itself principally to the Constitution of the Second Vatican Council on the *Church in the Modern World*, in which document the Council, conscious of the Church's fundamental mission to bring the Good News of salvation in Christ to all men, presents this salvation in Christ as a call of man in solidarity to his original destiny. This research therefore intends:

  i. To investigate this basic teaching of the Council document and so bring to light the important character of the element of solidarity in the total consideration of the salvation in Christ.
  ii. To analyse the cultural value of solidarity in the Dagara milieu, and their practice of it; and
  iii. To examine the nature of salvation, both in the Christian presentation of it and the concept that the Dagara have of it; and so, to see to what extent the Dagara culture of solidarity may be utilised, with the hypothesis that it is a true "pierre d'attente" for the achievement of the salvation proffered by Christ Jesus.

Plan of the Research: This book which has been conceived as an interdisciplinary – anthropological-theological – study, consists of three parts. The first part, which studies the destiny of man in the light of "Gaudium et Spes," will present in chapter one a historical background to the document. The aim of this is to uncover the principles, which can be called "the signs of the times" that guided the orientation of the Constitution, principally its pastoral intent, and which should therefore be maintained, or at least kept in mind in the practical application of what it proposes. The second chapter, which will attempt to interpret the document itself, will seek to identify the basic elements used by the document in its argumentations for the presentation of the message of salvation in Christ to the Modern man.

In part two, which will be divided into two chapters and will focus mainly on an evaluation of anthropological data, the value of solidarity in the Dagara culture and traditional beliefs will be examined as closely as possible and within the limits of this research. Thus, chapter three will study the origins and the role of solidarity in the moral life of the Dagara. This will make more evident the social and cultural values inherent in the Dagara practice of solidarity, which chapter four will endeavour to demonstrate within the Dagara social system.

Ultimately, part three, which will equally consist of two chapters will, in the light of the two preceding parts, examine the feasibility of the human moral value of solidarity such as it is practised in the Dagara context, passing from a stand-point of confrontation – with which previously non-Christian cultures have often been branded especially in the past – to one of mutual enrichment in the understanding and acccp-tance of Christian salvation. Hence chapter five will concern itself with the Christian understanding of salvation as it is chiefly presented in "Gaudium et Spes."

This will lay the background for chapter six, the final chapter, which will attempt to re-evaluate the Dagara con-cept of salvation in terms of solidarity and in the light of the salvation that Jesus Christ offers to man. The paragraphs that will conclude this research seek to summarize the premises of the thesis and further put in focus the pastoral objective of the Church and the place of solidarity in this objective so clearly pointed out by the Pastoral Constitution on the Church in the Modern World.

Sources: It remains to point out again that the sources that will be used in this research will be both theological and anthropological. In what is theological, the main source will be the Pastoral Constitution itself of Vatican II. In the study of the Constitution, the preparatory work that has been done on it, namely papal pronouncement and other documents, the draft constitutions, the Council debates on them and other materials that in any way help the uncovering of the basic principles on which the Constitution drew its inspiration, will be given due consideration. The English text of the promulgated Constitution itself is the translation edited by Walter M. Abbot and published by the American Press, 1966, except where it is otherwise indicated.

Scriptural quotations will be taken from "The New English Bible," Oxford University Press, 1970. The anthropological sources are from individual studies that have been made on the people concerned or in connection with them. I, however, remain the interpreter of the anthropological material on the grounds of my personal experience of belonging to the culture.

It is my hope that this research will contribute in its own modest measure to the re-examination of various human values found in different cultures so that human values inherent in previously non-Christian cultures may not be altogether rejected with what has often been considered to be in opposition to the Christian message of salvation. Such values have, on the contrary, something inherent in them that provide a valuable contribution to the acceptance of the Christian Salvation message of the Gospel. These so-called pagan values, which nevertheless derive from original human anthropology, may be seen as providing some pre-paration for the acceptance, indeed, of the message of the Gospel. As Thomas Aquinas has stated, "Grace builds on nature."

PART ONE

THE DESTINY OF MAN IN THE LIGHT OF "GAUDIUM ET SPES"

CHAPTER ONE

HISTORICAL SETTING OF AND INSIGHTS INTO "GAUDIUM ET SPES"

Announcement of the Council:
Vat. II and the Emergence of PCCMW

It is true that it was only on Christmas day, 25 December 1961, that Pope John XXIII officially announced, through the Apostolic Constitution "Humanae Salutis"[1] that he was going to call the Twenty-First General Council of the Church. However, for some, this was not altogether unexpected; for, already on 25 January 1959, i.e. barely three months after his election as pope, John XXIII had announced his intention of calling an Ecumenical Council in an allocution which he gave to an assembly of Cardinals in the Benedictine Monastery at Saint Paul's Outside the Walls.[2] During this allocution, which he was giving after the mass at the double occasion of the feast of the Conversion of St. Paul, Apostle to the Gentiles, and the closing of the week-long prayers for Christian Unity, both of which facts were alluded to in the homily of the mass,[3] the Pope suddenly announced in these words: *Venerabili Fratelli e Diletti Figli Nostri! Pronunciamo inanzi a voi, certo tremando un poco di commozione, ma insieme con umile risolutezza di proposito, il nome e la proposita della duplice celebrazzione: di un Sinodo Diocesano per l'Urbe e di un Concilio Ecumenico per la Chiesa Universale."[4]

At first instance, it may seem purely coincidental that this first public announcement of the Council was made at such a double celebration. Nevertheless, these very circumstances could not but lend some support to the speculations of theologians and others as to what was to be the principal task of such a Council.[5]

Certainly, the Holy Father must have had his principal preoccupation, and also other substantially important subsidiary reasons, for calling an Ecumenical Council of the Church. As he was to state later in his Apostolic Constitution *Humanae Salutis*, "It is a question in fact of bringing the modern world into contact with the vivifying and perennial energies of the gospel, a world which exalts itself with its conquests in the technical and scientific fields, but which brings also the consequences of a temporal order which some have wished to reorganise excluding God."[6] This preoccupation of the Pope was again expressed in a yet more concrete manner when in his opening speech to the Council he said; "The greatest concern of the Ecumenical Council is this: that the sacred deposit of Christian doctrine should be guarded and taught more efficaciously." Earlier in the same speech, he had expressed his hopes in the future of the Council in the following words: "Illuminated by the light of this Council, the Church – we confidently trust – will become greater in spiritual riches and, gaining the strength of new energies therefrom, she will look to the future without fear. In fact, by bringing herself up to date where required, and by the wise organisation of mutual cooperation, the Church will make men, families and peoples really turn their minds to heavenly things."[7] However, the general threat to the liberty and peace of the individual, and to the liberty and peace of all men, had reached such a point, both in Italy and the world in general at that time, in the eyes of the Pope that it became the cause of sadness and great anxiety both to him and to the entire Catholic Church.[8]

Though the causes for such sadness and the pre-occupation for John XXIII might not have been immediately individuated and identified further than the general threat to the peace and the liberty of the individual and of all, this situation in which the Church was living, all the same, needed a close examination and an attempt to arrive at some solutions. This, he judged, that only a general Council of the Church, under "the Spirit of the Lord," could seriously undertake if these causes were to be seen in their world-wide perspective. It is only then that the various angles of the problems can be examined to the required depth.

Nevertheless, this general concern for the peace and the liberty of all, expressed at the time by the Holy Father, did not trace clearly the theme the Council was to follow, nor did it forestall the speculations and diverse conjectures concerning the way it was to go. As Canon Moeller observes, there were two poles in the Pope's thought: Unity and the World.[9] But even these became more delineated only later on, and particularly in the Apostolic Constitution "Humanae Salutis" of 25 December 1961, which officially and publicly announced the Council to the world. Nevertheless, these were sufficient to give rise to the extremely varied speculations and reactions among journalists and commentators since between these two main poles there was room enough for various themes of which any single one could demand a full Council duration for a thorough deliberation.

The fact that the intention itself to call a Council was announced at the closing ceremonies of a week-long series of prayers for Christian Unity, and especially after a homily chiefly devoted to a strong appeal for Christian Unity itself, gave great support to those who perceived the Council in terms of Unity, even if the idea was quite amazing and perplexing, as Hans Küng's book *Council and Reunion* indicates.[10] Besides what might have been seen as perhaps the most outstanding theme that the Council could take, the theme of Ecumenism, a number of other themes, as Moeller points out, were spoken of. Thus, for example, the Episcopate and Laity; Liturgical reforms, and so on.[11]

However, as also observed by Moeller, others did not remain only on the level of speculating but moved on what the Council was to be; as he says, "From the very beginning, some people, especially from France and Latin America (Brazil), emphasized the importance of the Council in a world which had changed and grown to an enormous extent in the preceding fifteen years."[12] Yet, nevertheless, the history of Schema XVII, later known as Schema XIII, is a pointer to the fact that nobody was able to say for sure, particularly in those early moments, what was to be the one definite, clear and outstanding theme the Council was to adopt.[13]

As the Pope was to delineate in his Apostolic Constitution *Humanae Salutis*, it may be true that even at that early time when he announced his intention of calling a General Council of the Church amidst so much commotion, he had something more definite in his mind than just the general preoccupation with peace and liberty. There is a ground for thinking so, for immediately following the declaration of his intention to call the Council, the Holy Father continued: "For you, Venerable Brethren and Our Beloved Sons, there is no need of copious illustration of the historical and juridical significance of these two propositions (i.e., of the diocesan Synod for Rome and the Ecumenical Council for the Universal Church). They will happily lead to the desired and expected 'Aggiornamento' of the Code of Canon Law, which should accompany and crown these two endeavours by practical applications of the provisions of ecclesiastical discipline, which the Spirit of the Lord will be suggesting to us along the way."[14]

We can therefore say that John XXIII envisaged, at least, a Council which would in general bring the Church up to date in the world in which she exists, and in particular, would bring up to date the Code of the Church's Law which was in certain instances mistaken as the absolute rule for true Christian moral living, instead of the Word of God. This, we can surmise, the Pope might have thought, has been responsible for much of the alarming situation in which he then saw the Church in her relation to the world. So, we can say that, in the mind of John XXIII, the Council that he was calling was to be a Council of AGGIORNAMENTO.[15] Besides the explicit statement that Church Law was to be brought up to date, the Pope again did not specify. Thus, Moeller rightly remarks that the first session of the Council herself had to come before it was to be realised that, John XXIII, as he says: "From the very beginning had aimed at openness to the World".[16]

Among the sixteen Conciliar documents of the Ecumenical Council, Vat. II (four Constitutions, nine Decrees and three Declarations), the Pastoral Constitution on the Church in the Modern World (PCCMW) – "Gaudium et Spes (GSp)," is perhaps the one single document which has responded most to the hopes and aims of John XXIII. He, "from the very beginning had aimed at openness to the world," and this theme received most attention in his Apostolic Constitution formally announcing the Council. He devoted quite an important passage of it to this question of relation between the Church and the World.

This, we can, with much reason, say is precisely what the Pastoral Constitution has done despite whatever defects and faults critical study of it may find. The very origin of this remarkable document; remarkable both for its history and for its contents, bears full witness to the hopes of John XXIII which he expressed at the time he first publicly declared his intention to call the Council. He was confident that "the Spirit of the Lord will be suggesting to us along the way" what to do.[17] As Donald R. Campion remarks, it is the only major document which originated directly from a suggestion made from the floor of the Conciliar Aula. Much more, the fact that it aroused such universal interest right from the beginning, due to the basic human problems of our time into which it sought boldly to delve, makes it, in the words of Campion, "perhaps the most characteristic achievement of an essentially 'PASTORAL' Council."[18]

Indeed, if we would speak of the presence of the "Spirit of the Lord" in Vat. II, we would say that in the origin, preparation and gradual crystallisation of no other document was the movement and guidance of the Spirit so manifest as in the PCCMW. The history of the Constitution characterised by the enormous difficulties that it encountered all along its way, bear witness to this presence of the Spirit of the Lord right from the beginning as the Pope had wished. In addition, the general debater in the Council Aula, just as well as the deliberations of the various sub-commissions and commissions on this document are quite revealing in this regard.

The two dogmatic constitutions: Lumen Gentium (LGen) and Dei Verbum (DV) surely have central place among the Council documents, as they lead to a deeper understanding of the Church herself, and of the revealed Word of God, as respectively sources of the Church's doctrine.[19] Besides these two so fundamental constitutions among the Council documents, the Decree on Ecumenism, which officially marked a change of Catholic conception of, and attitude towards Christian Unity, definitely embraces a scope wider than just the Catholic Church. For recognising ecumenism as a movement for all Christian Churches, it seeks to promote unity among all who are Christians, and even opens the doors to others as well. Apart from these documents, the others deal with only particular elements within the Church herself.

It is in the line of the Decree on Ecumenism, and in fact, to a greater extent, that we can look at the PCCMW. It confronts the entire Church of Christ with the universal society of men in which this "Church of Christ" exists and preaches the presence of God's Kingdom. What is the relationship of the Church to the Modern World in its various expressions? It is the openness of this Constitution to all men that makes Robert McAfee Brown claim PCCMW as a message not only for Catholics, nor even for only Christians, but a message for the whole of humanity when he said: "Since 'the Church in the Modern World' is addressed not only to the sons of the Church and to all who invoke the name of Christ, but to the whole of humanity, (cfr. Art. 2 of GSp), this Council document is in a unique way the property of all men, and its significance may well be measured more by the degree to which it draws men together to implement its concerns than by the specific contents of its paragraphs".[20]

Origins of the Pastoral Constitution on the Church in the Modern World; "Gaudium et Spes"

In the above paragraphs, what we sought to do was to put into perspective the main objective of the Twenty-First Ecumenical Council called by John XXIII, i.e., the updating and presentation of the Message of SALVATION IN CHRIST in our Modern World, and this within the framework of our own research. Thus, we have tried to circumscribe, perhaps too briefly, how PCCMW can be said to have responded to the aims and hopes of John XXIII, and so, the particular place that it enjoys among the Council documents; having emerged as the Pastoral Constitution of the council which boldly confronts the Church of Christ with the World. We are fully aware that it is not the purpose of this research to make a historical survey of PCCMW.

However, to better understand the document, GSp, and its outlook on the destiny of man in the world today, in-depth examination of the document is necessary. But this cannot be done without greater effort to find out how the document came to be. It is in tracing its history that one can come to ultimately discover, at least, most of its ramifications in so far as the Salvation Message of Christ is concerned. It is thereafter that one can see, in its context, the **Dagara concept of salvation** insofar as **solidarity and co-responsibility** are contained therein, and how the message of the Salvation in Christ can be better made to appeal to them in their situation of existence. So, if this is the end to be achieved, the in-depth understanding of the Constitution, PCCMW, is imperative and cannot be ignored. Information on its historical setting, circumstances, and other influences leading to its definitive formulation help one to see and understand the extent of its ramifications.

The 'ensemble' of questions the Pastoral Constitution had to formulate into a coherent theme, contribute to a great extent a better understanding of these questions within the Church as the instrument of God's salvation of men in the world; so revealing as they do, the fundamental reasons of anxiety and the true concerns, therefore, including the salvation of **all peoples** as the primary concern of the Church founded by Christ for precisely that purpose.

The Debates at the End of the First Session and the Theme on the Church

It was at the 33rd General Congregation, on 4 December 1962, towards the end of the Session, that Cardinal (Card.)

Leon-Joseph Suenens made his famous speech on the floor of the Council Aula which was destined to give a definite orientation to the succeeding Sessions and work of the Council in general, and to indicate the main direction of the future Pastoral Constitution on the Church in the Modern World in particular.[21] On that day, 17 cards., archbishops and bishops spoke.[22] However, the speech of the Belgian Primate, was, as Campion remarks, one which spoke the mind of many of the Council Fathers.[23] This is evidenced by the practically equally remarkable speeches on the successive days, particularly those of Cards. Giovanni Battista Montini who was then Archbishop of Milan, and Giacomo Lercaro on the 5th and the 6th of December respectively. In their speeches, Card. Suenens' remarks were strongly re-echoed,[24] and he was even directly referred to by name.[25]

After having voiced sentiments of concern over the future course of the Council, Card. Suenens in his speech had gone on to speak of what should be central to the Council: "Ecclesia Christi, Lumen Gentium;" and he finished up by posing and attempting to give a response to that pertinent question: "Ecclesia Christi, quid dicis de teipsa?" For Suenens, the Council was, no doubt, "the Council of the Church" which has evidently two parts: (a) the Church *'ad intra,'* and (b) the Church *'ad extra'.* Thus, the question; **"*Church of Christ, what do you say of yourself?*"** demands not just a statement as answer by which the Council will simply identify and define Church's inner nature – Ecclesia *'ad intra'* – but demands also, and above, that the Council speak of the Church 'ad extra;' i.e., how the Church of Christ conceives herself in relation to the world of today in which she finds herself, and in which she has equally the obligation to proclaim Christ's message of **salvation**: a message which will continue to be relevant to all men in the modern world, with its diverse circumstances and settings.[26]

As it is fairly obvious, the first response to this fundamental question of the Belgian Primate, the Church 'ad intra,' is what the Council provided in the pages of the Dogmatic Constitution – **Lumen Gentium**. And the second part of the question is what the Pastoral Constitution – **Gaudium et Spes** – boldly attempted to provide.

Before this famous intervention of Card. Suenens, which eventually gave rise to the two separate Schemata, then known as schema XVII, devoted to the Church and the World, the Conciliar Preparatory Commissions had drawn up a total number of 70 Schemata to be dealt with by the Council. With the exception of a couple of Schemata, i.e., Schema VII which was to deal with Social Order, and a Schema on Ecumenism, all the Schemata were to be concerned with only matters within the Church herself. As Moeller explains, "The Commissions appointed corresponded to the standard dicasteries of the Curia and had intentionally made it plain that the Council was a domestic affair of the Church."[27] This however was unfortunate and aroused much concern among many Council Fathers who were looking forward to hear the Council say something about the Church in her relation to the world in which she exists. The Church is part of the world; she interacts with it, and she has to bear witness in it concerning Christ's salvation message. The world is that "vineyard of Christ" in which they themselves – the bishops of the Church – are working.[28]

John XXIII and the Pastoral Constitution

With Henri de Riedmatten and after him with Charles Moeller, we can affirm that the speech of Card. Suenens, which was made in the Conciliar Aula on 4 December 1962, was not just a reflection made on the spur of the moment, nor even prepared just the evening before. It grew out of a whole set of circumstances: speeches, studies and long reflections.[29]

Already, at the very first announcement of his intention to call the Council way back on 25 January 1959, John XXIII had expressed his concern for the situation of the Church in the world today as we had remarked. Yet again, in his Apostolic Constitution, "Humanae Salutis" of 25 December 1961, the relation between the Church of Christ and her relevance to the modern world showed itself again as the main concern of the Pope. "The Signs of the Times" must be discerned, but these signs can only be perceived as they are in and through the world of today.

Since after his intention to call a General Council of the Church was announced, the speeches and other documents of John XXIII gradually paved the way for and prepared the minds of many in the particular vision of the objective of the Council as was to be expressed later by Card. Suenens.

Whit Sunday Sermon: June 5, 1960

In his Whit Sunday sermon on 5 June 1960 in which he broadly outlined the main themes of the Preparatory work of the Council and the participation in the Council itself, John XXIII also asserted the world-citizenship of every Catholic for the fact that "Christ," as he said, "is the adored redeemer of the whole world."[30] If then, "each believer, as far as he is Catholic," is also a citizen of the world, as the Pope affirms, then the saving message of Christ which the Church presents to all cannot reach the individual believer in abstraction from this world of which he is also citizen; nor can he conceive this salvation coming to him from outside of the circumstances which constitute the world in which he lives and of which he is a citizen. Hence, a Council was designed that would seek to make Christ's saving message meaningful to all men and continue to be relevant to the believer as well as to open itself to the world in which men, including "the catholic," lives and by which he is continually influenced and formed.

The Speech of 11 September 1962 [31]

Yet precisely a month to the opening of the Council itself, John XXIII, on 11 September 1962, made a speech in which he mentions the distinction between the Church *'ad intra,'* and the Church *'ad extra'*. This distinction, we can already recall here, was to be the key point of the speech of Card. Suenens on December 4, re-echoed on the succeeding days by Cards. Montini and Lercaro.[32] In his radio-broadcasted speech, John XXIII stressed again, as in his Apostolic Constitution "Humanae Salutis," the necessity of the Church to look forward to the rest of the world:

"La sua ragion d'essere – come vien salutato, preparato ed atteso, - e le continuazione, e meglio e la ripresa piu energetica della risposta del mondo intero, del mondo modern al testament del Signore, formulato in quelle parole pronunciate con divina solennita, le mani distese verso i confini del mondo: Euntes ergo – docete omnes gentes – baptizantes eos in nominee Patris et Filii et Spiritus Sancti – docentes eos servare omnia quaecumque mandavi vobis (Mt. 28: 19-20). – "La Chiesa vuol essere ricercata quale essa e cosi nella sua struttura interiore – vitalita 'ad intra' – in atto di representare, anzitutto ai suoi figli, i tesori di fede illuminatrice e di grazia santificatrice, che prendono ispirazione da quale parole estreme, le quali esprimono il compio pre-eminente della Chiesa, i suoi titoli di servizio e di onore, cioe: vivificare, insegnare, pregare. – "Riguardata nei rapporti della sua vitalita 'ad extra,' cioe alla Chiesa di fronte alle esigenze ed ai bisogni dei popoli – quali le

vicende umane li vengono volgendo piuttosto verso l'apprezzamento e il godimento dei beni della terra, - sente di dover far onore con il suo insegnamento alle sue responsabilita: il 'sic transire per bona temporalia, ut non emittemus aeterna'".[33]

After this distinction of the Church 'ad intra' and 'ad extra,' the Holy Father went on further to bring out the evangelical necessity for the Church to turn towards the world, and the duty – mission – that she has to bring Christ to the world. "The world has its own problems, for the solutions of which she sometimes searches with anguish;" for man living in the contingencies of this world has his problems indeed: family problems, marriage problems, problems of children, of daily bread, his social and community duties, etc.[34] If then the Church would be truly turning herself towards the world in her duty to bring Christ to all, she cannot do so without facing up to all these problems which constitute the reality of the world in which man lives in these times.

As H. de Riedmatten indicates, this speech of John XXIII was in its turn inspired by a pastoral letter which the Archbishop of Malines-Brussels had addressed to his diocese in 1962.[35] "By chance John XXIII saw this letter and immediately informed its author that it expressed exactly the Holy Father's ideas about the Council. The same John XXIII then got Card. Suenens to produce 'a report on the organisation and aims of the Council's work'".[36] Thus Moeller, in the light of all this, also thinks that "it is not indiscrete now to state that the Allocutio of 11 September 1962 largely drew its inspiration from the second of these notes, so much so that John XXIII the next day made the Cardinal a present of one of his books as a sign of his agreement and gratitude".[37]

From all this, it can therefore be concluded that the intervention of Card. Suenens on the 14 of December 1962 in the Council Hall was not just made at the impetus of the moment, but rather after the occurrences of events which led to a more mature and reflected study of the situation of the Church in the world; and not without some positive encouragement on the part of the Holy Father himself. For Moeller, "it is no longer an unfounded hypothesis to affirm that the speech of 4 December was not made in the Council Aula without the Pope's prior knowledge, despite the serious state of his health at the time". As he justly adds, "These precise details are extremely important because the very idea of the Pastoral Constitution goes back to John XXIII's FUNDAMENTAL INTENTIONS FOR THE COUNCIL."[38]

The Opening Speech of the Council: 11 October, 1962

In this remarkable Opening Speech to the Council, John XXIII took up again his idea of a Pastoral Council that should open the Church to the world; lead the Church to appreciate the new order of human relations, through a positive outlook on the work of men, and to enter into a veritable dialogue with the world.[39] Rene Laurentin remarks in his study that "This speech is dominated by the eagerness to establish a very open dialogue between the Church and the World."[40] If we agree with Moeller, this speech is all the more important for the fact that John XXIII wrote it all himself; "No one stuck his nose in it."[41]

It was all this idea of a more open relationship between the Church and the world that was central in John's conception of a Pastoral Council, and which was so clearly interpreted in Suenens's speech which led to Schema XVII in which, for the first time, a General Council of the Church dealt with "material that concerned" the whole of mankind,[42] and not just the traditionally conceived scope of the Church with which such Councils usually exclusively deal.

Other Impulses that led to "Gaudium et Spes"

1. The Message of the Fathers of the Council to the World

A week after the opening of the Council, at the 3rd General Congregation, 20 October 1962, a message to the world by the Council Fathers was published. This message, which originated from the desire of many Fathers of the Council from several countries, and also of John XXIII himself, took up again and re-iterated the ideas, particularly that of dialogue with the world, expressed by John XXIII in his Opening Speech to the Council on 11 October. As Laurentin remarks:

"On a tone of conscience and not that of triumph, the Fathers proposed in this message the meaning of their effort; a renewal in Christ according to the Gospel, which implies 'Solidarity' with the 'poor,' involvement in the tasks of this world; solution to misery, to 'war,' to 'social injustices' and 'inequalities'".[43]

These are all aspirations which later found a more profound attention and examination in *"Gaudium et Spes"*.

2. The Definite Move Towards the Pastoral Constitution, GSp

The concurrence of the events, speeches and other documents which we have so far summarily examined in our research, and also many others which, due to the scope of our theme, we have not included here, built up finally to the decision to draw up a document which would be essentially Pastoral; facing up to the reality of the world and entering into dialogue with it. Nevertheless, it took two more definitive impulses to positively determine the main orientation, and to a certain extent, the content of the then future Pastoral Constitution.

a.   Questions from the Third World:

In his "History of the Constitution," Charles Moeller describes the impulse that given by the Latin American Bishop. Don Helder Camara. Then Auxiliary Bishop of Rio de Janeiro and also Secretary of the Brazilian Bishops' Conference, he was much informed of and very sensitive to the problems of the 'Third World'. Before and during those early days of the Council, he had constantly discussed these problems with visitors and continuously kept asking such questions as: "What ought we to do now?" In this perspective, he often criticized the excessive internal character of the Council discussion, and asked these truly pertinent questions: "Are we to spend our whole time discussing internal Church problems while two-thirds of mankind is dying of hunger? What have we to say on the problem of development? Will the Council express its concern about the great problems of mankind"? In a lecture in 'Domus Mariae, he asked yet another of those pertinent questions: "Is shortage of priests the greatest problem of Latin America? No! Underdevelopment".[44]

From these questions, which were surely questions shared by many Council Fathers, particularly those coming from the 'Third World,' it became obvious what the Latin American prelate expected the Council to concern itself about. The Church has to look now beyond her own narrow confines and to make the problems of the entire Community of men in this world her own; in fact, taking the problems of the whole of humanity upon herself (Is. 53). It is not the shortage of priests, for example, that is the most important problem facing the Church today, nor is it the status of the different categories of persons within the Church, nor of the various institutions that are the most important problems of the Church then. What the Council, in the mind of Helder Camara, should concern itself most with at that moment, were the problems of mankind; problems which made it difficult to see and to reconcile the reality of the world with that salvation proclaimed by Christ. The problems were how to reconcile the message of salvation, of which the Church is the bearer and the witness, with the real contingencies of the life in which men are constituted in our times.

This must concern the Church; and since in our times these situations assume so great an importance, so must they also become the first concern of prime importance for the Council. For, the Church cannot truly claim to be the bearer of Christ's message of salvation to men if she has nothing to say to these very same men in what one categorises as belonging to their "worldly situation" and so has nothing to do with the message of the Salvation in Christ, or being just peripheral to it.

b. Suenens and the Idea of the Church

Although, as we remarked, Card. Suenens had influenced very much, and even positively contributed to the 11 September Speech Pope John XXIII, the distinction 'ad intra' and 'ad extra' of the Church had meanwhile struck him much more than it did before, after the colloquia of Bishop Camara, and it was the depth of this distinction in his mind which was to enable him to refine it so well later. It was on 1 December 1962, in the closing address of a meeting that had taken place in the Belgian College in Rome, attended by about 50 bishops from different continents, that Card. Suenens spoke of the documents that the Council was to produce.[45] We can say that it was after this meeting in the Belgian College at which it was strongly stressed that this Conciliar speech of 4 December, proposing to group the documents to be produced around the two poles, 'ad intra' and 'ad extra,' gained its full and immediate maturation. It is common knowledge that after that meeting, Cards. Suenens, Lercaro, Lienart, Leger and Montini arrived at the same conclusions on the question of introducing some arrangement and interconnection into the Conciliar Schemata.[46] This fact can also be observed from the similarity in stress of the conciliar speeches of Cards. Montini and Lercaro who spoke in successive General Congregations after the 4 December speech of Suenens.[47]

With these speeches in the last General Congregations of the First Session of the Council,[48] the stage was set for the birth of Schema XIII. But before Schema XIII was born and finally approved at the very end of the last Session of the Council as the Pastoral Constitution on the Church in the Modern World,[49] there was yet the whole duration of "pregnancy" to live through, with all the dangers of possible "miscarriage" and of "abortion" of the yet rather delicate and unborn "fetus," and finally considering also the labours of childbirth itself. And there was also yet the general discussions which were to immediately precede the satisfaction and joy that was to be expressed by the so many at the "birth" of such a child: *Gaudium et Spes*". It was indeed the *"Joy and Hope"* not only of John XXIII, who by the way never lived to see it through, nor only of the Council Fathers and all those who worked so perseveringly on it, sometimes against do many odds, nor only of the faithful of the Church, but of *"all men of good will."*[50]

In the last part of the historical setting and insights to the Constitution that we are presently discussing, we shall briefly examine the works of the successive commissions and the subsequent development of the which finally, despite all the difficulties and, sometimes, open despair, flowered and matured into our Conciliar Document, "The Pastoral Constitution on the Church in the Modern World".

The Commissions and the Texts of Schema XIII

The history of Schema XIII, PCCMW, just like the document itself, is the longest of all the histories of the schemata of Vat. II. Starting right from the beginning of the opening Session of the Council, Schema XIII went through a long, difficult and uncertain journey till its final happy approval and promulgation on the very closing day of the Council.[51] Charles Moeller summarises this difficult journey of the document in this way: "Through five phases in which it had died, and five phases of resurrection, the dogmatic part of the text had overcome an incredible number of obstacles."[52] He attributes these difficulties that the document encountered to the complete newness of the text, the almost limitless mass of problems with which it had to deal, and also because of the large size of the Mixed Commission which was appointed to work on it. The final success of the Schema was due to men such as Card. Cento, whose enthusiasm, Moeller reckons, disarmed even the worst crises into which the Schema ran. Then others were: Mgrs. Guano, Philips, and Fr. H. de Riedmatten whose precise and concrete remarks were a constant inspiration, J.B. Hirschmann, R. Tucci, and Canon Hauptmann who overcame the last hurdle of having to re-write the whole text afresh. Ultimately, Card. Suenens so aptly formulated the idea on 4 December 1962 that it was able to arouse the interest of the Council Fathers and sustain that of the groups working on it till the very last successful end.

The Composition of Text I

We have already had occasion to remark that out of the 70 Schemata prepared by the Preparatory Commissions of the Council, there was no schema which, by itself, was devoted to the Church in the Modern World.[53] There was therefore no one particular commission from the beginning that was assigned the task drawing up a text that would speak of the Church in the Modern World as was to be done later. We have also already quoted the explanation of Moeller for this omission; for, the Commissions appointed corresponded to the standard dicasteries of the Curia.[54] And as a schema that would deal directly with "The Church in the Modern World" corresponded to none of the traditional dicasteries of the Curia, no one therefore thought, in the first place, that it would be in line with 'tradition' to draw up such a schema, and so, to appoint a particular commission to take care of it.

The history of Schema XIII, however, seems to have taken up from one of the 70 schemata originally prepared by the Preparatory Commission, Schema VII which was devoted to the Social Order.[55] As if because it was an after-thought, Schema VII itself, which did not have at this stage a commission of its own, had its theme diffused in the work of two separate commissions: the Theological Commission, which dealt with it in one of its preparatory schemata, "de Ordine Morali Christiano," and the Lay Apostolate Commission, which also dealt with the same material more concretely in the section of its preparatory draft entitled "de Actione Sociali in Specie."[56]

Both Commissions therefore treated the same theme, the 'Social Order,' but each one from its own point of view and with its own approach. The text of the Theological Commission, which had as its objective the enunciation of fundamental moral principles on which society can order itself as Christian, was rather static, while that of the Lay Apostolate Commission, which was oriented towards the promotion of Christian action in society, was more dynamic.

a.   *The Text of the Theological Commission*

The Theological Preparatory Commission had appointed a sub-commission composed of Mgrs. P. Pavan, A. Ferrari-Toniolo, Frs. F. Hurth, G. Grundlach, G. Jarlot, A.R. Sigmond, and E. Leo, who was relator for marriage, to work on the text. Moeller points out that this commission gave the text a rather classical stamp by emphasizing the objective character of the moral order. As he also remarks, although later revisions of this theological text which were always incorporated in successive drafts of the future Schema XIII never denied this objective character of the moral order, these later revisions nevertheless emphasised a more biblical, concrete and existential point of view.

In its last draft of the Schema entitled "De Ordine Morali Christiano,"[57] the Theological Preparatory Sub-commission to which the theological part of Schema VII on the Social Order (de Ordine Sociali) was entrusted, after insisting on the objective character of the moral order in the first chapter, defined in the second chapter the Christian Conscience as the place for the manifestation of the moral order. Then in the third chapter it went on to fight what it considered as the errors of "subjectivism and ethical relativism;" and finally in what can be called a logical sequence, concerned itself, in the fourth chapter, with sin and the possibility that the Christian has of advancing on the way of righteousness, and of his duty to do penance. After that, however, marked by the tone different from the first four chapters, chapter five anticipated in part what was to be the first part of Schema XIII: "De Ecclesia et Vocatione Hominis".

Chapter one of GSp (Schema XIII at that stage) in particular, entitled: "De hominae Personae Dignitate," directly recalls the fifth chapter of this last draft which was formerly chapter four in the draft presented to the Central Preparatory Committee of the Council in January 1962.[58] In this fifth chapter, what was to be said later in GPs art. 12 para. 4 already found full expression here. At this early stage, the central theme of man as the image of God had already found its way into the Conciliar text even if it was still rather abstract and conceptual in its outlook. It is present as the focal point, or rather, theme which was to be taken up again in the second and subsequent texts relative to Schema XIII.

b. *The Contribution of the Lay Apostolate Preparatory Commission*

While the Theological Subcommission dealt with specifically basic theological principles on the *Social Order* in its Schema, de "Ordine Morali," a Subcommission appointed by the Lay Apostolate Preparatory Commission and presided over by Mgr. F. Hengsbach, Bishop of Essen,[59] also produced a text: "De Apostolatu Laicorum in Actione Sociali," which we can say took care of the more practical application of our future Schema XIII.

This section of the Schema on the Apostolate of the Laity, entitled: "De Apostolatu Laicorum in Actione Sociali," was,[60] as Moeller judges, more positive in its view in regard to human action, while the idea of man as the image of God was relegated to a more marginal place without any explicit relation to the duty of establishing an earthly order in Christ.[61] After making the declaration entitled: "Ecclesia opera in Christiana Ordinis Naturalis Instauratione," in which the whole of the natural order is declared ordained to the supernatural and to the eternal salvation of man, and in which is also at the same time, acknowledged the intrinsic value of the natural order itself in as much as it is ordained to God, the Commission dealt with social action in general in the first part, then went into particular social actions. These include the family, education, the condition of women in social work and life, economic and social order, order in society, science and art, technology, the state, and finally international society.[62]

An Appraisal

If we consider the independent efforts of the two separate commissions which both treated, in their various ways, the same theme; the Social Order, Schema VII in the preparatory drafts,[63] and the fact that each of them functioned separately in its own capacity, it is not surprising that the texts which were produced were not without tensions between theological principles and sociological realities.[64] As Moeller observes, "In the end a text was successfully produced which while not too exclusively theological or lacking in direct reference to contemporary problems, was not exclusively sociological and theologically pointless."[65]

The difference and even the tensions between the two texts of the two Commissions could not have been altogether avoided.[66] Though these differences were to be very sensibly reduced in the final text of Schema XIII, these tensions between theological principles and practical social applications of them persisted throughout the stages of the history of the Schema.

The Second Text: Text II

1) It was in his speech of 4 December 1962, in which he criticized the method of the work of the Council and at the same time presented the two-poled aspect: "ad intra" and "ad extra" on the Church, that Card. Suenens clearly identified and put into greater perspective the proper approach to the problem that concerned the Church in the Modern World.[67] Cards. G.B. Montini and G Lercaro had, in the days that followed, expressed their support for the proposition made by Card. Suenens on the Church and the World,[68] and in their turn insisted on the necessity of speaking about Church as the Church of the Poor: "Mysterium Christi in Ecclesia semper fuit et est, sed hodie praecipue est Mysterium Christi in Pauperibus".[69]

2) This 'remise en question' of the method of work itself of the Council, and the proposed rearrangement of the schemata around the two poles: "ad intra" and "ad extra," brought the first Session of the Council to its close but ushered the Council itself into new hopes for its future course. New perspectives and perhaps horizons wider than the restricted internal Church, questions with which the first Session dealt could be perceived coming to the surface.[70] Were they ever to be materialised? That was the rest of the programme of the Council throughout.

3) *The Co-ordinating Commission*: During the inter-sessional period, Pope John XXIII had announced the formation of a Co-ordinating Commission and other measures intended for speedy results in the work of the Council. The first meeting of this Commission took place 21-27 January 1963 under the presidency of Card. A.G. Ciccognani then Secretary of State.[71] In this meeting, the Commission re-arranged the Schemata that had been prepared, around the main theme: "Ecclesia Christi, Lumen Gentium".[72] This was

the pivot on which the two poles, "ad intra" and "ad extra" of the Church, with all the Schemata surrounding each of them, were to hang. In this arrangement, the Schema devoted to "the Church in the World" became number 17 and was last of the texts.[73]

To facilitate its own work and still maintain the maximum unity necessary, the Co-ordinating Commission shared out among its members the work to be revised. The schemata were therefore divided among them and each member became responsible for a number of schemata for which he was also to be the "relator" before the General Assembly of the Council Fathers. It is thus that the Schemata: The Church, The Blessed Virgin, The Community of People, and The Social Order fell to the charge of Card. Suenens who had, at the end of the first Session, so inspiringly spoken on the Church and the perspectives that should be given it in the Council Vatican II.[74]

The Subcommission that was to work on the Schema under the charge of Card. Suenens was quickly summoned and set to work. It included such experts as Cannon F. Houtart, a sociologist, Frs. K. Rahner and B. Haring, both theological experts, Y. Calvez of "L'Action Populaire" in Paris, and a specialist in Marxism, Canon Lalande of Pax Christi, and Henri de Riedmatten, who was in charge of the offices of the International Catholic Organisations in Geneva. Their immediate task was to draft again the basic outline of the various chapters, rewriting them completely when necessary.

In the 21 to 27 January Meeting of the Co-ordinating Commission, Card. Suenens who was then the 'Relator' for "De Ecclesia" built his conception on the Schema in response to the following basic questions: "What above all is expected of the Council in this matter"? The response to this question was searched for within the Church in her totality, and more particularly within he traditional and hierarchically structured form. Hence it was felt that:

a. The Schema should show clearly a link between **Vatican I** and **Vatican II**. Thus, there should be a recall of what Vat. I said about the office of the Roman Pontiff and his primacy. Nevertheless, the doctrine of the primacy should be presented in such a way that it shows its pastoral and ecumeni-cal character and utility;

b. The Schema should illuminate the significance of the Episcopal Collegiality, the importance of which is affirmed by this "reunion" itself of the bishops in Council;

c. The Schema should show the significance of the Episcopate as such in itself;

d. The Schema should demonstrate the connection between the Episcopate and the Priesthood, declaring also the excellence of the ministerial Priesthood; and finally

e. It should affirm in a better way and indicate the place of the Laity in the Church.[25]

As it is evident, all this concerned a rather dogmatic treatise on the Church, and is what was actually developed in the pages of the dogmatic Constitution on the Church, "*Lumen Gentium,*" the Church 'ad intra'. The idea of the Church 'ad extra,' the Church in her relation to the human society in which she exists, cannot be considered independently of the nature of the Church, the "Ecclesia ad intra;" and this is indeed what binds the two Constitutions: **LUMEN GENTIUM** and **GAUDIUM et SPES,** so that, in order to have a true understanding of the **"*Ecclesia***

Christi" the two Constitutions have to be invariably considered as complementary.

However, to make our future Schema on the Church in the Modern World more relative, Card. Suenens, who was also the 'relator' for "De Ordine Morali," "De Ordine Sociali" and "De Communitate Gentium," suggested that the first two of these three Schemata, which have been previously worked upon in the preparatory work by the theological Subcommission and the Lay Apostolate Subcommission, respectively, be completely revised and fused with the new Schema "De Ecclesia Relate ad Personam Humanam". In this new Schema, the dignity of the human person was to be shown as an essential element of the moral order.

Hence, in the suggestion, chapter four of the Schema "De Ordine Morali," entitled "de Naturali et Supernaturali Dignitate Personae Humanae" and chapter one: 'de Fundamento Ordinis Moralis' of the same Schema were to constitute the introduction to the new Schema, while chapter two: 'de Conscientia Christiana,' chapter three: 'de Subiectivismo et Relativismo Ethico,' Chapter five: 'de Peccato,' and chapter six: 'de Castitate et Pudicitia Christiana,' were all to be left aside. In regard to "De Ordine Sociali" which became also part of this new Schema, Suenens thought it again better to entrust this part to a mixed commission of "de Doctrina Fidei et Morum" and "de Apostolatu Laicorum" to be revised to respond to the conditions of the modern times. Now it was left with the Schema "De Communitate Gentium". This was also thought best to leave in the hands of the same mixed commission which would also listen to lay experts in the matter.[76] At the same Meeting of the Co-ordinating Commission, Card. Suenens also proposed to incorporate as many of the preparatory texts as possible into the Schema – Schema XVII: The Church in the World".

The Mixed Commission, which numbered 60 members in all, although such a number guaranteed a wider represent-tation of views on the Schema, in some way hampered and made the work more difficult because of its size. For this reason, the combined schema was again divided into two parts: a more theoretical part presenting principles of which chapter one is the most important, then a more pastoral part which was to go into some concrete applications in various domains. At the end, this distinction was not maintained. Nevertheless, its influence on the final structure of the Pastoral Constitution remains evident; chapter one became part one of PCCMW and chapters two to six formed the nucleus of part two.[77]

Between February and May 1963, five successive versions were produced by the Mixed Commission. **The text of the first version** examined by the Mixed Commission on 11 March was composed in the period between February and March. Its first chapter which was partly composed by Danielou was remarkable as a whole, as Moeller asserts, "for its biblical and patristic perspective; its emphasis on the creation of man in the image of God, on the restoration of man in Christ, his glorification, the expectation of the resur-rection and the Kingdom".[78]

In the second version which was drafted between 14 March and 24 April, chapter four preserved practically the substance of the version before. The alteration of Labourdette's text on marriage, suppressing the paragraphs which spoke of mutual love in marriage, though done in order to base the doctrinal statements on so called "more objective norms," was to be the beginning of an argument that was to last throughout the whole Council.[79]

The Encyclical "Pacem in Terris" of John XXIII, which appeared in April 1963, and was widely acclaimed beyond the usual frontiers of Encyclicals, also had its influence on the development of the text. Father H. de Riedmatten, who had followed and taken part in the work of the Schema, said: "This was an instant of an important event which intensified the expectations of the nations in regards to the Council's action on these problems; it also put those drafting the text into a considerable quandary, for, they had the feeling that this document had already forestalled a very substantial part of the tasks which had been assigned to them." Some, Moeller adds, "wanted simply to take over themes of 'Pacem in Terris,' others favoured a theological explanation of the document." The first alternative was soon to be abandoned.[80]

A third version of the Text was worked upon and was drafted between 28 April and 14 May at the meeting of the Mixed Commission. Before the composition, some lay people were consulted. In fact, despite the reserved attitude that was shown by some bishops of the Theological Commission, Card. Cento who presided over the particular meeting insisted that lay people attend, and actually got fourteen laymen to attend.[81] As Moeller points out, numerous amendments to the text were owed actually to these laymen who took part in the discussions in spite of all the difficulties with which they were confronted. It was they who insisted on keeping the chapter on marriage when it was questioned whether it should be dropped. They also drew attention to the excessively literary character of the view of culture presented in the proposed text, and pointed out, in regard to culture, that it was better to expand the "description" of phenomena rather than try vainly to define them.

By combining the ideas in chapter one into groups, the number of articles were thus reduced. But more important still, the natural law point was thus better integrated with the biblical perspectives. The preface, which was also condensed, expressed in more reserved terms the role of the Church in the upholding of human dignity, the present situation which is marked by "hopes and fears" of the world, and the link thus established with *"Lumen Gentium"*. Moeller rightly remarks that this link thus established between the text and LGen, is of importance; "for, for the first time, it shows unmistakably that the future Pastor Constitution must be read in conjunction with the Dogmatic Constitution on the Church".[82]

The fourth version: The Mixed Commission had met several times between 20 and 25 May. However, few sessions were devoted to the examination of the text, due to the shortage of time. It had only managed to examine in detail the preface and chapter one, and the rest was entrusted to six sub commissions. By 25 May a short text was produced by the joint effort of the six subcommissions set on it. According to Moeller, this version was more theological in character and took better account of the element of sin and fragility.[83] Chapter one in this fourth version did indeed mark yet a novel attempt to compose a Christian doctrine of man based on the biblical truth of the image of God.[84] In domains such as culture, it was to be pointed out that the Church civilises by preaching the Gospel.

There was yet ***a fifth version*** to this Text II; It was this version which was finally submitted to the Co-ordinating Commission. This version which was composed between 25 and 29 May by members of the subcommissions still then in Rome, revised the Text of the fourth version. Some theologians who were very concerned about the objectivity of the moral law and the natural law had raised objections to the apparent absence of this in the text. It is in response to this that three sections were added in chapter one to article seven: "Lex naturalis est objective; Finis legis amor Dei et proximi; and thirdly, de Conscientia". This obviously marked a going back to the text of the second version, but deepened and enriched by the biblical and patristic outlook that has been given to it. The perspectives of the moral order and the natural law gave this last text of the successive versions of Text II a greater precision.

The Interim Texts

One would have thought that the last version of Text II had reconciled all the tensions and brought the combined schema to its perfection. But this seemed to have been only the beginning of the individuation of the difficulties yet to come, and not their solution. The chief dilemma was presented by the rather very concrete questions dealt with in chapters two to six when envisaged in the framework of the Council.[85] The Council found it difficult to spread its authority over such questions.

These seemingly irreconcilable difficulties almost brought about the division of the work into two separate parts: one to take care of the doctrinal text, and the other a more pastoral document which would enter into greater details but would have less authority.[86] However, at the third meeting of the Coordinating Commission on 4 July 1963, after Paul VI[87] had announced that the Council would continue,[88] Schema XVII, which then bore the title: "De Praesentia Efficaci Ecclesiae in Mundo Hordiena," was discussed. Cardinal Suenens, who was still in charge of the Schema and was thus the 'relator,' pointed out the importance of the text, making reference to the enthronement address of Paul VI in which the Pope had spoken of dialogue with the world of Today,[89] but went on to point out that though the fundamental idea of man as the image of God expressed in was quite acceptable, it did not permeate the six chapters of the text. He further indicated the lack of cohesion between natural law elements and the Gospel message, and in a final criticism, which interests us very much, he labeled the text as being too European in character, thus assuming very little account of the developing nations.[90] This criticism brought two results:

a. The establishment of a commission which was to draw up a new text in which would be expounded the general principles of the relationship between the Church and the world;

b. The formation of subcommissions charged with continuing the work begun in chapters two to six. Specialists, both clerical and lay were to be invited to help. On 18 April 1963, Dr. Lukas Vischer of the Faith and Order Section of the World Council of Churches (WCC) had written a letter to Mgr. Guano who was one of the three Bishops of the Laity Commission that was working on Schema XVII. This letter stressed the Lordship of Christ over both the Church and the World; a theme which was studied by the WCC after 1956. In it, he also criticized the ideas of natural law presented in the Conciliar text, rather placing the activity of the Christian in relation to that of the Risen Christ. After entering into other matters like ecumenism, marriage and 'responsible parenthood,' the letter concluded with a wish that a chapter on religious freedom be included.[91] This letter was duplicated, and Card. Suenens received a copy at his own re-quest.

The Malines Text: Interim Text 'A' (September 1963)

The setback suffered by Schema XVII in its last text – the fifth version of the Second Text – did not give it the death blow. The unfavourable remarks on it by Card. Suenens, as we have observed above, yielded two positive results: a) the establishment of the new commission to draw up a new text, and b) the formation of subcommissions to delve into the practical applications with the help of experts. This surely did guarantee another life-span to the Schema.

Meanwhile, from 6 to 8 September of 1963, Card. Suenens had assembled a small international group of theological experts in his palace at Malines.[92] The task before them was to sketch the dogmatic part of the Schema. After the first difficulties regarding where emphases should be laid; the new idea of man and eschatology according to the exegetes; religious freedom; man's consciousness of a wider world, a synthesis was gradually arrived at. Represented principally by Karl Rahner, it was thought that Christians do not necessarily have to accept the world as it is, but rather must try to build it up in the light of the principles of their faith. On the other hand, with Yves Congar, it was thought that it is "not necessary to reduce the role of humanity to that of a lay-brother in a monastery." With these two main views of the Christian and man in general, the synthesis of their task was attained: the presence of the Church in the world should be one of service, and not of power and domination. This presence should also, in fact, safeguard "the principle of free access to the Gospel without compulsion of any kind".[93] The text which was drawn up by Mgr. Philips thus stressed both the transcendence of the Gospel message and the great changes taking place in the world.

An analysis of this text, which we do not intend to make here, shows how far Schema XVII, the future Schema XIII, had progressed on its difficult journey. The stress on the transcendental aspect of the Gospel, together with the description of the tremendous changes in the world, fairly represented a much wider world view than the previous text which Card. Suenens had so criticized as "being too European". It marked an approach which showed a concern of the West for Eastern Eschatology, while also taking into account the concern of the West itself, by its far-reaching description of the changes in the world. The first part dealt with the evangelisation of the world, taking as its scriptural basis the missionary command in Mt. 28:18. Part two of the text which spoke of 'De Mundo Aedificando,' treated in first place the autonomy of the world; then of the unification of the world. And finally in part three, 'De Officiis Ecclesiae Erga Mundum,' Christian witness is brought out and its second half centered on 'diaconia' and 'communio,'[94] themes already studied by the WCC in the Montreal Meeting in July 1963, and which, even before then, were part of the content of Dr. Vischer's letter to Card. Guano on 18 April 1963.

At the meeting of the meanwhile enlarged Mix Commission on 29 November 1963, the Malines' text was presented. Though its good contribution was acknowledged, it was criticised for its purely theological perspectives. At the end, the text was not accepted by the Mixed Commission. That left the Commission in the air again, AND THE FUTURE OF Schema XVII was once more seemingly without prospect. There were not many alternatives left at this point. And a new text, the fourth which would be more pastoral and incorporating material of the previous texts, had to be drawn. But by whom this time?

The First Texts: Interim Text: 'B' (1 – 3 February 1964)

In this state of confusion, and in fact, of despair, a suggestion came from Mgr. Pelletier that a special commission be appointed and given the task of direction and of co-ordination of the work on the Schema. The suggestion was accepted, and Bishops Ancel, McGrath, Schroeffer and Wright who belonged to the Theological Commission, then Guano, F. Hengsbach, Ménager and Blomjious of the Laity Commission were appointed, with Fr. Häring as secretary.

Already at a meeting of a group of Council Fathers and experts of the Central Commission on 30 December 1963, an arrangement was reached in regard to the lines that the altogether new sketch to be drawn was to take.[95]

The draft was to begin from Gospel Truths directly concerned with the world that is to be built. "Pacem in Terris" had taken the lead in this direction and had its influence; for, the draft was to stress the dialogue and discernment of the "Signs of the Times" which is one of the main themes in "Pacem in Terris".[96] The Church must be present in the world as "The People of God," [97] and some foundations have to be laid by which it must respect the earthly realities.[98] Other facts that were to be dealt with by the new draft were the emerging new duties that confronted the faithful in the pluralistic society of which our modern world is made. Finally, and in fact, most important of all, the draft included, as one of its main objectives, consideration of man and human dignity which the other themes dealt with, and on which many others were to find their basis.

The new text was drawn up by Fathers B. Häring and Sigmond. By the middle of January 1964, chapters one and two which dealt with man's inalienable vocation, and the Church in the service of God in the world, were ready. This text which was revised and expanded was presented to the Commission on 21 January for discussion in Zurich.

The Zurich Meeting of the Commission took place from 1 to 3 February. The entire text, which was composed in French and had as title: *"La participation active de l'Eglise a la Construction du Monde,"* could be summarised thus: the introduction consisting of five articles, the rest of the text sought to express the Council's solidarity with the whole of humankind. Its opening phrase: ***"Joy and sorrow, hope and anxieties"*** which so beautifully expressed this solidarity with all of mankind, was to be retained in its substance throughout subsequent versions including the final text, the Latin rendering of which – *"Gaudium et Spes"* – was to give the Constitution its name. The subsequent articles of this introduction also treated mankind's progress (art. 2); formulated some fundamental questions (art. 3); described the audience to whom the document was addressed (art. 4); and expressed the concept of the Church as man's servant (art. 5)[99]

The rest of the Text then took up again, in chapter one: *Man's Integral Vocation*, but on yet a more biblical and concrete level than was in Text II. Chapter two under the title: *The Church in Service of God and the World*, expounded art. 5 of the introduction, the mission of service to which the Church is called. In chapter three, entitled: *The Attitude of Christians in the World of Today*, the Text discusses in art. 18, 'true love of the poor and of Poverty,'[100] and included an article on the spirit of dialogue. Chapter four: *The Tasks of Christians*, concerned itself with such themes as 'Starving Mankind' (art. 20); 'War and Disunity among Nations' (art. 21); 'Personal Dignity of Man and the Family' (art. 22); and concluded with an article on 'Man's Spiritual Unrest' (art. 23). This last article, as remarked by Moeller, concentrated more on ethical than on the socio-economic aspects of man, and was thus to be the focal theme of the chapter on culture in the final text.[101]

In all, there are three things which characterise this first Zurich text and mark the degree of progress attained in the history of the Schema.

    a. The general intention of the text was **Biblical**, and in this direction the text had gone a good way towards success.

b. The deeper ***sociological outlook*** taken by the text, even if still general, is evidenced by its concern for the concrete situations in which the Church exists today.

c. Thirdly, and not the least important, are the ***ecumenical*** perspectives of the text. Earlier, we spoke of the letter which Dr. Lukas Vischer of the WCC wrote to Bishop Guano who was one of the three bishops of the Laity Commission to work on the Schema XVII together with the Subcommission from the Theological Commission.[102] This was before the Malines' Text. However, as it has been pointed out by Moeller, this letter had practically no influence on Text II which was then being drafted at the time. He further asserts that it did however have influence in the Zurich Meeting in February 1964,[103] In fact, Mgr. Guano himself and Canon Moeller, who both took part in the Zurich Meeting and played an important part in the revision of the text, had had a long discussion with Dr. Vischer at the beginning of February in Glion on the contents of that letter.[104] Now again, Dr. Vischer who had, on 21 January, received the full version of the Zurich text, had another long discussion with Mgr. Guano, Fr. R. Tucci and Canon C. Moeller on this text.[105] All these deep insights shared between Dr. Vischer and members of the Commission responsible for the draft could not but show the ecumenical interest and even collaboration in the drafting and of this Zurich Interim Text.

With the definite imprint of these three points on this first Zurich Text, Schema XIII, still then Schema XVII, again aroused some enthusiasm. Though this Text in its actual version was not the one presented to the Mixed Commission, and later, to the Central Commission, Schema XIII had taken from this text its more definitive form, and the future of the Schema looked again brighter and more hopeful at this point of its history than a year before, in May 1963.

The Zurich Text: Text III

We have already referred to the above Interim Text as the first Zurich Text. Although this text marked fresh hopes for Schema XIII, these hopes had yet to be consolidated. This is what the Second Zurich Text was to do.

After the First Zurich Meeting of 1 to 3 February 1964, a group of experts: Frs. De Riedmatten, Häring, Sigmond and Tucci revised the text according to the suggestions given at the Meeting, and also taking into consideration the suggestions coming from Dr. L. Vischer in the talks he had had with various members of the Commission on the First Zurich Text. De Riedmatten and Häring made respectively two Latin translations of the text which was to be submitted to the Mixed Commission for discussion in March.[106]

a. *Discussions on the Second Zurich Text*

The Mixed Commission in its Meeting, after criticising the Latin style of the text as being too journalistic, however, expressed the need of using a style which would be doctrinally precise yet at the same time also capable of drawing the interest of all people. In regard to the content, the discussion centered on two main points:

> i. Some expressed, with insistence, that it was best the Schema remained centered human problems in the way in which they are raised;
> ii. Others, on the other hand, criticised the text, that it "integrated the temporal into the spiritual

far too easily," and argued on dogmatic grounds, that the text should first remind people of the Christian truths. At the end, it was agreed to revise of whole of chapter four which dealt with "The Tasks of the Christian" so that a profound dogmatic basis may be given to all the matter, including the material relegated to what, for some time, was called the appendix chapters.[107]

b.   *"The Signs of the Times"*

Before the Meeting of the General Commission took place, 28 to 29 April 1964,[108] the first three chapters of the text that were discussed and criticised by the Mixed Commission at its Meeting on 4, 9 and 12 March were completely revised by the drafting committee. As Tucci obverses, a new paragraph which dealt with the theme, "Signs of the Times"[109] was introduced. The introduction of this new theme was certainly made as a result of the remark made by the Protestant observers in regard to the Interim Zurich Text. They had criticised the chapter of this Interim Text as having not taken sufficient account of the dynamic character of history. To supply what was deficient, they presented the idea of the Church in the temporal order as a 'sign'. This sign is constituted by the temporal action of the Church called in a world where ***good and evil*** are in constant conflict. Thus, they spoke out emphatically that the Church has to bear witness; and instead of speaking of failure, Christians should speak of the "Sign of Hope".

The treatment of this theme was relatively new to the text, and so drew immediate attention. In fact, the theme on the "Signs of the Times" became the most importance advance registered by the Second Zurich Text. Its final revised version which was discussed at the Mixed Commission's

Meeting of 4, 5 and 6 June 1964, requested that the "Signs of the Times" be brought to feature, not only at the beginning of the Text, in the Preface, but also in every chapter.[110] Thus in each chapter there would be a presentation of the 'signs of the times;' i.e. what the world tells us in regard to the subject discussed in the chapter. The study of the 'signs of the times' should then be done with great discernment, starting first with the positive signs and coming only later to those signs which are negative.

While on one hand some WCC observers in a letter of 29 May 1964 had criticised the absence of the biblical eschato-logical meaning of the expression, "Signs of the Times," in the text in which it was used; on the other hand, the new paragraph quickly became a truly great stimulus in a search for a better description of the state in which the world was.

c. *The June Meeting of the Mixed Commission on the Revised Text*

The impetus generated by this new paragraph on "The Signs of the Times" continued, and a specially selected Sub-commission, known as "The Signs of the Times" met regularly every week to study the theme. Suggestions came from various experts all over and also from Observers of the WCC.[111]

At the Meeting of the Mixed Commission which took place on the 4, 5 and 6 June, the text revised with the help of the experts and other persons was presented for dis-cussion.[112] The development in regard to "The Signs of the Times," as Tucci summarises, was remarkable throughout the entire text:

i. Christ as light of the world, introduced in a final paragraph of the preface, marked a genuine Christological orientation;
ii. Common descent as basis for human solidarity is in this way better distinguished from unity in Christ;
iii. Also, the hierarchical function of the Church got a better distinction from that of the individual Christian;
iv. While the tension usually existing between "living for God's Kingdom" and the "building of the earthly city" received a more carefully studied and nuanced treatment.
v. Even the non-paternalistic tone itself was a registration of a great progress in attitude towards the realities of the actual times.

The Commission decided unanimously that the text be submitted to the Co-ordinating Commission after a few amendments were made. This marked a break-through for the Schema. The Co-ordinating Commission meeting on 26 June decided to send the text to the Council Fathers. It obtained Pope Paul VI's approval on 3 July, and in a general rearrangement of the Schemata, it became number XIII, the last again on the list of the documents sent to the Council Fathers in 1964.[113] The text contained only 25 articles, because the rest of the material, which was later to be re-integrated with the main text, was considered at this time, as still being too fluid to be covered by the same Conciliar Authority as these 25 articles, and was therefore relegated to a place in the appendix chapters

We are not going into the efforts here, which were made outside the group officially commissioned to work on the Schema. Nevertheless, we cannot pass over in silence without a mention of at least this fact, because of the influence these efforts did have on the official text. These included among others, the Encyclical *"Ecclesiam Suam"* of Paul VI, his first encyclical which was published on 6 August 1964.[114] The third part of the Encyclical dealt extensively with dialogue between the Church and the world in which she finds herself. This surely had an immense influence on, and gave a great encouragement to, those who were still toiling on Schema XIII.[115]

Before the text was ultimately sent to the Council Aula for debate, the Central Subcommission,[116] which still wanted to forestall some otherwise unnecessary objections, took measures to further improve the text as much as possible. It is in this perspective that at its Meeting of 10 and 12 September 1964, a new dogmatic subcommission was created, with Mgr. Garrone as its president and Mgr. Philips its secretary. This subcommission was in addition to The Signs of the Times' subcommission which had already been functioning.[117]

Beside the contribution made towards the perfection of the text by these two subcommissions, the Central Subcommission took yet a further preventive step "unique in the history of the Council documents;" it sent, at the beginning of the session, a list of amendments to the already printed text. It also sent with that a statement, giving guidelines for the future revisions of the text.[118] Beside the amount of time that was saved by this action on the part of the Central Subcommission, greater precision and clarity was also thus brought to the text.

Schema XIII in the Council Aula

The first debate on Schema XIII in the Council Aula came on 20 October to 5 November, and again on 10 November 1964. It was at the 105th General Congregation. As Caprile attests, Card. Cento presented Schema XIII: "De Ecclesia in Mundo Huius Temporis".[119] Mgr. Guano who was the 'Relator' read the report of the Mixed Commission which had approved it on 13 October. Moeller summarises the report of Mgr. Guano in these words: "The purpose of the text, he said, was to show the Church turning her attention to the great problems of our times in the light of her specific mission of preaching Christ, and her recognition of human values. Mgr. Guano explained the meaning of the terms used. The word 'Church' here means the whole people of God, not only the Hierarchy, while the 'world' is understood in its totality as loved by God but also affected by sin. Man is viewed in his earthly situation and in his Christian vocation. He pointed out the chief difficulties, especially that of striking a balance between the principles of the Gospel and the description of contemporary problems. He referred to the Appendix chapters and recalled that they have the full authority of the Commission". [120]

Then followed the debate: "Man diskutiert darueber bis 5. November und auch noch am 9. und 10. November". In all, there were 169 interventions.[121] Card. Meyer made a very important intervention in regard to the theological aim of the Schema. He spoke on how the community of redemption formed the link between Church and the world. However, beside general criticisms of the text as being too admonitory (Card. Lienard), too European (Card. Lercaro), also lacking greater realism (Card. Leger), and a remark on the newness of both its theology and the problems with which it dealt, the discussion ultimately came to centre on four points:

a. The reason for the text's silence on atheism;
b. What reason the Church had to speak of earthly things; she could fail in her eternal task if she neglected earthly things;

   c. Personal, family, and racial discriminations; and

   d. Fourthly, culture, development, peace and atomic weapons.[122]

Moeller points out that the most important intervention made on culture came from Card. Lercaro who declared that this section must become the core of the entire Schema. "Culture in fact is a 'fundamental medium,' a 'form' involved in each and every content expressed in words, symbol, ritual or any other means".[123] Card. Lercaro also pointed out how the Church's "paideia" is practically exclusively bound to western "organon," and concluded by urging the Church to recognize her "poverty," in the field of culture, and to convince herself that her irreplaceable contribution is found in the realities of Holy Scripture.[124]

This first debate on Schema XIII in its conclusion concerned itself very much with peace, war and the atomic weapons. But before it was over, a happy decision, on the fate of the Appendix chapters, was made. As Moeller remarks, keeping them separate from the main text helped deepen and widen the theological perspective of the Schema. But their re-integration to the main text, as he also was quick to point out, gave them such doctrinal authority which they would never have enjoyed were they to have remained as appendix material only.[125]

Despite whatever criticisms that the text might have been subjected to in the Conciliar Hall, the overall impression was quite positive and even marked the greatest success so far achieved by the Schema. Considering its history, which in certain moments found the very continuation of the Schema threatened and even in several occasions actually came to the point of being abandoned altogether, the fact itself that it did actually come before the General Assembly of the Fathers for their consideration, signified a big victory for it. Without even prospecting the final success that it was to obtain, the awareness of its importance and the interest that it had thus aroused at that point, not only among the Council Fathers, but also among many outside of the Council and even outside and beyond the normal traditional sphere of interest of the Church's Council, could already be said to be by no means a meager measure of this breakthrough and success.

The Ariccia Text: Text IV

The immense success which the Schema XIII finally attained in the General Assembly in November 1964 did not, however, signify its final victory. There was still a lot of work to be done to bring it up to the expectation of the majority of the Council Fathers. This is what was undertaken immediately by the Central Subcommission.

To broaden still further the spectrum, and so ensure that as varied aspects as possible of the matter on the Schema were included and reflected in the consideration, the Central Subcommission had enlarged itself considerably since after its 10 to 12 September 1964 meeting, and for the first time, laywomen and nuns also took part in the Commission's discussion as auditors.[126]

The work was shared out among seven commissions[127] with introductions that each subcommission should divide its work into three parts: a) description of facts; b) theological principles; and c) practical applications. In view of the wide audience for whom the text was intended, it was agreed that the style was to be one easily accessible of understanding to all: believers and non-believers alike.

Outside of the ordinary commission meetings, individual and small group initiatives were necessary to speed up the work, as time was short.[128] Thus Moeller informs us that on his way back from Rome on 12 January 1965, he stopped in

Paris, and that in the course of a working session he had with Canon Haubtmann, they agreed on the basic lines of the comments the Fathers had made and how they were to be accounted for in the revised texts.[129]

In this working session, Canons Haubtmann and Moeller had examined the criticisms of the text debated upon by the Fathers from 20 October to 10 November and had quickly drawn up a sketch. Carefully considering the criticisms, they were to

a. Present the Church as the "People of God;"
b. Define what the term "the world" means; and
c. Present the "People of God" in this "world" as journeying towards a kingdom, thus involving a historical orientation.

This means that the Church is related to the rest of the world and human society in different ways, and this relationship is what must be considered in the circumstances and concreteness of the historical moment in which both Church and world exist.

To present this idea, they found that it was necessary to work out a Christian anthropology. This would mean taking up again from the debated text the image of God which did not suffer unfavourable criticism from the Fathers. As the majority of the Fathers had insisted, the text was to be addressed to the whole of mankind. The theme on "the Signs of the Times" would thus have found its full use. At the same time, it would have to be borne in mind that today's problems, as Moeller himself saw them, "are not merely connected with the change in technical and economic order, but also with ethical and moral discovery".[130]

It was the text, revised on these lines by Canons Haubtmann and Moeller, which was to be submitted to the

Central Subcommission at the meeting in Ariccia on 31 January to 6 February. The Dogmatic Subcommission which was presided over by Mgr. Garrone, had by the end of this meeting succeeded through introducing a new chapter to present a total view of man, which was otherwise threatened by the isolated and unrelated manner in which man, society and the world were presented previously. The unified view and presentation of man was possible at this last moment thanks to the theme of man as image of God, which could find a true relevance in every chapter, and could thus become the unifying essential factor throughout the text. Moeller asserts that this theme includes a relation both to God and to the neighbour, and dominion over the world; and that this triple subdivision in addition, "brought out man's total vocation: embodied spirit, existing in a society, situated in history, in the centre of a universe for which he is responsible as God's viceroy."[131]

The Central Subcommission, together with presidents of the subcommissions and some experts, met in Rome from 8 to 13 February 1965 to examine the work done. At this meeting, the descriptive section of the text was considered to be too optimistic, sociological in character, and once more, occidental. Successive revisions of the text followed till the meeting of the Mixed Commission which also took place in Rome from 29 March to 8 April.

This meeting according to Tucci's description of it, was dominated by Mgr. Philips who was well known for his wide theological competence, his command of the Latin language and his conciliar and parliamentary experience.[132] He got approved a time-table and a method of discussion which saved a lot of time, by combining into one answer the replies to several questions that were submitted by the Council Fathers.

At this same meeting, a report was also made explaining the new text which had come out as a result of the suggestions and amendments the Fathers had made to Text III in October-November 1964 during the third Session. At the suggestion of Mgr. Philips, the description of man's situation in the world of today was entitled "Introductory Statement," for the reason that the Council could not commit its authority to descriptions of facts which were sure to change with time. Finally, this meeting of the Mixed Commission, which ended with practically unanimous approval of the text, also voted in favour of retaining the term "Constitutio Pastoralis" for the document as was suggested by Mgr. Guano earlier, and later taken up Canon Moeller.

At this point of its history, with this approval of Text IV by the Mixed Commission, Schema XIII had cleared yet another of the so many hurdles bestrewed on its way. Surely, it had yet to get the approval of the Co-ordinating Commission, and to withstand the further criticisms in the Conciliar Aula before attaining its final triumph and promulgation. However, for the present, the future looked yet brighter and more certain of absolute success than any time in its history. The work was now entrusted to an Editorial Committee.[133]

From 9 April to 4 May, the Committee worked in Rome, Paris and Louvain. Not only was the language multiply checked, but the whole text was carefully revised and improved upon as a result of ever new light. Canon Moeller, who attended the Congress of International Catholic Organizations (OIC) in Vienna from 22 to 26 April, could thus use the very interesting conclusions of the Congress for the enrichment of Schema XIII and, in particular, of the chapter on Culture. In fact, the chapter on Culture gained more and more importance with the successive revisions, and it gradually turned out to be most closely connected with the doctrinal part of the Schema. In fact, Culture is a fundamental factor at the base of all political, economic, social and international realities. Some of the Fathers even wanted to place this chapter on culture at the head of the second part. But it was too late then to alter the order of chapters again, as Moeller indicated.[134]

By the end of April, the text was ready, and was entitled ***"Schema XIII: Constitutio Pastoralis De Ecclesia in Mundo Huius Temporis"***. The opening words of this revised text were no longer *"Gaudium et Luctus"* as they were from the Zurich Text, but they became ***"Gaudium et Spes"***.[135]

It was the two presidents of the Mixed Commission, Cards. Cento and Ottaviani, who on May 4th gave the document to Mgr. Felici, Secretary General of the Council, to be submitted to the Co-ordinating Commission. The Commission met on 11 May, and Card. Suenens who had been responsible for the Schema since the beginning, gave a report. The Co-ordinating Commission approved the text, and it got the approval of Pope Paul VI on 28 May. The Text could thus once more make its appearance in the Conciliar Aula.

The Fourth Session and the Emergence of Text V

The Fourth Session of the Council opened on 14 September 1965. However, it was not before 21 September, at the 132nd General Congregation that Schema XIII made its way into the Council Aula again.[136] The Fathers had just finished the debate on Religious Freedom when Mgr. Garrone who, since 14 September had taken Mgr. Guano's place at the express wish of the Pope, read the report on Schema XIII.[137]

The text debated upon was the Ariccia Text, Text IV, after all the revisions that it had then undergone. Already, before the text came into the Conciliar Aula for the debate on 21 September, the German Bishops had at a meeting on 17 September criticized the first part of the text as being too static. Their contention was that the doctrine on man and the world presented by the text needed to be supplemented, and that the temporal and historical character of man needed more attention than was given it in the text. They also found the doctrine on sin inadequate and accused it of naturalism, optimism and of oversimplification of some problems. The French and Belgian Bishops defended the text. While they admitted its imperfections, they pointed out on the other hand that the fundamental purpose was not so much the presentation of the whole of Christian doctrine but the illumination of the problems of civilization in the light of the Gospel, and "to apply a doctrine of man to the problems of the world." In his defence of the text, Mgr. Garrone affirmed that the "anthropology of the Schema is progressive, but it is not distorted".[138] In his ever-concrete way of perceiving problems, Mgr. Philips drew attention to the novelty of the venture that Schema XIII was, and indicated the dilemma by which the Schema was beset: for, the Schema had to use the Church's language, yet in such a manner that those outside the traditional orbit of the Church, and for whom the message of the Schema was also intended, could hear, understand and feel that the Church seriously addressed them with a certain understanding of their problems, and, at least, had interest in them. "The method is pedagogical".

This discussion was a great help and of much importance for the fate of the Schema in the debates on it that were to take place from 21 September to 9 October. The text was accepted as a basis but would have to be improved upon.

So, Mgr. Garrone, with all the insights that the various points and remarks of this 17 September meeting had yielded, insisted in his 'relatio' that "the central theme and the vital principle of the whole Schema was the problem of men," and further pointed out that "the text aimed at tracing a few essential lines of the Christian anthropology which so many of the Conciliar interventions during the Third Session had demanded."[139] The debate which then ensued examined each chapter. One of the most important amendments which was introduced by the German theologians was again on the use of the term 'world'. They requested that it be indicated to mean the human society in this world, but that it, at the same time, signify this same world which has fallen into disorder and is dominated by the Devil, yet, nevertheless, will ultimately be restored through the death and resurrection of Christ. In Part One, chapters 1 to 3, the term 'Church' was to be defined to mean "the People of God," while in chapter 4 it was to refer to the hierarchy.

The comments and amendments proposed to the text in this debate were numerous.[140] However, thanks to the very efficient set-up by Mgr. Philips, which had proved its worth in other instances, the work of the revision of the text, to answer to the expectations of the comments and the amendments proposed, was quickly organized and no time was lost. The revised text was even shorter than the one before, and according to the summary of Tucci, there was no substantial changes in it. Even parts which were recently introduced, and were thus completely new, stood substantially unchanged.[141]

"Gaudium et Spes": The Pastoral Constitution on the Church in the Modern World; The Final Text and Promulgation

Schema XIII had now its last hurdle to cross. Text V which was the result of the revision of the previous Text debated upon by the Fathers in the General Congregation from 21 September to 9 October, was ready once more to make its appearance in the Council Hall. The work of revision had taken just a little over a month, i.e., from 9 October to 13 November, on which latter date the text was again presented to the Fathers. The votes taken on Text V had reflected, as Tucci indicates, a high degree of satisfaction among the Fathers,[142] even though 'non placet' votes went as high as 144 in the last chapter on the section on war.

Nevertheless, the total number of the 'modi' proposed at this debate ran so high that at the 'expensio modorum,' the Subcommission had to examine and take into consideration some 20,000 'modi'. All the proposed amendments again focused on three points: atheism, marriage and the section on war.

a. On atheism, some of the Fathers wanted Communism condemned, at least, with a reference note to papal documents.

b. In regard to marriage, the controversy which resulted thereupon from the amendments introduced, including the 'modi' sent in by the Holy Father, was finally resolved by the introduction of the famous footnote 14 of chapter one of Part II, which said the question will be assigned to a committee for further study and the final decision, based on these studies, be left to the Pope.[143]

c. As to what concerned the section on war, the American Bishops who were anxious that a quotation from "Pacem in Terris" used in a footnote of the text would make it difficult or even impossible for some governments to defend freedom in the world, intervening wherever it is threatened, proposed at this last moment some amendments in this section.[144] This degenerated into a last minute crisis for Schema XIII, and Moeller believes that this crisis, which could have caused adverse results in the final vote on the entire Pastoral Constitution, was fortunately surmounted by an explanatory note proposed by Mgr. Garrone, and accepted by the Mixed Commission.[145]

The examination of these proposed amendments and their incorporation into the text were voted upon by the Fathers on 4 December. The result was extremely favourable,[146] and the amended text thus became Text VI of the Schema XIII. Two more final votes were taken, one on 6 December and the very last on 7, at the 9th public Session of the Council. It was after this vote that ***"GAUDIUM ET SPES"*** was promulgated together with three other Council Documents: *"De Libertate Religiosa," "De Activitate Missionali Ecclesia,"* and *"De Presbyterorum Ministerio et Vita"*.[147]

Assessment

With the promulgation of PCCMW on 7 December 1965, the long and difficult journey of Schema XIII, which we have sketched in the above paragraphs and pages, could be regarded as having come to its end. But looking at it in another light, this journey would seem only to have begun. Though it may be difficult to give an adequate resume which would indeed embody all that the Constitution may stand for in its depth, nevertheless, a few perspectives which have come out as a result of this long and arduous research of the Schema in the midst of the original Schemata of the Second Vatican Council called by John XXIII, cannot be left unremarked by way of some short personal note of observations and assessment.

The Expectations and Hopes of John XXIII

From our study, it seems obvious that the motivation which pushed John XXIII to call the **Twenty-First General Council** of the Church has been clearly one of pastoral concern, as strongly indicated by Rene Laurentin.[148] It is not the nature of the Church – the structures of it, the position of its different categories of persons and dignitaries, nor the proper role of each of the institutions within the Church herself; neither is it for the purpose of defining more dogmas – that moved John XXIII to summon the Council, even though these also came in one way or other into the deliberations that took place; but rather, his great concern to study how the message of salvation in Christ, of which the Church is the Sacrament and Instrument, can be effectively presented and positively responded to by all men in the contemporary world. For, Christ's message of Salvation is for men at all times.

This diachronic view which belongs to history in general, belongs also and necessarily to the historical evolution of the message of salvation. But any effective presentation of the message of salvation cannot be made without the synchronic aspect of history for the reason that each historical epoch in which humans live has its own peculiarities, and these peculiarities cannot be ignored without a great risk of incomprehension of the message to the human beings of that epoch. This comprehension is the goal of all catechesis and the reason for all pastoral activities of the Church.

This chief reason which led John XXIII to call **The Twenty-First General Council** of the Church is clearly manifested in the opening words of his Apostolic Constitution of 25 December 1961, in which he publicly announced the Council:

Humanae Salutis Reparator Christus Jesus, qui, antequam in Caelum ascenderet, a se electis Apostolis mandatum dedit, ut Evangelii lumen gentibus universis inferent, iisdem partier, ut credito ipsis muneri autoritatem et fumamentum aderet, illud prolixe poolicitus est: Ecce ego vobiscum sum diebus usque ad consumationem saeculi.[149]

John XXIII's motive for the Council was therefore to search, with this perspective in mind, for a means adapted to the time of history in which man is living today, through which the message of salvation in Christ may be presented to him. This meant **"aggiornamento,"** bringing the Church up-to-date, as he had said when he first spoke of the Council to the Cardinals in the Benedictine Monastery of Saint Paul's Outside the Walls on 25 January 1959.

In order to bring "the light of the Gospel to all people," the Church has to face the realities of the times – *signa temporum* – of the particular people to whom she is bringing this message, so as to be able to enter into a genuine dialogue with the world. These were the hopes John XXIII had cherished, and for which he was calling the Council; hopes which we believe were partially, if not to a far greater extent than we dare to affirm, responded to in this document produced by the Council, and which so properly bears the name: PASTORAL CONSTITUTION ON THE CHURCH IN THE MODERN WORLD.

Asserting the True and Fundamental Meaning of Man

In the successive texts that we have just studied, the main question which has articulated itself throughout has been one of trying to formulate, in terms which take into account the historical present in which man lives, but always based on the light and truth of God's word, the true and fundamental meaning of man; seeking to state the relevance of the world to the human being.[150]

The Salvation that Christ presents to man through his Church transcends the order of this world. Yet man who is to be saved, is and remains a child of this world; lives in particular environments and circumstances offered him by this world, and is himself part of this world insofar as he is part of the order of creation. How will the Church present a Christian cosmology, and for that matter, a Christian anthropology which offers the true view of history and the universe in the perspective of the plan of Salvation?

Every human being is caught up in a historical movement. Yet as a created being which forms part of the order of creation and, therefore, contingent in relation to the whole historical movement of the universe, he cannot look at this history of which his own salvation history is part, only diachronically. He has also to consider the reality that he lives in a definite time which, though part of the global historical movement, is all very particular to him. Thus, the Church, which presents diachronically the Salvation of Christ, has also to take into consideration in this historical moment of the universe, the particular epochs of it which have to be viewed synchronically; i.e. she has also to present this message in the light of the particular time of the global historical movement in which she is presenting it. Without this perspective, there is no hope of reconciling the transcendental goal to which man is ultimately called from within the world he now lives. Yet this should be possible if at all the Lord of Salvation is also the Lord of History. Thus, the search for the fundamental meaning of man cannot be attained without considering the synchronic aspect of history in which the individual is seen in relation to the particular circumstances in which he exists.

The Place of the Constitution Among the Council Documents

It does not seem that the importance of the Pastoral Constitution on the Church in the Modern World for Vat. II can be exaggerated. It is true that if the Schema had ever proved to be a failure at the end, the material that was gathered and regrouped in it could have been re-distributed somehow, and various documents created with it, as some members had already suggested in the darker moments of its history.[151] But the question remains as to whether such documents would ever have had the same synthetic, clearly related doctrinal exposition, and hence, authority and impact as did finally PCCMW.

The more one digs into the various questions into which the document went in its preparation, and all the difficulties that it encountered in seeking realistic answers to them, the more one realizes the central place that PCCMW occupies among the Council Documents. Moeller puts it in another way when he says:

"The further away one moves from the Council, the more one recognizes how important it is that GSp is one of the four great Conciliar texts with the dogmatic Constitutions on Revelation and the Church, and the Constitution on the Liturgy. That is the very heart of the Council."

But to insist more on the importance of GSp, The Pastoral Constitution on the Church in the Modern World, he further notes:

"*Lumen Gentium* is founded on *Dei Verbum*; *Gaudium et Spes* is rooted in LGen and in addition is directed 'ad extra,' to use Card. Suenens' words again, not only beyond the Church but even beyond the sacred domain to that world of men and the created universe for whose Salvation the Church is sent."[152]

Without the doctrinal foundations laid down in the first part of the Constitution, and so, without the Constitution as it is, the "rapprochement" of the salvation message with the Modern World would have been simply difficult to make; and the more so, particularly in the domain of culture which is proper and basic to each people.

The Suitability of the Title

In our view, it is unquestionable that a better title than: "Pastoral Constitution on the Church in the Modern World" could have been chosen. For, the Constitution which actually seeks to convince modern man that the salvation in Christ is relevant to him, and so, indicates the way to this salvation with the light of the Gospel, is truly and deeply pastoral. In it, the Pastors of the Church, united in Council, manifested their concern for the sheep of Christ; not only for those within the traditionally defined limits of the fold, but also for all others who, though they may yet be outside these traditional limits, are nevertheless all invited to it where all will find their salvation. For Christ himself said: "There are other sheep of mine, not yet belonging to this fold, whom I must bring in; and they too will listen to my voice" (Jn. 10:16).

This concern of the Pastors, therefore, manifests itself not only in the alarm raised by the gradual loss of the meaning, and thus the loss of the use of some traditional practices and uniformity, but also and positively in the quest for the meaning and understanding of the new circumstances that are proper to the historical epoch in which man lives (signs of the times), and to read all these signs in the light of the saving message of the Gospel.

The opening words of the Constitution which gives it its more popular name, "Gaudium et Spes," could not have been more fitting and more providential. One could indeed say they are an inspiration of the Holy Spirit under whose guidance John XXIII placed the Council right from the beginning.[153] "Gaudium et Spes" not only sums up so well the history of the Constitution which has been so pregnant with good news for all men – yet many a time in its drafting it was reduced to just mere hopes – but also very accurately describes in those three words the contents of the entire Constitution which fills all of humankind with much joy and greater hopes for the future, and man's salvation, no matter in which peculiar environments and circumstances they are living.

The debates regarding the themes, content, wording and literary style of the document ended with the overwhelming vote that it received in its favour, and its promulgation on 7 December 1965. But, in reality, this was not the end of the history of the Constitution; rather, in a certain way, it only marked then the beginning proper of its history. For, the document laid down, and reaffirmed doctrinal and moral foundations in the light of the Gospel, which should guide man in the times and circumstances that he is living, to the salvation that Christ proclaims to all men through his Church.

In the next chapter, we shall briefly examine what basic intuitions GSp offers, in view of re-examining them in a definite and particular context where human beings who believe that they are also invited to the salvation in Christ, live in circumstances and exigencies proper to them, but in which they believe also that their values are nevertheless relative to, and valid for the same SALVATION THAT CHRIST PROFFERED.

Chapter One Endnotes

<u>1</u> John XXIII, Constitutio Apostolica "Humanae Salutis," 25 December, 1961, <u>AAS</u>, 54 (1962), pp. 5-13.

<u>2</u> Giovani Caprile says, however, that the first courageous mention of the Council was made by John XXIII on 2 November 1958 as attested by Mons. Capovilla, and again to Don Giovanni Rossi on 9 January 1959 before his public announcement of it to the Cardinals at Saint Paul's Outside the Walls. Cfr. G. Caprile, *Il Concilio Vaticano II*, (Vat. II), Vol. 1, Part I, Edizioni "La Civilta Cattolica," Roma, 1959, pp. 3, 40-4; See also p. 437: Avvertenza".

<u>3</u> John XXIII, "Homily," 25 January 1959, <u>AAS</u>,51 (1959), pp. 70-4.

<u>4</u> John XXIII, "Solemne Allocutio," 25 January 1959, AAS, 51(1959), p. 68; cfr. Rene Laurentin, L'Enjeu du Concile, vol. 1, Edition du Seuil, Paris, 1962, p.97.

<u>5</u> C. Moeller, "History of the Constitution," *Commentary on the Documents of Vat. II*, Herbert Vorgrimler (Ed.), 5 vols., Burns and Oates, London, 1969, p.1; (German Original*: Das Zweite Vatikanische Konzil, Dokumente und Kommentare*, Part III, Herder, Freiburg, 1968 (241-592), English translation by W. J. O'Hara); cfr. R. Laurentin, op. cit., pp. 156 ff.

<u>6</u> John XXIII, "Apostolic Constitution: Humanae Salutis," *The Documents of Vat. II*, 1966, p. 703. The Latin text reads as follows: "Siquidem id ab Ecclesia nunc requiritur, ut virtutem perennem, vitalem, divinam Evangelii in venas iniciat eius, quae hodie est, humanae communitatis; quae gloriatur quidem de rebus a se recens in artium doctrinarumque provincias invectis, sed eius patitur socialis disciplinae damna, quam quidem, posthabito Deo restituere conati sunt". Cfr. AAS, 54 (1962), p. 6.

<u>7</u> John XXIII, "Opening Speech to the Council," *The Documents of Vat. II*, Walter M Abbott, (Editor), Guild Press, New York, 1966, pp. 713 and 712 respectively. The Latin texts are respectively the following: Quod Concilii Oecumenici maxime interest, hoc est, ut sacrum christianae doctrinae depositum efficaciore ratione custodiatur atque atque proponatur;" cfr. <u>AAS</u>, 54 (1962), p. 790; "Huius ergo Concilii lumine illustrata, Ecclesia

spiritualibus divitiis, ut confidimus, augebitur atque, novarum virium robur ex illo hauriens intrepide futura prospiciet tempora. Nam, opporunis inductis emendationibus ac mutua auxiliatrice opera sapienter instituta, Ecclesia efficit, ut homines, familiae, nationes reapse ad ea, quae supra sunt, mentes convertant," <u>AAS</u>, 54 (1962), p. 788.

<u>8</u> John XXIII, "Homily of January 1959," op. cit. p. 72.

<u>9</u> C. Moeller, op. cit., p. 1.

<u>10</u> H. Kung, *Council and Reunion,* London – New York, Sheed and Ward, 1961, (Translated from the German, *Konzil und Wiedervereinigung,* Verlag Herder, Freiburg); cfr. Also R. Laurentin, *op. cit. vol. 1*, Paris, Editions du Seuil, 1962, pp. 97-113.

<u>11</u> H. Kung, *The Living Church: Reflections on the Second Vatican Council*, London – New York, 1963; See also C. Moeller, *op. cit., p. 1.*

<u>12</u> C. Moeller, History of the Constitution, op. cit. p. 2.

<u>13</u> The intervention of Cardinal Suenens on 4 December 1962, towards the end of the first Session of the Council, can be taken as an indication of the fact that up till then it was not yet definite as to what orientation the Council was to be given. Cfr. Acta Synodalia Sacrosancti Concilii Oecumenici Vaticani II (ASSCO Vat. II, vol. I, Periodus Prima, pars IV, Typis Polyglottis MCMLXXI (1971), pp. 222 – 7, cfr. R. Laurentin, op. cit., vol. 1 pp. 97 ff.

<u>14</u> John XXIII, *Solemn Allocutio of 25 January 1959*; AAS, 51 (1959), pp. 68-9. (my own translation).

<u>15</u> Ibid., p. 68; see also R. Laurentin, *op. cit.,* p. 164.

<u>16</u> C. Moeller, *op. cit.*, p. 7.

<u>17</u> John XXIII, *Solemn Allocutio, January 1959*, op. cit., p. 69.

<u>18</u> Donald R. Campion, *The Church Today; An Introductory Comment to PCCMW*, The Documents of Vat. II, Walter M. Abbott, Ed., Guild Press, New York, 1966, p. 183.

<u>19</u> A. Dulles, *The Church: An Introductory Comment to the Dogmatic Constitution on the Church,"* The Documents of Vat. II, Walter Abbott, p. 10.

<u>20</u> R. McAfee Brown, "The Church Today: Response," *Documents of Vat, II*, p. 309, Dr. Robert McAfee Brown was a

Protestant Observer at the Council, (Second Session), and has written the book, *Observer in Rome,* in which he describes bis daily experiences as observer at the Council. He was professor of Systematic Theology at Union Seminary, New York, and has been after that, Professor of Religion at Stanford University.

21 Cfr. ASSCO. Vat. II, vol 1, Periodus Prima. Pars IV, pp. 222-7.

22 Il Concilio, La Civilta Cattolica' (19 January, 1963), vol. 1 pp. 180-1; see also ASSCO. Vat. II, op. cit., pp. 215-63. The Council Fathers who spoke on that day included cards.: Joseph Fringe of Cologne, Villelmus Godfrey of Westminster, Leon-Joseph Suenens of Malines-Brussels, Augustine Bea, Antonius Bacci, Michael Browne; Archbishops Emile Blanchet (France), Raphael Rabban (Syria), Emile Guerry (Cambray, France); Bishops Raphael Gonzalez Moralejo (Aux. of Valencia, Spain), Carolus Maccari (Italy), Thomas Holland (Coadj. Portsmouth England), Albert Devoto (Goya, Argentina), Joseph Vairo (Gravina-Irsina, Italy), Francis Hengsbach (Essen, Germany), Michael Doumith (Maronite, Liban), and Joseph Descuffi Smirne, Turkey).

23 D.R. Campion, op. cit., p. 184.

24 See ASSCO. Vat. II, op. cit., pp. 291 – 4, 327 – 30.

25 Ibid., loc. Cit.

26 Ibid., pp. 223-4

27 C. Moeller, "History of the Constitution," Commentary on the Documents of Vat. II, H. Vorgrimler, Editor, vol.5, Burns and Oates, London, 1969, p.2; cfr. Also, Laurentin, op. cit., vol. 1, pp. 144-9.

28 For the expression of such concern about the absence of this second orientation of the Council, and also of expectations, confer the following: "Was erwarten Sie vom Konzil?," *Wort und Wahrheit,* Special number, 15(1961) pp. 569-718; "Voeux pour le Concile," in *Espirit,* December 1961, pp. 673-874; "Qu'attendons-nous du Concile?" in the series *Etudes Pastorales,* (1961); H. Kung, *Council, Reform and Reunion,* Sheed and Ward, New York, 1961; B. Klopenburg, *Concilio Vat. II,* Prima, Segunda, Sessao Preparaca (1962- 4); R. Laurentin, op. cit., pp 151ff.

29 Cfr. C. Moeller, op. cit., pp. 7 ff.

30 G. Caprile, *Il Concilio Vaticane II,* Vol. 1/1, Edizioni "La Civilta Cattolica," Roma, 1966, pp. 187-92; "Il Concilio Ecumenico resultera della presenza e participazione di vescovi e prelati che saranno la viva rappresentanza della Chiesa Cattolica, sparsa nel Ondo intero. Alla preparazione del Concilio dara prezioso contributo un'accolta di persone dotte, competentissime, di ogni regione e di ogni lingua. E' questo ormai un principio entrato nello spirit di igni Fedele, appartenente alla Santa Chiesa Romana: di essere cioe e di ritenersi veramente, in quanto cattolico, Cittadino del mondo intero, cosi come Gesu del Mondo intero e l'ardorato Salvatore: Salvator Mundi. Un buon esercizio di vera cattolicita e questo, di cui tutti I Cattolici devono rendersi conto e farsi come un precetto a luce della propria mentalita, e a direzione della propria Condotta nei rapport religiosi e sociali" (pp. 188-9).

31 John XXIII, *"Radio Broadcast,"* 11 September 1962.

32 Cfr. *ASSCO. Vat. II, op. cit.,* see footnote 3. above.

33 John XXIII, *"Radio Broadcast," op. cit.,* p. 680.

34 *Ibid.,* p. 681.

35 C. Moeller, *op. cit.,* p. 8

36 *Ibid.,* p. 8.

37 *Ibid.,* p. 8; see R. Laurentin, *op. cit.,* vol. 2 (Bilan de la Premiere Session), p. 15.

38 C. Moeller, op. cit., 8

39 R. Laurentin, *op. cit., vol. 2,* pp. 13-5: Presentement la bonne providence nous conduit vers un nouvel ordre de rapports humains qui, a travers le travail des hommes, et souvent en dehors de leur attente s'oriente vers l'accomplissement de ses desseins supremes et inattendus.

"... La doctrine authentique sera exposee suivant les methodes de recherche et de presentation dont use la pensée modern. Autre est la substance de la doctrine antique contenue dans la formulation dont elle est revenue. .... "L'Eglise doit regarder le present, les Nouvelles conditions et formes de vie introduites dans le monde, et qui ont ouvert de nouveaux Chemins a l'apostolat Catholique".

40 R. Laurentin op. cit., vol. 2., p.8

41 C. Moeller, op. cit., p.8.

42 Cfr. *"Gaudium et Spes*," art. 2; see also R. McAfee Brown, op. cit., pp. 309 ff.

43 R. Laurentin, op. cit., vol. 2, pp. 22-3

44 C. Moeller, op. cit., pp. 10-1.

45 Ibid., p. 11.

46 Ibid., loc. Cit.

47 See ASSCO. *Vat. II,* pp. 291-4, 327-30. Cardinal Montini, after he had stressed the bond that exists between Christ and his Church, went on to show his agreement with the Schema proposed by Cardinal Suenens on the Church and the World. Cardinal Lercaro on his part expressed his agreement with the Belgian Primate's proposition and laid strong emphasis on the necessity of speaking of "the Church of the Poor".

48 The First Session of the Council was formally closed on 8 December 1962, feast of the Immaculate Conception. The last General Congregation which was the 36th, took place on the 7th of December. Cards. Montini and Lercaro had made their speeches on the 5th and 6th respectively, i.e. at the 34th and 35th General Congregation. Cfr. ASSCO *Vat. II, op. cit.*

49 The title of the Constitution was voted upon on 4 December 1965, four days before the solemn closing of the Council, which took place on 8 December, again on the feast of the Immaculate Conception. The vote on the entire Constitution was taken on 6 December at the 168th and the last General Congregation, and the final vote, on 7th December. For the details on the results of the votes, see C. Moeller, op. cit., pp. 73-4; also R. Laurentin, *Bilan du Concile Vat. II,* (vol. 5 of L'Enjeu du Concile), 1966-71, Editions du Seuil, Paris.

50 John XXIII, in the address of his Encyclical, "Pacem in Terris," *AAS,* 55(1963), 20 April 1963.

51 C. Moeller, "History of the Constitution," *Commentary on the Document of Vat. II*, H. Vorgrimler, (Editor), vol. 5, Burns and Oates, London 1969; A. Wenger, *Vatican. II, Chronique de la Ie, IIe, IIIe et IVe Sessions*, 4 vols., (1963-6), Paris, Centurion; R. Tucci, Introduzione Storico-dottrinale alla Costituzione Pastorale, *"Gaudium et Spes," La Chiesa e il Mondo Contemporaneo nel Vat. II,* Brescia, 1966, pp. 17-134; R. Laurentin, *L'Enjeu du Concile, 4*

vols. et Bilan du Concile Vat. II, Seuil, Paris; L. A. Dorn and G. Denzler, *Tagesbuch des Konzil,* Nurnberg, J. M. Sailer; H. de Riedmatten, "Histoire de la Constitution Pastorale de l'Eglise dans le Monde de ce temps," (1967); G. Caprile, Editor, Il Concilio Vat. II, 5 vols, Edizione "Civilta Cattolica," 1965.

52 C. Moeller, op. cit., p. 70.

53 Cfr above, Section II, subdivision A: "The Debates at the end of the First Session and the Theme on the Church".

54 Cfr. footnote 27 above; see also D.R. Campion, op. cit., p. 183

55 As remarked earlier, this Schema is one of the only two Schemata which went beyond the walls of the Church.

56 Cfr. *Acta et Documenta Concilio Oecumenico Vaticano II Apparando (ADCOVat. II),* Series II (Preparatoria), vol. III, Pars I, Typis Polyglottis Vaticanis, 1969, pp. 24-53 (De Ordine Morali), and pp. 247-75 (De Ordine Sociali). See also ADCOVat. II, Series II (Preparatoria), vol. II, Pars II, Typis Polyglottis Vaticanis, 1967, pp. 28-96 again for the Schema "De Ordine Morali". This draft of the Schema was the one presented to the Central Preparatory Commission of the Council on 15 January 1962 for discussion. In a later draft under a cover entitled: *"Schemata Constitutionum et Decretorum (SCD),* the Sub-commission added the term "Christiano" to the title of the Schema 'De Ordine Morali,' so that it then read: "De Ordine Morali Christiano;" cfr. *SCD,* Series Prima, Typis Polyglottis Vaticanis, 1962. It came out with other schemata on 13 July 1962 and was distributed to the Fathers for the September discussions.

"De Ordine Sociali," which was put as second schema in what the Commission considered Appendix material, was composed of seven chapters: (i) De Ordinis Socialis Fundamento et Vitae Socialis Principiis; (ii) De Dominio Humano et Privata Proprietate; (iii) De Indole Laboris Humani; (iv) De Justa Laboris Remuneratione; (v) De Agricultura et Agricolis; (vi) De Pace Sociali Tuenda; and (vii) De Relatione inter Rem Publicam et Oeconomiam.

57 Cfr. *SCD,* Series Prima, Typis Polyglottis Vaticanis, 1962. This draft of the Schema released from the Vatican together with

others on 13 July 1962, and distributed to the Fathers for the discussions in September, had five chapters instead of the six presented to the Central Preparatory Commission on 15 January of the same year. The five chapters were the following: (i) De Fundamento Ordinis Moralis Christiani; (ii) De Conscientia Christiana; (iii) De Subiectivismo et Relativismo Ethico; (iv) De Peccato; and (v) De Naturali et Supernaturali Dignitate Personae Humanae.

58 The earlier text of the Theological Subcommission which was presented to the Central Preparatory Commission on 15 January for discussion, had a slightly different sequence of chapters from that of the July text discussed in September of the same year. Chapter One: De Fundamento Ordinis Moralis to which the term "Christiani" was added in the September text, retained its place. So did chapters two and three: "De Conscientia Christiana" and "De Subiectivismo et Relativismo Ethico" respectively. Chapters four and five, however, exchanged places so that chapter four: "De Naturali et Supernaturali Dignitate Personae Humanae" of the January text became chapter five of the September text. Cfr. *ADCOVat. II,* Series II, vol. II, Pars II, Typis Polyglottis Vaticanis, 1967, pp. 28-96, or *ADCOVat. II,* Series II vol. III, Pars Prima, 1969, pp. 24-53; and compare them with *SCD,* Series Prima, Typis Polyglottis Vaticanis, 1962, pp. 74-96.

59 Mgr. F. Hengsbach was later to become the Reporter for the part II of the Schema.

60 Cfr. ADCOVat. II, Series II (Preparatoria), vol. III, pars II, pp. 364-88.

61 C. Moeller, op. cit., p. 6.

62 Cfr. ADCOVat. II, loc cit.

63 The Schema on the Social Order, number VII in the mass of the original schemata prepared by the Preparatory Commission of the Council, was the only schema to contain the ideas that were to be later expressed in the Pastoral Constitution. They were the main ideas of this schema which were later taken up in the Schema XVII devoted to the Church and the World, later re-numbered XIII in July 1964. Cfr. Tucci, *op. cit.,* p. 26.

64 However minimal it might have been, the success to bring about a certain coherence between the texts of the two separate Commissions was due to the fact that the three persons: Mgrs. P. Pavan, Ferrari-Toniolo and Jarlot served in both sub-commissions, theological and Lay Apostolate, that worked on the Schema. Their knowledge of the two approaches therefore must have helped to avoid most of the outstanding tensions that were bound to arise. Cfr. ADCOVat. II, Series II.

65 C. Moeller, op. cit., p. 3.

66 Cfr. Text of the Theological Preparatory Commission, 'Schemata Constitutionum,' Series IIIa, pp.5-44; also, text of the Commission for the Lay Apostolate, *Schemata Constitutionum*, Series IV, pp. 137-73, (1962).

67 ASSCO Vat. II, vol. 1, Periodus Prima, pars IV, Typis Polyglottis Vaticanis 1971, pp. 222-227.

68 ASSCO Vat. II, op. cit., pp. 291-94.

69 Ibid., pp. 327-8.

70 R. Laurentin, op. cit., vol. 2, p. 97.

71 G. Caprile, *Il Concilio Vaticano II, vol. 2*, pp. 326 ff.

72 C. Moeller, *op. cit.*, p. 12.

73 R. Tucci, *op. cit.*, p. 26

74 The responsibility of the various schemata was shared out thus: **Card. Ciccognani** had care of the Oriental Churches and Ecumenism; **Card. Lienard**: Revelation and the custody of the deposit of Faith; **Card. Spellman**: Chastity and Marriage (in their moral aspects); **Card. Urbani**: The Apostolate of the Laity, Faithful's Associations, the Clergy, Instruments of Social Communication and Marriage (under its sacramental aspect); **Card. Confalonieri**: Seminaries, Missions, Academic Studies and Catholic Schools; **Card. Dopfner**: Bishops and governments of the dioceses, Pastoral care, and Religious; and finally to Card. Suenens came the schemata: The Church, The Blessed Virgin, The Community of People, and The Social Order. See G. Caprile, Il Concilio Vat. II, vol. 2, p. 325.

75 G. Caprile, op. cit., p. 327.

76 Ibid., p. 329; cfr. also C. Moeller, op. cit., p. 13.

77 The combined schema was divided in the following manner: chapter One - *De admirabili Vocatione Hominis secundum Deum*; chapter two – *De Persona Humana in Societate*; chapter three: - *De Matrimonio, Familia et Problema demographico*; chapter four – *De Cultura Humana*; chapter five – *De Ordine Oeconomico et de Justitia Sociali*; and chapter six – *De Communitate Gentium et Pace*. Cfr. G. Caprile, op. cit., vol. 2, p. 329; also C. Moeller, loc. Cit.

78 C. Moeller, op. cit., 13-4

79 Cfr. Debates of the General Congregation on the fifth Text of Schema XIII, from 13 November to 7 December1965, in ASSCO Vat. II, Typis Polyglottis Vaticanis, Vol. IV. Cfr. however, C. Moeller, op. cit., p. 14.

80 See C. Moeller, op. cit., p.14.

81 Ibid., p. 15, footnote 17. Note: Cardinal Cento who was president of the Commission for the Apostolate of the Laity, was co-president of the Mixed Commission with Cardinal Ottaviani, who was also president of the Theological Commission, See C. Moeller, op. cit., p. 37.

82 *Ibid.*, p. 16.

83 *Loc. Cit.*

84 Credit to the structure of this version goes to the united effort of several theologians: Mgr. Garrone, Frs. Y. Mgr. Delhaye and Canon Charles Moeller; See Moeller, op. cit., p. 17.

85 Ibid., p. 17.

86 H. de Riedmatten, *Histoire du Schema XIII* (Manuscript of a study, p. 17; See also C. Moeller, *op, cit.*, p 18 note 18.

87 John XXIII died the evening of 3 June1963, and Cardinal C.B. Montini was elected pope to succeed him; cfr. *AAS, 55(1963)*, pp. 433-566; see also G. Caprile op. cit., vol. 2, pp. 421 -584.

88 The announcement that the Council would continue was made on 27 June, 6 days after Paul VI was elected pope. Cfr. *AAS, 55(1965)*, pp. 581 and 621.

89 Paul VI, "*Coronatio Summi Pontificis*," 30 June, AAS, 55(1963), pp. 616 ff,

90 G. Caprile, op. cit., Vol. 2. P. 466; cfr. also C. Moeller, op. cit., p. 19.

91 For a summary of the letter of Dr. L. Vischer, see C. Moeller, op. cit., pp. 20-1. Dr. Vischer himself gives his views on the Council in an article he wrote, entitled: "Überlegungen nach dem Vatikanischen Konzil," in Polis, 26(1966), pp. 58-73. Caprile speaks of the Conference held by the WCC at Yale Divinity School in 1957 at which the common vocation of man was already discussed, and Christ as the point of Unity of all; cfr. Caprile, op. cit., vol I, part II, p.12.

92 The group consisted of Mgrs. Cerfaux, Philips, Prignon, Canons Delhaye, Thils Dondeyne and Moeller, and Fathers Y. Congar, K. Rahner, B. Rigaux and R. Tucci; see R. Tucci, *Introduzione storico-dottrinale alla Costituzione Pastorale "Gaudium et Spes,"* pp. 39-43.

93 C. Moeller, op. cit., p. 22.

94 C. Moeller, "History of the Constitution," *Commentary on the Documents of Vat. II*, H. Vorgrimler, (Editor), pp. 23-5.

95 Members of the Central Commission present at this 30 December meeting were: Mgrs. Guano, Blomjious, Frs. B. Häring, Sigmond and R. Tucci who took part as experts. Mgrs. Hengsbach, Schroeffer, Ménager, Renard, Hien and Ancel sent in suggestions. Cfr. C. Moeller, op. cit., p. 26. Caprile gives the list of the various commissions in vol. I, part I, of Il Concilio Vat. II; see pp. 193, 195, 210, 245.

96 John XXIII, "Encyclical 'Pacem in Terris,' AAS, 55 (1963), pp. 257-304; The third part of the Encyclical 'Ecclesiam Suam' of Paul VI, his first Encyclical, assuming the theme of dialogue in his Enthronement Homily of 30 June, was yet to be his greater encouragement to the theme of dialogue in the Schema. Cfr. AAS, 56 (1964), pp. 609-59.

97 Cfr. LGen, chapter 2,

98 Cfr. the Malines Text, Interim Text A, where it speaks of "De Mundo Aedificando;" here the autonomy of the realities of the world are recognised by the Text.

99 This theme was already approached in the Malines' Text. See the Malines' Text above, Interim Text A.

100 Cfr. The Speech of Card. Lercaro: The Church as Church of the Poor, *ASSCO Vat. II, vol. 1, Part IV*, pp. 321-30.

101 C. Moeller, *op. cit.*, p. 30.

102 Cfr. *The First Zurich Text*; Interim Text B.

103 C. Moeller, op. cit., p. 20.

104 Canon C. Moeller reports that Fr. B. Häring, who had drafted the original text with Fr. Sigmond for the discussion in Zurich, had also taken part in this discussion with Dr. Vischer at Glion. See C. Moeller, op. cit., p. 20. However, in a discussion which the present author had with Fr. B. Häring in person on the subject (12th April, 1975), the latter said he could not remember having taken part in this particular discussion in Glion, although he had also had some very intensive and fruitful discussions with Dr. Vischer concerning the same matter in other different encounters.

105 C. Moeller, op. cit., pp.32-3.

106 The Mixed Commission's Meeting referred to here is that of 4,9 and 12 March 1964; cfr. C. Moeller, p. 34.

107 Ibid., pp. 34-5

108 Members of the Central Commission who took part in this meeting were: Mgrs. Ancel, Hengsbach, Ménager, Schroeffer, Glorieux, Canon Moeller, Frs. Y. Congar, Delos, B. Häring, Hirschmann, Sigmond, and Tucci. Mgr. Kominek and the three laymen: Messrs. M. de Habicht and Vanistendael, and Professor Ruiz Gimenez sent in suggestions. Cfr. C. Moeller, op. cit., p. 35, footnote 32.

109 The expression as it is used here goes back to "Pacem in Terris" of John XXIII. See Encyclical, "Pacem in Terris," AAS, 55 (1963), p. 291. In fact, it goes back even further ; John XXIII himself had already used it with direct reference to its biblical sense in his Apostolic Constitution, "Humanae Salutis," of 25 December 1961; see AAS, 54 (1962), p. 6.

110 R. Tucci, op. cit., p.58; cfr. also C. Moeller, op. cit., p. 37.

111 C. Moeller, op. cit., pp. 35-6.

112 Card. Cento of the Laity Commission and Card. Ottaviani of the Theological Commission co-presided over this Meeting of the Mixed Commission.

113 Cfr. Footnote 73 above, and its relevant reference.

114 Paul VI's Encyclical "Ecclesiam Suam," *AAS*, 56 (1964) pp. 609-59. Moeller enumerates others whose activities must have contributed significantly in this line; cfr. C. Moeller, op. cit., pp. 38-9. Daniel

115 Cfr. Footnote 96 above.

116 Moeller lists the members of the Central Subcommission present for the September Meeting as follows: Card. Koenig, Mgrs. Ancel, Blomjious, Charue, Dearden, Garrone, Guano, Hengsbach, McGrath, Ménager, Roy, Schroeffer, Wright; Experts were: Mgrs. Ferrari-Toniolo, Glorieux, Pavan, Philips; Canons Thils, Delhaye, Hauptmann, Moeller; Frs. Benoit, Congar, Danielou, De Riedmatten, Gagnebet, Häring, Hirschmann, Lebret, Medina, K. Rahner, Rigaux, Semmelroth, Sigmond, Thomas, Tucci; Laymen were de Habitch, Larnaud, Manzini, Sugranyes, de Franch and Vanistendael. Cfr. op. cit., p. 39, footnote 42.

117 See above number **4)**: The Second Zurich Text: Text III, subdivision c). "The June Meeting of the Mixed Commission on the Revised Text". Its members included Mgrs. McGrath, D'Souza, Canon Delhaye, Fathers Danielou, Gagnebet, Lebret, and Tucci. A number of other persons representing various parts of the world were invited to take part in the work. Moeller points out that it was this Subcommission "which drafted the important documents which made possible, in Ariccia in February 1965, the composition of what was to be the Introductory Statement of the Pastoral Constitution;" cfr. C, Moeller, op. cit., p. 40

118 G. Caprile, *Il Concilio Vat. II*, vol. 4, p. 243.

119 C. Caprile, "Die Chronik des Konzils," in *Das Zweite Vatikanische Konzil*, H. Vorgrimler, (Editor), Herder, 1968, vol. 3 p. 644.

120 C. Moeller, "History of the Constitution," *Commentary on the Documents of Vat. II*, H. Vorgrimler, Burns and Oates, London, vol. 5, 1969, p. 41.

121 G. Caprile, "Die Chronik des Konzils," *op. c it.*, footnote 119 above.

122 A. Wenger, *Vatican II, Chrlnique de la I, II III, IV Sessions*, vol. 3, pp.393-447.

123 C. Moeller, *op. cit.*, p. 43.

124 Cfr. *ASSCO Vat. II*, vol. 4, Periodus Tertia, part IV, Typis Polyglottis Vaticanis. Cfr. G. Caprile, *II Concilio Vat. II*, vol. IV, Terzo Periodo (1964-1965)

125 C. Moeller, *op. cit.*, p. 44, footnote 56.

126 R. Tucci, *op. cit.*, p. 78. Members of the enlarged Central Subcommission, beside Card. Cento and the 23 other Council Fathers, were Mgrs. Charue, Dearden, Frannie, Heuschen, van Dodewaard, P. Fernandez, Castellano, De Silva, Petit, P. Moehler; Clerical Experts were: Mgrs. Ferrari-Toniolo, Geraud, Higgins, Klostermann, Lelande, Prignon, Ramslaar, Thils, Worlock; Canons Haubtmann, Moeller, Dondeyne, Heylen, Houtart; Fathers Calvez, Goggey, Congar, Danielou, de Riedmatten, Debarle, Labourdette, Lebret, Lio, Martelet, Mulder, Schillebeeckx, Semmelroth, Sigmond, Gagnebet, Girardi, Grillmeier, Häring, Hirschmann, Tromp, Tucci, and van Leeuwen; Lay Experts were Prof. Colombo, M. de Habicht, Prof. De Konninck, J. Folliet, Keegan, Prof. Minoli, Ruiz Gimenez, M. Scharper, Prof. Swiezewaki, M. Vanistendael; then including Miss Belosillo, Miss Goldie, Monnet and Vendrik; also among were Srs. Guillemin and Mary-Luke. Secretaries to the enlarged Subcommission were Fr. Dalos and Miss Besson. Cfr. Moeller, op. cit., 49, footnote 66; See also Tucci, op. cit., notes 73-74.

127 The seven Subcommissions among which the work at Ariccia was shared were: a) The Dogmatic Subcommission; b) The "Signs of the Times" Subcommission; c)Subcommission of the Dignity of the Human Person; d) Subcommission for Marriage; e) Subcommission for Culture; f) Subcommission for Economic and Social Life; and g) Subcommission for Political Life. Later, a new chapter was introduced, the chapter on International Community and Peace, and a new subcommission appointed to take care of it. The Subcommission for the Dignity of the Human Person was divided up between this new subcommission and the Subcommission for Political Life. Cfr. Moeller, *op. cit.*, p. 52.

128 At this meeting on 30 December 1964, the Co-ordinating Commission had laid down a time-table for the work, and Schema XIII's revised version had to be submitted in March, to be

approved by the Pope before it could be distributed to the Council Fathers at the beginning of June in the following year.

129 C. Moeller, *op. cit.*, p. 47.

130 *Ibid.*, p. 48.

131 *Ibid.*, p. 51.

132 R. Tucci, *op. cit.*, p. 95.

133 Members of the Committee included Mgrs. Guano and Charue, and Canons Haubtmann and Moeller.

134 C. Moeller, *op. cit.*, p. 57.

135 R. Tucci, op. cit., p. 97.

136 G. Caprile, "Die Chronik des Konzils," *op. cit.*, p. 648.

137 C. Moeller, op. cit., 61.

138 The German Bishops present at the meeting mentioned were Volk, Reuss and Hengsbach. Fr. K. Rahner also took part. On the French and Belgian side were Mgrs. Ancel, Garrone, Musty, Philips and Elchinger; also, Canon Haubtmann and Frs. Danielou and Y. Congar were present. It was Mgr. Elchinger who organized the meeting. Others who took part were Semmelroth, Hirschmann, Schillebeeckx, Ratzinger, Moeller and Heylen. Cfr. C. Moeller, op. cit., p. 59-60.

139 C. Moeller, op. cit., p. 61.

140 Canon Moeller notes that it filled almost 500 large pages of single-spaced typescript. Ibid., p. 62'

141 R. Tucci, op. cit., pp. 120-5; see also A. Wenger, op. cit., vol. 4, pp. 262-82. R. Laurentin, *L'Enjeu du Concile,* (Bilan du Concile Vatican II), vol. 5, pp. 96-102.

142 R. Tucci, op. cit., pp. 123-5.

143 This note here-referred to is no. 173 in the English translation of the Documents by Walter M. Abbott. See *the Documents of Vat. II,* The American Press, 1966, p. 256.

144 Walter M. Abbott, *op. cit.*, Footnote 263 on the Pastoral Constitution (PCCMW). In the Latin text the note referred to is note 4 in chapter V of Part II.

145 Cfr. Walter M. Abbott, *op. cit.,* In footnote 264 Abbott makes allusion to this explanatory note suggested by Mgr. Garrone. The next two paragraphs after the allusion to "Pacem in

Terris" embodies this explanatory note. See A. Wenger, *op. cit.,* vol. 4, pp.276-80

146 R. Laurentin, *Bilan du Concile Vat. II: L'Enjeu du Concile,* vol 5, pp. 41 ff.

147 G. Caprile, "Die Chronik des Konzils, op. cit., p. 651. The vote on the entire Text VI, of Schema XIII, now "Gaudium et Spes," took place at the 168th General Congregation on 6 December. Out of the 2373 votes, 2111 were favourable, 251 "non placet" votes, and 11 invalid ones. For the promulgation vote 7 December, 2309 out of 2391 Fathers that voted were in favour, (placet), 75 against (non placet), and 7 invalid ones.

148 R. Laurentin, op. cit., vol. I, p. 161.

149 John XXIII, Constitutio Apostolica "Humanae Salutis," AAS, 54(1962), p. 5.

150 Canon C. Moeller also recognizes "the problem of Man" as the central theme and vital principle of the whole Schema; see op. cit., p, 61.

151 Cfr. R. Tucci, *Introduzione storico-dottrinale alla Costituzione Pastorale,* "Gaudium et Spes," op. cit., 101-3. See also C. Moeller, *op. cit.,* p. 58.

152 C. Moeller, *op. cit.,* p. 70.

153 John XXIII, "Solemne Allocu5io" 25 January 1959, AAS, 51(1959), p. 69.

CHAPTER TWO

SOME BASIC INTUITIONS OF THE CONCILIAR DOCUMENT "GAUDIUM ET SPES"

Man's Call to a Unique Destiny

If we return to the speeches and the debates which took place in the Council Aula from 4 December 1962 to the end of the first Session, the truth of the affirmation that "in one way or another the entire work of the Council is centered about the theme of the Church" cannot miss being seen.[1] The Dogmatic Constitution on the Church, LGen, presents with Conciliar authority the Church's actual understanding of her own nature, as Dulles asserts.[2] But the Church which is centered upon is not the one considered in terms of structures and of government as was the case in the First Vatican Council, but "the Church as a people to whom God communicates Himself in love;"[3] 'The People of God,' the Church as the newly established instrument through which God calls all men to Himself.

From this interior vision of herself, what can be called the overall theme of the Council becomes evident: God communicating His divine love to man, to the whole of mankind; to His "People;" to His Church. He did not do so only once and for all in history, but He continues to communicate His love to man even today, in the various environments and circumstances in which He finds man, and wherever He finds him.

The Pastoral Constitution takes up this theme of the Church, however, not centering its deliberations this time on the nature of the Church, the Church *'ad intra'* as has done

LGen, but examines this Church as the People of God to whom God communicates himself, and through her as the instrument of salvation, continues to communicate himself to and with all mankind today; assessing the relation that man who is thus communicated to in love[4] and called by God, has with the rest of the created contingencies that surround him and constitute the world in which he lives. This becomes the deliberation on the Church *'ad extra,'* and thus permits GSp to form a truly one whole with LGen. Looked at in this way, the relevance of the comment made by Moeller on the preface of Text II of Schema III becomes even more intelligible when he said: "

> It expressed in a more reserved way the role of the Church in preserving human dignity, the present situation marked by the hopes and fears of the world – this is the seed of the 'Introductory Statement' of the final text – and the link with LGen. This last point is of some importance, for, for the first time, it shows unmistakably that the future pastoral constitution on the Church must be read in conjunction with the Dogmatic Constitution on the Church.[5]

So, God has communicated himself in love to his Church, to his People; and through the Church as an instrument he continues to communicate himself to everyman in every epoch of history and in every place under every culture. In communicating himself to man, God invites man to his love, a love which is unique and much higher than man can comprehend; a love which is divine, a love in which, and by which he calls man to himself, and thus to man's own ultimate salvation, his destiny.

This call to such a unique end is addressed to man through God's own "WORD," and this address is made to man within the circumstances which constitute his world, and in the particular historical moment in which he exists. Ratzinger (now Pope Emeritus Benedict XVI), criticizing the division between theology and philosophy established by the Thomists at the beginning of article 12, considers it as a juxtaposition which is no longer adequate; for, as he contends; "there is, and must be a human reason in faith; but which human reason is always conditioned by a historical standpoint so that reason pure does not exist".[6]

The Constitution GSp, which in its pastoral intent seeks to present in modern times this unique destiny to which man is called by God in love and which invitation to salvation is made explicit in Jesus Christ, endeavours to do so in such a manner that its relevance to this particular moment of history in which individual persons and groups live may not be obscured. As is pledged in the preface:

> The Council brings to mankind light kindled from the Gospel, and puts at its disposal those saving resources which the Church itself, under the guidance of the Holy Spirit, receives from the Founder. For the human person deserves to be preserved; human society deserves to be renewed. Hence the pivotal point of our preservation will be man himself, whole and entire, body and soul, heart and conscience, mind and will (GSp preface, art. 3).

The Good News of Salvation which Christ, the "Word of God" proclaimed over two thousand years ago in Palestine, is not limited just to that time alone, nor for that matter, to any other particular time in history; neither is it intended for only a particular people, geographically or otherwise. For, Christ himself gave this commission to his disciples: "Go forth therefore and make all nations my disciples, ... and be assured, I am with you always, to the end of time" (Mt. 28:

19-20). So, although people may be living in different circumstances and in time different from those in which this message was first proclaimed to man, this invitation to the unique end is addressed to them as well. The only particularity of it is that each man is invited and called in his own time in history which is also Salvation History, and is addressed within the social, cultural and physical conditions in which he is constituted.

This is a basic intuition perceived and made clear by Vat. II; and in its endeavour to make this relevance of man's call by God perceptible also to the modern man, GSp entitles its very first part which studies man in the context of the Church, the Sacrament of Salvation, "De Ecclesia et Vocatione Hominis".[7] Here, GSp goes directly to the "raison d'etre" of this vocation of man in the light of Holy Scripture when, immediately after describing the situation of man in the modern world, his hopes and anxieties often caused by the profound changes in all orders and conditions of his life,[8] it turns to the theme on "De Humanae Personae Dignitate," a theme which is most fundamental to his calling in love by God.

Before its 'Introductory Statement,' in the three first articles which served as preface, GSp asserts the intimate bond of solidarity that exists between the Church and the 'ensemble' of the human family. In the very opening article which begins the preface and in which both the theological and human aspects of joy and hope are expressed, a neat emphasis is subsequently laid on the followers of Christ, making it clear that "the joys and hopes, the griefs and anxieties" of all mankind are also those of Christ's followers who form his Church, the visible sign of God's calling and also the sacrament of salvation to which mankind is called.

These followers of Christ, the community of the faithful has, as Moeller comments, "received the message of salvation in order to announce it: 'nuntium Salutis omnibus proponendum acceperunt'".[9] Thus beside the close link with, and in fact continuation of, LGen,[10] GSp in this very first article also demonstrates the close link which the community of the faithful has with mankind in its history. So, this first article, to quote from Moeller again, "takes up a series of themes from LGen in relation to believers in Christ in their diaspora condition within the perspective of human history which, in a mysterious sense manifested by the prophets, is also History of Salvation, or Salvation History".[11]

Chapter one of the first part begins immediately to delve into the underlying reason for which man has a most unique vocation and destiny. After sin and man's disgrace, God does not cease to repeat his unique call of man through the person of his Son – Christ. The message which Christ brings thus becomes the message of salvation; a continued call of man to the unique and ultimate goal for which he was created and destined.

The fact that this unique call of man by God in communicating himself to man through Christ is affirmed in the preface itself of GSp. Expressing the joys and hopes, the griefs and anxieties that Christians share with the men and women of their time, the document did not lose time in turning to what is its whole objective; the call of man to Salvation. "United in Christ, they are led by the Holy Spirit in their journey to the Kingdom of their Father, and they have welcomed the news of Salvation which is meant for everyman".[12] GSp realises that even from the very din that pervades our world today, man does not cease to pose those fundamental questions which regard himself, certain events that occur to him in life, including death, and what follows this earthly life. In its introduction, it reaffirms the Church's belief in the role of Christ in man's salvation as already affirmed by the chief of the Apostles, Peter, over two thousand years ago (Acts 4: 12):

> The Church believes that Christ who died and was raised up for all (2 Cor. 5:15), can through His Spirit offer the light and the strength to measure up to his supreme destiny. Nor has another name under heaven been given to man by which it is fitting for him to be saved. ... In her most benign Lord and Master can be found the key, the focal point, and the goal of all human history. [13]

In searching for the true ground for which man is so uniquely called by God, who communicated and continues to communicate Himself to him through Christ, GSp presents no ground so fundamental as the very dignity of man. If man has a particular calling, it is because of his dignity. This is what the Constitution discusses in its very first chapter, in Part One; for, God created man in His own image (Gen. 1: 26,27; Ps 8: 5-6; Wis. 2: 23; Cor. 11: 7; Col. 3: 10; Eph. 4: 24; and Mt. 19: 4); and so, man's dignity comes from the fact that he shares in GOD'S OWN IMAGE.

At the very beginning of its history,[14] GSp perceived the image of God in which man is created as the source of his dignity and therefore the underlying reason for his unique call. God, who is beyond the limit of any earthly existence, in creating man to His own image, gives to him and calls him to an existence similar to His own; one which goes beyond the limited existence of man himself and of any that the world can offer him. This is why the destiny to which man is called is *supernatural, eschatological* and beyond his otherwise limited nature as a creature.

The fact of sin which has come in to disrupt, as may be said, God's original plan, and thus to jeopardise this original destiny for which man was created, and the situation of disgrace in which it left man in the world, are discussed in the subsequent articles after this affirmation of man's dignity.[15] In the midst of this chaos and infidelity to his true and supernatural goal brought about by sin and expressed in atheism, man can still be guided to the true significance of his being and of his actions, and to the meaning of the events in his life including the last one, death and what is beyond, thanks to the moral conscience which "is the most sacred core and sanctuary of man".[16]

After sin, it is "only in the mystery of the incarnate Word" that the mystery which surrounds man and the whole significance of his calling, and that of the Church as well, take on light (GSp art. 22). This must be stressed in view of man's sinfulness. "Christ, the final Adam, by the revelation of the mystery of the Father and His love, fully reveals man to man himself and makes his supreme calling clear" (GSp art. 22). So, in Christ, GSp affirms with Saint Paul man's reconciliation to God (2 Cor. 5: 18-9; Col. 1: 20-22). He is called back to his supreme destiny. Through the Spirit of Christ, man can again call God "Abba, Father" (Rom. 8: 14-15). Through Christ, man is redeemed from the disgrace of sin and is called to salvation, to his supreme destiny. As the chapter concludes: "Such is the mystery of man, and it is a great one, as seen by believers in the light of Christian revelation. Through Christ and in Christ, the riddles of sorrow and death grow meaningful. Apart from his gospel, they overwhelm us. Christ has risen, destroying death by his death. He has lavished life (salvation) upon us so that, as sons in the Son, we can cry out in the Spirit: Abba, Father!" (Rom. 8: 15).

Reaffirmation of the Dignity of Man

Nowhere in our modern times is the affirmation of the dignity of man found so strongly and unequivocally asserted as in GSp, which bases its teaching on this subject on the concept of human dignity in Scripture.

Human Dignity in Scripture

In Holy Scripture, the dignity of man has always been in one way or another asserted. Certain passages, however, assert it more emphatically than others, but this assertion is found throughout Holy Scripture.

1. *In the Old Testament (O.T.)*

In the O.T., man's dignity is more evidently proclaimed by the Prophets, who never ceased in one instant or the other to preach against all discriminatory practices and injustices against the under-privileged, the slaves, the widows, the orphans and the strangers. The Prophet Malachi, for example, announces the judgement God will make on his people on the last day: "I will appear before you in court, prompt to testify against those who wrong the hired labourer, the widow and the orphan, who thrust the alien aside and have no fear of me, says the Lord of Host" (Mal. 3: 5). God will testify against all these accused people because of the wrong they do against the dignity of the other. It is because of their dignity as human beings that all these cate-gories of persons have **rights**. And when these rights are arbitrarily abused, when others do not respect these rights, then it is their dignity that has been disregarded.

The Prophet Amos decries the crimes, and especially the injustices, perpetrated both by Israel and her neighbours, and for which they are all equally punished: "For crime after crime of Israel I will grant them no reprieve, because they sell the innocent for silver and the destitute for a pair of shoes. They grind the heads of the poor into the earth and thrust the humble out of their way.... ." (Amos 26).[17]

These are all considered as moral practices dishounorable to the human person so highly elevated in the eyes of God, and which crimes therefore called for punitive intervention on the part of God. They were seen ultimately as a dishonour to the dignity of God Himself who has created man in His own image, and therefore, given him a share in His own dignity.

2. *In the New Testament (N.T)*

The New Testament affirms the dignity of all men still more forcefully. The fact that Christ is God's Son, and so God himself made man for man's sake, is at once an affirmation and a measure of the greatness of the dignity of everyman. If by creation in the image of God man attains a divine dignity, by the mystery of the Incarnation this dignity is reasserted much more than ever. For, as it is affirmed in GSp itself, "by his incarnation the son of God has united himself in some fashion with every man" (art. 22).

Man is truly dignified in the eyes of God. Even after sin, God has sent man His only Son out of love for man.[18] In God's Son, man attains the greatness of being the sons and daughters of God as Christ has taught us,[19] and even joint-heirs with him.[20] To further demonstrate what man is worth before Him, God has not spared His Only Son. As Paul tells us through his letter to the Romans: "Even for a just man one of us would Hardly die, though perhaps for a good man one might actually brave death. But Christ died for us while we were yet sinners, and that is God's own proof of his love towards us" (Rom. 5: 7-8).

Here we do not intend to enter into the scriptural and, perhaps, the patrological and neo-scholastical problems that Ratzinger thinks are involved in the text when it starts from the text of man as being made in the image of God.[21] For us, it is sufficient to assert from the fact that if God's love which goes so far as to make man in His own image, and calls him his own son, and even heir through Christ, and if this is not something that should give man some pride and great dignity in his being, then it is difficult to conceive of any other reality or type of relationship that would give man a more genuine dignity. Christ invites everyman to be as perfect as their heavenly Father is perfect,[22] and he further identifies himself with everyman when he considers anything done to any one as being done to he himself.[23] Man's dignity therefore comes from God Himself who created man in His own image and continues to foster particular relations with him through His Holy Spirit.

The Pastoral Constitution and the Dignity of Man

As stated above, this dignity of man which has always been upheld by Sacred Scripture, and so particularly articulated beyond any doubt in the N.T. as the reason for God's continued relationship with man, is again strongly reaffirmed in various degrees throughout the Pastoral Constitution, GSp, and more explicitly so, in chapter one of the same Constitution, which appropriately gives it the title, "The Dignity of the Human Person". In this chapter, the Fathers of the Council see in man's dignity, the fundamental reason for which man is so specially called by God to a destiny which is beyond his status as a creature. It clearly points out right from the beginning that the dignity which man enjoys comes from the fact that MAN IS MADE IN GOD'S IMAGE.[24]

Joseph Ratzinger, commenting on art. 12 of the Constitution, says that the Council text does not accept the theory of Karl Barth which holds that "the image and likeness of God" consists in the relation between man and wife, which would thus be a pure analogy; but that it however brings the existence of humanity, man and woman, into undefined connection with human likeness to God, and thus shows man as a social being who essentially exists in relationships. He concludes by affirming: "the circle of solidarity is open to a third, who is wholly other, God. And that, for the Council, is the content of the doctrine that man is made to the image of God. Man stands in immediate relation to God; he does not merely have to do with God indirectly through his works and his relations with his fellow men. He can know and love God himself".[25] If man in his relation with God stands so close and immediately to Him who is so sublime and dignified, man himself can enjoy no lesser dignity than what the fact of this relationship brings to him.

In another development, it can be inferred that GSp also finds the dignity of man as coming from the fact that he is 'made' of body and soul.[26] Through his body, man shares in the rest of the material creation around him. But the capacities of his soul : dignity of mind, truth and wisdom, and the moral conscience inscribed in him by God,[27] enable him to rise superior to and above matter; and despite the reality of sin and its effects, to perceive the glory of God and his own infinitely great vocation. No other earthly creature has this nobleness in it besides man.

Christ is the new man; "the image of the invisible God" (Col. 1: 15; 2 Cor. 4: 4) has restored to man the divine likeness in which he was made. This is the dignity of man, and it is the dignity which GSp lodges so well in the fact that the person of Christ, who, being "the image of the invisible God," made himself perceptible to man through his Incarnation,[28] and this is what is reaffirmed again and again by the document. It is by reason of the exalted dignity proper to the human person, of which "there is a growing awareness," that every man has rights as well as duties in the society in which he lives.[29] And the essential quality of men (cfr. art.29), reverence for the human person (art. 27), and love even for the enemies (art.28) would have no basis if not because of this dignity that all men share,

Furthermore, it is precisely on the grounds of this dignity of all men, coming from man's divine calling and destiny, and by reason of which everyman enjoys fundamental rights and duties, that "every type of discrimination, whether social or cultural, whether based on sex, race, colour, social condition, language or religion, is to be overcome and eradicated as contrary to God's intent'.[30] So if this fundamental principle is accepted, not even in the name of Christianity could one single culture claim such absolute concordance with God's intent that others must fall only to second place, and can be discriminated against as inferior, and worst of all, as incapable of incarnating the gospel message in them or as possible means by which this message of invitation that God extends to all through Christ could be lived

The nobility of marriage and the family which GSp discusses in the opening chapter of Part II, reduced to its most simple terms, is but a forceful supposition of the dignity of man.[31] And most especially, human culture – which we shall have further opportunity of exploring in this study – would have no real basis whatsoever for its existence, nor proper justification for its development in the varying conditions in which people live and grow, if it had not been for man's dignity endowed by his calling and unique destiny. As the opening paragraph of chapter two of the second Part suggests, human life and culture are bound together, and it is not possible to conceive the very person of a man, no matter whatever dignity may be attributed to him, arriving at full and authentic humanity without a culture particular to him.[32] For, "human culture necessarily has a historical and social aspects, and the word 'culture,' often takes on a sociological and ethnological sense. It is in this sense that we speak of a plurality of cultures" (art. 53).

From the above remarks, therefore, it can be concluded here that GSp does really reaffirm in no uncertain terms the dignity that belongs to every human being. This dignity, as chapter one of the document clearly asserts, has its foundation in the image of God in which man was created, and so, called to a particular destiny, a destiny which goes beyond the horizons of his being as creature;[33] a destiny which, after sin, becomes salvation of man through Christ who, by the Spirit, renews man entirely from within, achieving even "the redemption of the body" (Rom. 8: 23).[34] Besides, this dignity which everyman possesses also guarantees the rights and the duties of the individual and social groups, making no abstraction of the global fact, but rather taking into consideration the "Kairos" in which both the individual and the society are existing, and in the light of which "Kairos" – "signs of the times" – man's destiny which now depends on the message of salvation, proclaimed by Christ, must be interpreted as present.[35] This conferred dignity also becomes the basis of mutual respect and concern for one another between persons, binding them together in **solidarity** and thus making everyone **responsible** for the other, and all **co-responsible** for the particular destiny for which all were created, and to which all alike have been 're-invited,' or called back to through the message of Christ which saves.

Reading therefore into the document, one comes to the conclusion that GSp reaffirms SALVATION IN CHRIST AS A

MESSAGE ADDRESSED TO ALL MEN, since all are endowed with that same human dignity. In what regards the practical answer to this message inviting man to salvation, it is true that the Church is tied to her origin, Jesus of Nazareth whose testimony she has to continue. But, as Ratzinger comments, "because 'the Lord is Spirit' (2 Cor. 3: 17) and remains present through the Spirit, the Church has not only the chronological line with its obligation of continuity and identity, she has also the moment, the 'Kairos,' in which she must interpret and accomplish the work of the Lord as present".[36] By virtue of the dignity which the individual enjoys and shares with every other person, man's answer to the call to salvation also becomes a reality which he undertakes **solidarily** and **co-responsibly** with every other man, so that perceived from this angle, salvation and the attainment of it is a **solidary** and **co-responsible** engagement incumbent on all.

However, with the buzz of the modern world in which man finds himself immersed, one must acknowledge that this reality is not always so obvious to him; nor are all its implications in his daily life and activities usually so easily perceptible.

The place where this human solidarity and co-responsibility manifest itself more concretely, effectively and, indeed, perceptibly is in the immediate society in which the individual is inserted and surrounded by the contingencies of life through a given accepted morality, and is bound by cultural ties. This includes the technological world around him in which he lives and works, and in which these cultural ties are built and developed. Such *solidarity* and *co-responsibility* cannot therefore be validly inquired into without consideration of the *'signs of the times'* prevalent in the given **'Kairos'** and the given *immediate society.*

In the paragraphs that will follow immediately, our main task will be to examine, however briefly, the moral import of some areas we shall depict, where human solidarity and co-responsibility are seen by GSp as human **values** which have their ramifications and, indeed, find their ultimate import on the dignity, vocation, destiny and SALVATION ITSELF OF MAN.

HUMAN RELATIONSHIPS: A REALITY OF SOLIDARITY AND CO-RESPONSIBILITY

Man called in Solidarity and in Brotherhood with his Fellow Men

Among the values that people share, very few can be so universal and common to all as the innate tendency to solidarity. Men have the inborn inclination to associate more freely and to act more in solidarity with those with whom they share their social stratum and cultural interests. This is more so evident today, when people, growing more aware of their rights as well as their duties in their societies[37] would act in solidarity with others to defend these rights, conscious that the abuse of the rights of one jeopardises their own, and is in fact the abuse of their own rights. Thus, the defence of the rights of others becomes a duty on the interest and preservation of their own rights. Hence a duty in which all are co-responsible.[38]

Reasserting one of the oldest definitions of man, GSp holds that man is essentially a social being and that it is only through his relationship with others he can live and develop his potentialities. [39] To substantiate this claim, the document quotes Gen. 1: 27, and sees in the companionship of Adam and Eve, the two first created persons "the primary form of interpersonal communion,"[40] that type of interpersonal companionship which has indeed made the interdependence of all men in every part of the world today so much more obvious and urgent.

If this "primary form of interpersonal communion" of the two first created persons can be interpreted as the naïve interpersonal companionship which so urges the inter-dependence of all men in the world today, the reality more fundamental to this fact must not be left out of sight: i.e. that this "primary form of interpersonal communion" had a deeper end in view and was to lead both persons together either to their "death" or to their "life". And as Genesis tells us, they both fell together (Gen. 3).

Therefore, this innate solidarity which urges men to come together and to act together in defence of their rights con-ferred on them by their dignity does not, and should not, be allowed to remain only on the level of the technical end of the social development of man. In fact, this new urge to solidarity can only be seen in its proper light in the globality of man's final destiny which is his complete salvation, "life" together, and not "death". This point is neatly brought home when the Council document, speaking on the community of mankind, says: "One of the salient features of the modern world is the growing interdependence of men one on the other, a development very largely promoted by modern technical advances. Nevertheless, brotherly dialogue among men does not reach its perfection on the level of technical progress, but on the deeper level of interpersonal relation-ships. These demand a mutual respect for the full spiritual dignity of the person;" and continuing the same theme but now with specific reference to Christianity, it adds: "Chris-tian revelation contributes greatly to the promotion of this communion between persons, and at the same time leads us to a deeper understanding of the laws of social life which the

Creator has written into man's spiritual and moral nature" (GSp art. 23).

If the human solidarity promoted by modern technical advance can only reach its perfection through the mutual respect for the full spiritual dignity of the person, this means that the value of the human solidarity itself reaches, and can be made to operate on, a far superior level than just only the technical progress required by the modern world. That is to say, human solidarity also comes in necessarily on the plane of man's salvation. Because of the fact that all men are called to the same destiny, and because of their common dignity which gives them rights, and which rights can only be enjoyed through mutual respect, co-operation and solidarity in their moral actions become indispensable if they are to respond positively to the invitation to salvation: the destiny for which they were created.

The authors of GSp express this human solidarity and brotherhood in salvation in the following words: "God, who has fatherly concern for everyone, has willed that all men should constitute one family and treat one another in a spirit of brotherhood. For having been created in the image of God, who 'from one man has created the whole human race and made them live all over the surface of the earth' (Acts 17: 26), all men are called to one and the same goal, namely, God Himself" (art. 24).

So, this solidarity among men, which finds its immediate perceptibility in the technological society today, attains its full meaning and reality only in man's response to the final destiny to which he has been called. Indeed, the social life fostered by man's innate aptitude to be solidary with others is not, as GSp sees it, superadded reality to the being of man; rather, through his relationship with others, "through reciprocal duties, and through fraternal dialogue he develops all his gifts and is able to rise to his destiny".[41]

The call to salvation and the response to it as an act of solidarity is a theme that is sufficiently clear throughout GSp, and particularly in the second chapter of Part One. But this reality is much more strikingly present in the last five paragraphs of the chapter in which the Council Fathers see in the Incarnation of God's Word an example 'par excellence' of an act of solidarity. Thus, they hold: "God did not create man for life in isolation but for the formation of a social unity. So also 'it has pleased God to make men holy and save them not only as individuals without any mutual bonds, but by making them into a single people, a people which acknowledges him in truth and serves him in holiness,'[42]. So, from the beginning of Salvation History He has chosen men not just as individuals but as members of a certain community" (art. 32, para. 1).

It is this communitarian character that Christ developed in his work, particularly by sharing in the human fellowship through his flesh. He founded through his Spirit, a new community of brotherhood after his death and resurrection. "This solidarity," the Fathers concluded, "must be constantly increased until that day on which it will be brought to perfection. Then saved by grace, men will offer flawless glory to God as a family beloved of God and of Christ their Brother."[43]

Otto Semmelroth in a commentary on this part of the text says it is every sector of the human life that has been raised in Christ into a living unity with God. As he points out:

By the foundation of the Church as a mysterious body in which all members are interrelated and their unity is not diminished by hierarchical and personal differences, man's social solidarity is confirmed and sacramentally represented on the plane of salvation". Further on, he admits that "even in the Christian order of salvation the solidarity of a freely accepted community is not assured once and for all. It has to grow and be preserved against perpetual threat until it reaches its fulfilment. And the latter is not a heaven of many individuals, but perfect corporate glorification of God.44

In conclusion, he holds that God is not glorified where solidarity with other human beings is neglected.

Indeed, a further analysis of the value of human solidarity and brotherhood set forth by PCCMW could be gone into. However, even this limited analysis imposed by the scope of the study here still permits one to conclude validly that the technologically social solidarity and brotherhood, desirable and actually manifested among people, finds its true fulfilment in man's ultimate destiny. The call of man to salvation cannot be answered to and achieved only individually. The individual is called in solidarity with others, and it is with them that he has to answer to it.

Yet it must be sadly admitted with Piet Schoonenberg that human solidarity in this sphere has not always been given its due emphasis, precisely when it comes to this plane: sin and salvation. In his book "Man and Sin" he writes:

Both Scripture and Magisterium of the Church have emphasised human solidarity with respect to sin. Yet, as that dogma (i.e. the dogma of Original Sin) is generally presented, solidarity does not come much to the fore in it. It affirms a mysterious bond between each individual child and the first father of the race, while the sins of his own parents, of his environment and the great sinful decisions of the past generations have no share in it.45

One thing is clear, and Bernhard Häring put it in focus when he said: "We are forever caught in a vicious circle of discussion in legalism and situation ethics unless we break through to a radical comprehension of man's life as a final choice between the ***solidarity of salvation*** and the ***solidarity of corruption***"[46] Further on, he proposes:

> If we consider tradition and doctrine on the point of sin, and Original Sin in the light of solidarity especially in view of fundamental option between the saving solidarity in Christ and the solidarity of corruption without Christ, we can avoid the danger of fatalism and all temptation to hand the full weight of sinfulness around the neck of the poor 'first Adam' in order to excuse ourselves.[47]

The history of 'Man' therefore lies between two tensions: solidarity in sin and perdition, or solidarity in salvation in Christ; and salvation for the individual is to be achieved only through solidarity and co-responsibility in action (charity) with other people. This appears to be a genuine insight which penetrates into the theme of solidarity and brotherhood which runs through all the chapters of the Pastoral Constitution on the Church in the Modern World, be it on one level or other.

Solidarity and Its Mutual Recognition: Basis of the Individual Personal Dignity

In the ordinary Human relationship, the dignity of the individual person has no meaning nor guarantee unless if it is recognised and respected by others. But this respect for and recognition of others' dignity is often allowed to be blurred by other values far inferior to it. This wrong perspective is at the same time remarked and put right by GSp when it establishes, or at least gives suggestions for the establishment of the rightful relationship between man and his activity throughout the world. "A man is more precious for what he is than for what he has. Similarly, all that men do to obtain greater justice, wider brotherhood, and more human ordering of social relationships, has greater worth than technical advances... Hence, the norm of human activity is this: that in accord with the divine plan and will, it should harmonize with the genuine good of the human race, and allow people as individuals and as members of society to pursue their total vocation and fulfil it" (art. 35 para. 2 and 3).

Unless the individual would recognise in human activity that he and his neighbour share the same destiny and have to work in solidarity towards it, it will not be long before a way is given to "that spirit of vanity and Malice which transforms into an instrument of sin those human energies intended for the service of God and man". For, "when the order of values is jumbled, and bad is mixed with good, individuals and groups pay heed solely to their own interest and not those of others".[48] Therefore, though it may seem somehow para-doxical, the dignity of the individual can only be respected in the day to day engagement of people when the individual lets himself be guided by the rule of mutual recognisance that the others have and share the same lofty teleological values with him, and which can only be obtained through their common solidarity effort. This applies not only to persons as indivi-duals, but also to whole cultural groups which, not very un-commonly, consider their own narrow interests and refuse to see any value, or very little, if at all, in the others.

Going beyond the Ordinary Economic and Political Activities of Man to His Teleological Calling

In chapter four of Part Two, with which the present article is concerned, the Council Fathers faced two of the starkest realities of life, and more particularly of the present age. They categorised this part of the document under the title, *'De Quibusdem Problematibus Urgentioribus,'* (problems of special urgency) and complex nature, that the Council made an honest attempt to illumine with the ideals proclaimed by Christ, persuaded by the hope that "by these ideals Christians may be led and all mankind enlightened, as they search for answers to questions of such complexity".[49] At first instance, the very title given to this part of the document seems to indicate that the problems dealt with belong only to the day to day activities of man without further reference. But the real point and depth intended and reached by the document in these points become most obvious as one delves more profoundly into them.

If there is any field in modern man's life where human solidarity as a value is most manifest, it is surely in man's economic-political activities and life. Drawing attention to this fact at this point of the study does not seem to add something very peculiar to the analysis we have already made; nevertheless, once having established the depth to which the value of human solidarity goes – reaching to the very heart of human destiny itself, salvation,[50] - it is surely not an insignificant thing to indicate now the role that the same value can and does play on these levels at which man is engaged daily, if that will make its connection with this deeper level, which should be its ultimate end, more explicit.

1. *The Economic Activity of Man*

In a first apercu, every economic activity that man undertakes has as its end the satisfaction of the material needs of man. In his economic activity, man uses and adapts matter for his own service, thereby carrying out the injunction by

God on him to dominate and rule the earth together with all its contents Gen, 1: 28).

But beside the encounter that man makes with created matter which he uses and adapts in his economic activities, the realm of economy has also become the place of encounter between man and man. Man, through the work that he does for the satisfaction of his needs, comes into an inevitable encounter with other men, and a necessary relationship develops as a result. The nature of this relationship depends very much on what man thinks and is convinced of his own destiny. This, in passing, is where Christianity and Marxism, or more generally, believers and non-believers meet one of their fundamental differences if not their **fundamental difference**. For the one who believes in the destiny and call of man that has been described or even circumscribed above, this relationship between men through man's economic activities has a deeper significance that just a mere satisfaction of temporally immediate and material needs, or production for the sake of production.

This is the obvious reason why GSp, which is concerned with man's ultimate destiny and salvation, could not, without grave default, pass over in silence this realm which touches and influences so profoundly man's morality here and now in his society, but has teleological repercussion for him.

It is true that the nature of man's relationship with others through his economic activities has received some attention from the Magisterium of the Church as well as particular individuals in the Church in various times throughout the centuries. St. Thomas, for example, considered the purpose of created things as common to all;[51] and other Fathers and Doctors of the Church preached that everyone has the right to have a share of the earthly goods, and that men are obliged to come to the relief of the poor.[52] As to what regards official Magisterium teaching on man and his socio-economic activity, the notable taking of position on the issues involved started, in modern times, with the encyclical *"Rerum Novarum"* of Leo XIII. Other encyclicals and papal pronouncements teaching the subject followed until the encyclical *"Mater et Magistra"* of John XXIII, which came out just a year before Vat. II itself.[53]

But if one takes the principle ideas advanced in *"Rerum Novarum"* and in *"Mater et Magistra,"*[54] though the teaching of *"Mater et Magistra"* already marks quite an improvement on that of the former,[55] the links between every single one of man's economic activity and his call to salvation remain rather latently expressed when compared with the same issues in GSp. In *Mater et Magistra*, John XXIII, after expressing continued concern for social and economic problems, recalls the teaching of *Rerum Novarum*: that work is not a commodity and that labour agreements should be governed by justice and charity. And also after recalling the reaffirmations of Pius XI in Quadragesimo Anno of the right to private ownership of property, and the organization of economic affairs in accordance with the common good, he then sought, in his own teaching, to maintain a balance between individual freedom and the ordering activity of the State, and to declare that *individual men are the foundation, cause and end of all social institution.*

It can be said with justification that it is from this last part of the encyclical of John XXIII that GSp perceives all of man's economic activities, not just as an end in themselves, but in the perspective of man's total vocation. Thus, the text announces at the very opening of the chapter on man's socio-economic life: "In the socio-economic realm too, the dignity and total vocation of the human person must be honoured and advanced along with the welfare of society as a whole. For, man is the source, the centre and the purpose of all socio-economic life".[56] The economic activities of man are, therefore, to be directed in the service of man and in such a manner that God's plan for mankind may be realised (Mt. 16: 26; Col. 3: 17); 57 and again, it is in this that man's solidarity and co-responsibility, as is worthy of his dignity, can find concrete expression.58

For PCCMW, it is the dignity and the vocation of man to his peculiar destiny and salvation, revealed and proclaimed by Christ, that should be the factor ruling all of man's economic engagement. If, as it has been remarked above, men, due to their common destiny and vocation are bound together in solidarity, there is no reason why their economic activity which finds its full meaning in their total vocation should not be the co-responsibility of all. This is, indeed, penetrating the daily contingencies of man's economic life to its very core; and in so doing, the value of human solidarity, by reason of his vocation, again becomes evident, and the world-wide interdependence of peoples in the field of man's economic activity demonstrates clearly and bears witness to this interdependence and brotherhood among men for the achievement of the destiny to which man is called.

2. *Politics as a Pointer to Human Solidarity and Co-responsibility*

After what has been concluded on man's economic activity, there remains rather little to be said on the meaning of his political activity as the two spheres cut across one another in many instances and deal with the same things, at least as far as the scope of this study is concerned. In fact, what is said above of man's economic activity applies to the political activities as well, for, the two do really concern the same fundamental reality and are thus experientially co-related. Indeed, man in his political activity endeavours to regulate the relationship into which he has entered with others through his economic activity. Politics, therefore, must also find its ultimate goal in the total vocation of man.

Therefore, after describing modern politics, in which "a keener awareness of human dignity" is remarked,[59] the document sets forth the nature and goal of politics; underlining the insufficiency of the individuals and smaller groups in the matter of establishing fully human condition of life and attaining the 'common good'.[60] Oswald von Nell-Breuning distinguishes the two senses in which the term 'common good' is used: a) as a value in itself, and b) as a means to an end. He maintains that it is usually in the second sense that the Church uses the phrase.[61] If one therefore takes this second sense, which is, nevertheless, an immediate object of man's political activity, it can be justifiably asserted that 'as a means to an end,' it is intended for and directed towards man's total vocation and destiny: man's salvation. This fact again demonstrates politics to be the responsibility of all and calls for the participation of everyone.[62] Solidarity participation can be demonstrated especially by responsible choosing of the leaders of the political community or society.

In the critical view of Nell-Breuning,[63] democracy, in which the people are convinced of their common destiny and where the power therefore flows upwards from the people, has been shown great reserve by the official Church where authority flows from above downwards, 'from the visible representative of Christ who does not receive his office from the people.' Yet, as he observes, Catholic Theologians, particularly Spanish scholastics of the 16th century,[64] had maintained the principle of the sovereignty of the people. However, as Nell Breuning continues in his comment, though GSp does not go so far as to formally endorse the sovereignty of the people, i.e., the principle of the democratic structure of the State, it nevertheless assumes it as the point of departure in dealing with the political life of man.

Church and State may therefore differ and look at politics from two different points of view, "Yet by a different title, each serves the personal and social vocation of the same human being," and thus "this service can be more effectively rendered for the good of all, if each works better for wholesome mutual cooperation, depending on the circumstances of time and place. For man is not restricted to the temporal sphere, while living in history he fully maintains his eternal vocation" (art. 76, para. 2).

This strongly suggests that all politics should be oriented towards the eternal vocation of all men; i.e., salvation, whole and complete. And this is therefore an activity that should be undertaken in solidarity and in mutual co-responsibility with all others. For it is truly a means to the achievement of man's greatest common good, above which there can be no other as it is his ultimate destiny, his SALVATION. It is on this title that the Council can claim for the Church the right to pass judgements in matters touching the political order,[65] using only those helps which accord with the gospel and with the general welfare as it changes according to time and circumstances.

Marriage and the Family as Foundations of Human Solidarity in Society

In describing the nature of clan as what he calls a society of "mechanical solidarity," Emile Durkheim asserts that it is a 'family' in the sense that all the members who compose it are considered as kin of one another, and that they are, in fact, for the most part consanguineous. He therefore consequently holds that the affinities the community of blood brings about are principally those which keep them united.

He considers that they sustain relations with one another; in fact, relations which can be termed domestic, since they are also found in societies whose familial character is uncontested in such matters as collective punishment, collective responsibility; and where private property is concerned, mutual inheritance.[66] Chapter six of the book referred to here seeks to distinguish between two types of solidarity in the human society. He calls one "the mechanical solidarity," which we have already referred to above, and "the organic solidarity". He describes the society characterized by the latter type of solidarity as a society with different organs, each of which has a particular role, in turn formed of differentiated parts and of social elements of different nature arranged in different manner.

In Durkheim's view, which is supported by present-day sociological data, the second type of sociological solidarity – organic solidarity – is prevailing more and more over the former. This type of balance in favour of Organic Solidarity in society is due to the change of structure of society itself, caused by the flow of people from countryside into the cities and the movement of people from one place to another for reasons of work and employment. Hence the building of new environmental conditions which favour this type of society today.[67]

From the description which Durkheim gives of the two types of social solidarity, he sees that what he calls "the mechanical solidarity" strives on and is sustained by 'family' bonds termed 'domestic relations'. The solidarity of this type therefore, comes from marriage and the 'family'. The two social solidarities which are described here are therefore distinguished: one by the family ties and affinities which characterise it, and the other by the interrelation of different organs of diverse social elements "coordinated and subordinated one to another around the same central organ which exercises a moderating action over the rest of the organism".[68] As Durkheim himself admits, the so-called "mechanical solidarity," which we will prefer to call "family or clan solidarity" in our context here, "still enjoys a special situation, and, if one chooses so to speak of it, a privileged position".[69]

These remarks of Durkheim lend weight to the particular attention given by the Council to marriage and the family in its consideration of the urgent problems in our modern society. Surely, the clock cannot be turned back so that the "family solidarity" based on Clanic society becomes again the preponderant society with the qualities of solidarity proper to it. But it is still a fact that family solidarity remains the nucleus and basis of any solidarity at all in most societies even today; and even the so called "organic solidarity" in society has its roots in "family solidarity," and can be perceived as a progressive perfecting of the latter. In this light, PCCMW, in perceiving the nobility of marriage and of the family, rightly situates the two-fold reality in its proper perspective, and through it as an example, demonstrates the profound nature of human society as a whole in the light of its vocation and ultimate destiny.

After a short description of the situation and some problems pertaining to marriage and the family in the modern world,[70] the document turns to the sanctity of married life and the family, and the growing intimate union of persons that it inspires.[71] By the mutual love of the spouses, which yields as first fruit love and solidarity among the members of the family, Christ's saving presence in the world will be manifested to men, particularly those of the immediate society in which the family lives. In fact, as an evolutionary vision on the Church's traditional concept of the aims of marriage, GSp perceives marriage not just as an institution solely for procreation.[72] It looks far ahead of the temporal realities of marriage and family themselves to that eternal destiny of all men of which every true marriage in the light of Christ's ideals should signify and be instrument of.[73]

If one affirms with the Council that the family is the foundation of the society (GSp art. 52 para. 3), it would be taken as also implied that it is the foundation of the solidarity that should exist in the society of men, all of whom have the same calling and destiny. The Constitution GSp explains that in the family "the various generations come together and help one another to grow wiser and to harmonize personal rights with the other requirements of social life" (Art. 52, para, 3). It is in this light that Bernhard Häring sees the solidarity of parents and children, in regard to salvation, as a mutual responsibility.[74] This responsibility should not remain within only the limited walls of the "restricted family," but must, as the same commentator insists, extend to the society as a whole. To bring home the duty of responsibility between groups, he remarks that both society and the State must also make it their business to organize social life in ways which will further the family.[75]

In conclusion, one can say that in the perspective of the last paragraph of the chapter which recalls the image of the living God in the spouses and their dignity as persons, is summed up, through the sacraments of marriage, the occasion for man to his ultimate destiny in solidarity with the rest of mankind through Christ. The moral life of solidarity expressed in the love of the spouses between themselves and between and between all the members of the family, proclaims and bears witness to these truths. It is in this way that the Christian family, as Häring maintains, is called to manifest to the world and the entire human society the true nature of love, fecundity, unity, fidelity and solidarity.[76] Together with the organic groups of society, the family as nucleus of the society, be it in its 'restricted' sense or 'extended' form, is solidarity co-responsible for the achievement of the salvation in Christ to which the individual is called.

This discourse on marriage and the family as foundation of human solidarity in society would lose its real force and impact, when it comes to the practice, if the diversity of the various cultural backgrounds and peculiar situations in which the individual marriages and families exist, would not be recognised and taken into serious and realistic consideration in the Christian moral propositions presented here by the by the Council. It is the extent to which the Council in GSp recognises this diversity in the human culture that the next paragraphs of this study will try to assess.

Conspicuous Recognition of the Diversity of Human Culture

Robert Tucci, commenting on chapter two of the second part of PCCMW, which dealt with "The Proper Development of Culture," remarks that relations between Church and Culture did not feature expressly in any of the Schemata drafted by the various commissions in the preparatory phase of the Council; and that even though the need of the theme had become apparent in the Commission for the Lay Apostolate, it was relegated to a place in the appendix, for lack of time.[77]

However, as it is known, the fundamentality of the theme became more and more evident itself, and in fact, gradually imposed itself as basic to the Pastoral Constitution as the successive drafts enter more and more deeply and concretely into the various situations which truly constitute the reality of the modern man. For this gradual realisation of the fundamental role of culture by the Council, the theme on the "signs of the times," the most remarkable outcome of the Second Zurich Meeting, is responsible.[78] As Moeller sums it up in his discussion on the Ariccia Text (31 January – 14 September

1965), "the chapter on culture gradually turned out to be the most closely connected with the doctrinal part of the Schema. Culture is in fact a fundamental factor at the base of all political, economic, social and international realities".[79] Thus GSp, which was directed to all men immersed in these realities, would have indeed failed miserably had it not been able at the end to see the basic importance of an attentive and careful evaluation of culture. Actually, at the end, some members of the commission responsible for the draft even wanted to place the chapter on Culture at the head of the second part of the entire Constitution, when this part was re-instated as integral part of the main text and no longer just as an appendix material. It was only the limitedness of time at this late moment which made this rearrangement of the text no longer possible.[80]

From this historical development of GSp itself, one sees the gradual recognition of human culture as a whole, and the place that it holds as a value in the evangelization of the various peoples and social groups which come invariably under one cultural tradition or another. They are these cultural traditions which, though with the interrelations of peoples in the modern societies, continue to influence from the bottom the political, economic and social morality of the various peoples to whom the message of Christ is being brought.

The decree, "Ad Gentes" (AdGen.) of Vat. II which restates the Church's divine Mission to all nations as "Universal Sacrament of Salvation,"[81] and also relates God's universal design for the salvation of the whole human race through Christ,[82] recognises that the gospel message has to be preached to all men of all nations who "who are formed into large and distinct groups by permanent cultural ties, by ancient religious groups, and by firm bonds of social neces-sity".[83] This clearly admits the diversity of culture in the human race; a diversity which is a result of historical events, geographical circumstances and economic and social conditionings which have grouped people together in these different cultural traditions. AdGen even sees the planting of the church in a given human community as being attained "when the congregation of the faithful, already rooted in social life and considerably adapted to the local culture, enjoys a certain stability and firmness."[84] The decree AdGen therefore, leaves no doubt as to the fact that it is within the culture of the people that the missionary can bring the gospel of salvation to any particular people; "They (the missionaries) will thereby gain a general knowledge of peoples, cultures and religions, a knowledge that looks not only to the past, but to the present as well. Anyone who is going to encounter another people should have great esteem for their patrimony and their language and their customs" (AdGen art. 26, para. 2).

In fact, as B. Häring has accurately expressed it, the morality of evangelisation really does consist in evangelising the morals of the different cultures which regroup people together.[85] They are the various cultures of people into which the Gospel Message has to enter, purifying them of all that is contrary to what leads to salvation in Christ, and uplifting and perfecting them as grace perfects nature.[86] The Sacred Congregation for the Propagation of the Faith had already recognised the values that can be found in every culture,[87] and later papal encyclicals have been attentive to this point as well.[88] In this case, the gospel which encounters an already existing morality becomes the norm of moral judgement in the particular culture lived.[89]

Although Vat. II has recognised and given place to cultural plurality either implicitly or explicitly in most of its documents,[90] nowhere else has it so conspicuously done it as in GSp where a whole chapter is devoted to culture. In the very introduction of the chapter, the document states the necessity of culture for the authentic development of man, and describes culture in its general sense as all those factors by which man perfects and unfolds his multiple spiritual and bodily qualities. As this involves progress, human culture, therefore, necessarily takes on a historical and social aspect; thus, very often giving the term itself a sociological and ethnological meaning; the sense in which the Council speaks of a plurality of cultures.

Though the Fathers see that modern conditions in which men live have brought about a change in man's social and cultural dimensions, giving wide openness to different cultures, on the other hand, they recognise that "In every group or nation there is an ever increasing number of men and women who are conscious that they themselves are artisans and authors of the culture of their community"[91] The modern conditions of living can also create anxieties about the influences to which the various cultural heritages are open; "What must be done to prevent the increased exchange between cultures which ought to lead to a true and fruitful dialogue between groups and nations, from disturbing the life of communities, destroying ancestral wisdom, or jeopardizing the uniqueness of each people"? (Art. 56, para. 2).[92]

Speaking of faith and culture, GSp sees the mystery of the Christian Faith as a furnisher of incentives and helps by which the Christian is led, not only to things above but also to an energetic discharge of his duty of constructing a more human world, and especially towards discovering the full meaning of his activity; a meaning which gives human culture its proper place in the integral vocation of man.[93] All the values inherent in the various human cultures can be already a preparation for the acceptance of the gospel message. In this light, the many links between the message of salvation and human culture become evident. As the Council itself affirms in GSp, "God, revealing Himself to His people to the extent of a full manifestation of Himself in His Incarnate Son, has spoken according to the culture proper to different ages" (art. 58. Para, 1).

In the light of the above paragraphs, once can conclude that the Pastoral Constitution recognises beyond any ambiguity the values inherent in the diverse human cultures. The fact that it sees in the various cultures values that provide preparation for the gospel message, and also admits a necessary link between the message of salvation and human culture, is an acceptation of the tremendous riches inherent in each culture which can be exploited to the benefit of all mankind called in solidarity to salvation. It also demonstrates the autonomy of these human values maintained and nourished through culture.

Culture, like man himself, is involved in a historical process: a historical movement of which God Himself is the Lord. As such, it must progress and continually renew itself. The gospel message which comes into the dialectical movement of history, to "re-call" all men to their original destiny, should not, and does not destroy the individual culture and its values, but rather gives to all men the right to a more human and perfected culture which favours and promotes the personal dignity of each without discrimination of any kind.[94] For, as Peter said: "I now see how true that God has no favourites, but that in every nation, the man who is Godfearing and does what is right is acceptable to Him" (Acts 10: 34ff; Gal. 2: 6, 3: 28; Rom. 10: 12). It is, therefore, the gospel message of Christ and the true witnessing to it which elevates and purifies all the different cultures in which it is preached,[95] thus making them all one. For, by the same norm of the gospel, men of the all different cultures are made acceptable to the one and the same God, who created them all in His image, and destined them to the same end, despite

119

their differences and legitimate cultural autonomy. This reality is, indeed, conspicuously recognised by the Council in the Pastoral Constitution, GSp.

A Synthesis in View of Practical Application

With this interpretative re-reading of GSp and the formulation of what has been called basic intuitions in the second chapter, the work set out to be done in this first part of the research can be considered as accomplished. In the first chapter, after a brief description of the Council in general, and that of GSp in particular, there was recalled historical development of the Schema XIII up to its promulgation as the **Pastoral Constitution on the Church in the Modern World**.

In the four major points into which chapter two is divided, GSp is re-read with a definite hypothesis in mind. This hypothesis has been to put into focus what has been considered as the basic intuitions of the document. Absolutely considered, the intuitive elements offered by the Pastoral Constitution are certainly multiple, and many more different ones from these presented here could have been identified, considering the depth and riches of the document as a whole. However, this has been rather a question of a choice of material due to the particular and restricted orientation of the study. For our purpose, the option has been postulated and guided by the theme itself under study and research, and one could therefore not possibly identify and describe here all the intuitive values contained in the document without getting too far out of the particular scope of values that which one intended to study.

The Destiny of Man

In the light of what has been re-read in GSp, the fundamentally basic intuition of the document on which all others depend could be defined as the destiny of man. Unlike the rest of the created beings in the world, it is only man who is said to have been create in God's own image (Gen. 1: 27). This fact manifests the unique and singular destiny to which man is called. The reality of this is further brought to light in the mystery of the Incarnation, when God's own Son, who is indeed, "the image of the invisible God" (Col. 1: 15), became man, sharing all man's conditions with him – except, of course, sin (Rom. 8: 3; Gal. 4: 4; Phil. 2: 7; Heb. 2: 17).

The Incarnation took place after man, through sin, had made insecure this original destiny to which he was called in creation. It is, in the present economy of salvation, to restore to man and to proclaim to him that – in the infinite love and mercy of God – he can yet attain destiny for which he was originally created, that Christ became man. So, through his Incarnation man is 'recalled' to his original destiny, to SALVATION THROUGH CHRIST.

Other Values reaffirmed by the Incarnation

But Christ by his Incarnation does not only make man's original destiny possible again for him. Also, "by his Incarnation, the Son of God has united himself in some fashion with every man," as the Council affirms.[96] The mystery of the Incarnation thus, paradoxically, puts into greater light the following two realities:

First: The solidarity and brotherhood in which all men are bound. For, by becoming man, Christ has entered into solidarity with man, thus, reaffirming God's design in which He created man and called him to the one and the same destiny. Through his Incarnation, Christ became brother to all men since he came to proclaim to all men the same message of salvation, and thus put into perspective again man's solidary destiny. Furthermore, by his entering into brotherhood and solidarity with all men through his incarnation, Christ has made it possible to all men to call God their Father; for, all become thus enabled to receive the Spirit which was promised, and thus through the Spirit all can become the sons and daughters of God.[97]

Second: The dignity that was conferred on man by his being created in the image of God also achieves new freshness. As brothers and sisters of Christ, a fact made possible by Incarnation, man shares in his dignity as son of God, and in the Son of God-become man, man acquires again, at least a part of that dignity which belongs to God. It is in fact this re-elevated dignity of man which makes human solidarity more conspicuous and more urgent since sharing the same dignity as brothers in Christ becomes an exigency to cooperate in solidarity towards the continuous preservation of this dignity.

So, man has a definite vocation, a unique destiny for which he was created, and to which he has been recalled in Jesus Christ, after sin. This call which is to salvation is addressed to all men. This means the individual has to answer to this call to salvation in Christ **not alone, but in solidarity with his fellow men**. For, since he shares the same vocation and dignity with them, his personal salvation on the context of "the world" depends on others just as that of others depend on him. Thus, each person becomes responsible to a certain extent, not only for his own salvation, but also for that of the others. In this light therefore, salvation becomes a **mutual co-responsibility** of all.

This solidarity and co-responsibility among men is not a reality only in reference to man's ultimate destiny. It already finds expression in man's life here in the world in which he works with all other men, constructing a more human world.[98] Karl Rahner and Herbert Vorgrimler have defined theology as 'an undistorted hearing of God's Word with a view to salvation, ultimately in the service of salvation itself'.[99] This when understood and viewed under the aspect of the individual's encounter and relationship with God, rejoins in one way or another man's total vocation and destiny. For, theology is also a discourse on God that should lead to faith in Him; and this faith has four essential dimensions of which the 'world' in which man lives is one.[100] It is in this world that man's response to his call to salvation is made. If it is so, this world, with all that it implies, in particular its values, has to be taken seriously, and its autonomy recognised. This autonomy is what is recognised by the Pastoral Constitution of the Church in the Modern World.[101]

Furthermore, as GSp is aware, God in His saving relationship with man has taken account of the different circumstances in which man may be found in the world, and also the traditions which he has built up due to these circumstances throughout history. For, God, as the document says in article 58, "revealing Himself to His people to the extent of a full manifestation of Himself in His Incarnate Son, has spoken according to the culture proper to different ages".

This is where the message of salvation finds its link with the world; for, the world of a given society or people means its culture which, through these historical circumstances and tradition, has come to establish its moral values and norms, and determines its whole way of life. It is into this world and no other that the message of salvation proclaimed by Christ, the Son of God who recalls man to his destiny, has to come, elevating and perfecting the values which already exist therein, and using them to lead its people to salvation, to that particular destiny for which man was originally created.

This light shed by GSp has its relevance here: this analysis of it announces and defines the second part of the research undertaken here; a reappraisal of the Dagara values of solidarity and co-responsibility in view of this salvation proclaimed in and by Christ. It is the validity of these moral values among the Dagara, and the manner in which they can be tapped as valuable instruments for realizing the salvation proclaimed by Christ that the next part of this Anthropo-logical-Theological research will be exploring.

Chapter Two Endnotes

1Avery Dulles, "The Church;" An Introductory Comment to the Dogmatic Constitution on the Church, The Documents of Vat. II, Walter M. Abbott, (Editor), Guild Press, New York, 1966, p. 10.

2 Ibid., p. 11.

3 Ibid., p. 12.

4 Ibid., p. 12.

5 C. Moeller, "History of the Constitution," *Commentary on the Documents of Vat. II*, H. Vorgrimler, (Ed.), 5 vols. Burns and Oates, London, 1969, vol. 5, p. 16

6 J. Ratzinger, "The Dignity of the Human Person," Commentary on the Documents of Vat. II, Vorgrimler, (Ed.), 5 vols., Burns and Oates, London 1969, vol. 5, p. 110.

7 Part one of the document covers from Articles 11 to 45 of the Constitution.

8 "Gaudium et Spes," Articles 4-10.

9 C. Moeller, "Preface and Introductory Statement," *op. cit.*, p. 87.

10 "The Dogmatic Constitution of the Church," *Lumen Gentium*, chapter two.

11 C. Moeller, *op. cit.*, p. 87

12 *Gaudium et Spes*, art. 1.

13 Cfr. *Gaudium et Spes*, art. 10.

14 *Schemata Constitutionum et Decretorum*, Series Series Prima, De Ordinis Morali Christiano," Chapter V, De Dignitate

Personae Humanae, Typis Polyglottis Vaticanis, 1962, pp. 92-6; see also C. Moeller, *op. cit.*, pp. 4-5.

15 Cfr. Gaudium et Spes, arts. 13-21.

16 Ibid., art. 16.

17 Amos cries out against both Israel and her neighbours against the way certain classes of people were looked down upon as having no dignity, (Amos chapter 2). The law of Yahweh applies both to Israel as well as to the foreigner living in the midst of Israel, cfr. Is. 56: 1-7 etc., and this because all men enjoy the same dignity, being all created by the same Yahweh who made man only a little less than angles (Ps. 8: 5).

18 Jn. 3: 16.

19 Mt. 6: 7-14; cfr. also Rom. 8: 15 and Gal. 4:6.

20 Rom. 8: 17; Gal. 4: 7; Tit. 3:7.

21 J. Ratzinger, op. cit., p. 121

22 Mt. 5: 48.

23 Mt. 25: 31-46.

24 Cfr. *Gaudium et Spes*, art.12.

25 . Ratzinger, op. cit., pp. 122-3.

26 GSp, art. 14.

27 Ibid., arts. 14, 15, and 16.

28 Ibid., art. 2.

29 Ibid., art. 26.

30 Ibid., art. 29.

31 Ibid., arts. 47-52.

32 Ibid., art 53.

33 Ibid., art. 12.

34 Ibid., arts. 13 and 22.

35 J. Ratzinger, *op. cit.*, p. 116

36 Ibid., loc. Cit.

37 Gaudium et Spes, art. 26.

38 The Trade Unions today, for example; the English Trade Unions, are examples of solidarity action in defence of human rights in the industrial camp. The Encyclical "Mater et Magistra" of John XXIII, *AAS*, 53(1961), pp. 401-69, recognizes this solidary action of people in defence of their legitimate rights against the employer.

39 Cfr. GSp, art. 12. The social nature of man and dependence is expressed again in art. 25. St. Thomas Aquinas, referring to the second book of Physics and the fifth book of Metaphysics of Aristotle, admits the ends of man as two-fold: individual and communitarian, i.e., solidary. Cfr. *Summa Theologica*, I-II, q. 1, 8, ad. 2.

40 In the English translation of the *Documents of Vat. II*, edited by Walter M. Abbott, the footnote 25 of GSp links the fact of creation of "male and female" with the concept of marriage, considered as fundamentally an interpersonal communion". There are other angles from which this could be looked at. Here it is this "primary form of interpersonal communion " from the point of view of solidarity which it provides between human beings that is looked at.

41 Cfr. GSp, art. 25.

42 LGen *art*. 9.

43 GSp, art. 32, para, 5.

44 Otto Semmelroth, The Community of Mankind, *Commentary on the Documents of Vat. II*, H. Vorgrimler (Editor), 5 vols. Burns and Oates, London, 1969, vol. 5, pp. 180-1.

45 Piet Schoonenberg, Man and Sin, Sheed and Ward, London, 1972, p. 98.

46 B. Häring, *Sin in a Secular Age*, Academia Alfonsiana, Rome; MS, of a book, 1973, p. 103.

47 Ibid, p. 107. Cfr. also I. Schabert, "Solidaritaet," in Segen und Fluch im Alten Testament und seiner Umwelt, Bonn, 1956.

48 Cfr. GSp, art. 37, para. 3.

49 Cfr. Preface to Part II of *Gaudium et Spes*.

50 Cfr. 'A' above, "Man called in Solidarity".

51 Saint Thomas, *Summa Theologiae, II- II, q. 66, 2*. Here St. Thomas considers the purpose of all created things as common to all people.

52 GSp, art. 69; see also footnote 223 of W. Abbott on the same document. St. Thomas also discusses the question in Summa Theologiae, II-II, q. 32, a. 5.

53 Leo XIII, "Rerum Novarum," *AAS* 23(1890-91), pp. 651 &ff.; Pius XI "Quadragesimo Anno," *AAS*, 23(1931), pp. 190ff.;

Pius XII, "Allocutio to Catholic Association of Italian Workers" *AAS*, 51(1959), p. 358; John XXIII, "Mater et Magistra," *AAS*, 53(1961), p 450. It is interesting to note that "Rerum Novarum" of Leo XIII which was the first official Church pronouncement in modern times on this matter, came 24 years after the publication of the first volume of *"Das Kapital"* of Marx. The latter was published in 1867.

54 John J. Murphy, "Rerum Novarum," Master pieces of Catholic Literature, ed. Frank N. Magill, Harper and Row, New York, 1965, pp. 699 and ff. Also, James C. Rauner, ibid., pp. 1106-1110.

55 To really understand the language and tone of any encyclical so as to interpret it rightly, one cannot neglect especially the social background against which it was conceived and written.

56 Cfr. GSp, art. 63; also art. 67, para. 2.

57 Ibid., arts. 64, 66 paras. 5, 69, para. 1.

58 Ibid., arts. 65, 67, para. 2.

59 Ibid., art. 73.

60 Ibid. art. 74

61 Oswald von Nell-Breuning, "The Life of the Pollical Community," in Commentary on the Documents of Vat. II, ed. H. Vorgrimler, 5 vols., Burns and Oates, London, 1969, vol. 5, p. 318.

62 Cfr. GSp, art. 75.

63 O. von Nell-Breuning, op. cit., pp. 320-21.

64 Most outstanding theologians at that time, who spoke out on the question were especially Francesco de Vitorio (1492-1546), Melchior Cano (1509-1560), Francesco Suarez (1548-1617). Cfr. L. Vereecke, *Storia della Teologia Morale in Spagna nel XVIe Secolo e Origine delle 'Institutiones Morales,'* MS, Academia Alfonsiana, Rome, 1972/73.

65 Cfr. GSp, art. 76 para. 7.

66 Emile Durkheim, On Morality and Society, ed., Robert N Bellah, University of Chicago Press, Chicago, 1973, pp. 63-5.

67 F. Houtart and J. Remy, *Eglise et Société en Mutation*, Mame, 1969; F. Houtart, *Sociologie et Pastorale*, Fleurus, 1963; Schmeller, in *Revue d'Economie Politique*, 1890, p. 145, quote by

Emile Durkheim in *On Morality and Society, op. cit.*, p. 74; Alvin Toffler, *Future Shock*, Pan Books Ltd., London, 1971.

68 E. Durkheim, op. cit., p. 69.

69 Ibid. loc. Cit.

70 GSp, art. 47.

71 Ibid., art. 48.

72 Ibid. art. 50 para. 6.

73 Ibid. art. 51 para. 5.

74 B. Häring, "Fostering the Nobility of Marriage and the Family," *Commentary on the Documents of Vat. II*, ed. H. Vorgrimler, op. cit.,

75 Ibid., loc. Cit.

76 Ibid., p. 237.

77 Robert Tucci, "The Proper Development of Culture," *Commentary on the Documents of Vat. II.*, H. Vorgrimler, ed., op. cit., vol. 5, p. 246.

78 Cfr. above, chapter one, paragraph on "Signs of the Times".

79 C. Moeller, "History of the Constitution," Commentary on the Documents of Vat. II, vol. 5, p. 57.

80 Ibid., loc. Cit.

81 Vat. II, "Decree on the Church's Missionary Activity," Ad Gentes, art. 1; see also LGen, art. 48.

82 AdGen, art. 3.

83 Ibid., art. 10; also art. 26 para. 2.

84 Ibid., art. 19.

85 B. Häring, *Evangelisation Today*, Fides Publication, Notre Dame, Indiana, 1974, part two.

86 St. Thomas, *Summa Theologiae*, I, q.1, 8, ad 2; I, q. 2,2, ad !

87 Sacra Congregatio de Propaganda Fide, "Instructio circa Prudentiorem de Rebus Missionalibus Tractandi Rationem," *AAS* 6(1939), pp. 269-70. It is this awareness of the value of other cultures that must have led to the abolition of the Missionary oath for those missionaries going to China the same year, 1939.

88 John XXIII, "Mater et Magistra," *AAS*, 53(1963), p. 283.

89 B. Häring, *op. cit.*, pp. 45ff.

90 Cfr. Vat. II, "Constitution on the Sacred Liturgy," *Sacrosanctum Concilium*; a liturgical adaptation or celebration in

a particular given cultural society may remain only an empty ritual and void of any meaning if it has no relevance to the cultural group in which it is performed. The liturgical adaptation urged by the Constitution of the Liturgy therefore presupposes a recognition of the diversity of cultures, Cfr. Ad Gentes, which is more explicit on the point.

91 *GSp*, arts. 54, 55.

92 As Walter Abbott remarks in footnote 183 of PCCMW, (see p. 261 of edition used and quoted above), the danger here sometimes assumes the form of a cultural colonialism. John XXIII points out an aspect of this danger in "Mater et Magistra" in noting the false values sometimes exported by economically advanced nations together with their economic and technical aid to others.

93 Cfr. GSp, art. 57.

94 Ibid., art. 60.

95 Ibid., 59 paras. 3; also art. 52 para. 1.

96 Ibid., art. 22.

97 Jn. 1: 12; Rom. 8: 14-15: Gal. 3: 26-29, 4: 4-7: cfr. also, GSp, art. 23.

98 GSp, art. 57.

99 K. Rahner, and H. Vorgrimler, *Concise Theological Dictionary*, Burns and Oates, London, 1965, p. 456.

100 The four dimensions of faith here are: God, man himself, the world with all its values and particular circumstances in which man lives, and then the Church, the community of lawfully constituted society through which Christ's message continues to be proclaimed to the rest of mankind, and which herself bears witness to the eschatological fullness of the revelation in Christ.

101 Cfr. GSp, art. 57 paras. 2 and 3; also art. 59 para. 3, where the affirmation is more explicitly made.

PART TWO

THE VALUES OF SOLIDARITY IN THE DAGARA CULTURE AND THEOLOGICAL THOUGHT

CHAPTER THREE

ORIGINS AND ROLE OF SOLIDARITY AND CO-RESPONSIBILITY IN THE DAGARA MORAL LIFE

Introduction

If in revealing Himself to man, God, through His Incarnated Son, has spoken according to the culture proper to different ages,[1] it is an unmistakable indication that God takes the conditions[2] in which everyman is found, seriously, and wants that His message attains man in those conditions. GSp has recognised the variety of these conditions in which different men have been constituted; and thus, after reasserting the universal mission of the Church to all peoples, affirms, nevertheless, that the Church, continuing to proclaim and bear witness to the message of God's Incarnate Son, "can enter into communion with various cultural modes, to her own enrichment and theirs too" (GSp art. 58). In fact, not only 'can' the Church enter into communion with the various cultural modes, but actually has to use these already existing modes in which the person is found to explain, spread and deepen Christ's message.

To enter into this communion with the various cultural modes and to use them properly to proclaim and expound Christ's Message, the condition in which the person to be attained lives, cannot be ignored without frustrating consequences to both the person himself as such, and to the message itself; i.e., it will only result in a failure to truly 'purify and elevate' his morality as was intended. Hence a corresponding sterility and ineffectualness on the part of the message itself will occur, as the message which has no concrete application to his life will be seen as irrelevant to him.

It is for this reason that the present study which wants to investigate the validity of the cultural values of the **Dagara Solidarity and Co-responsibility in view of the Christian Message of Salvation** cannot achieve its purpose without, at least, a summary description of, and some reflection on, the people whose values are here being investigated in view of the Christian Message attaining them through these values.

It is true, and has to be remarked from the beginning, that the research undertaken here is not a geographical study of the Dagara, neither does it pretend to seek to make a historical investigation of them; nor does it seek to present purely and simply a sociological structure of them. If I would consider a brief treatment of any of these aspects here as necessary, it will be for the reason that once someone speaks of a "people," even theologically, or rather should we say, especially theologically, one cannot discuss them in abstraction of their particular "Umwelt," i.e., the 'time and 'space' in which they live. These are major factors which underlie and contribute essentially to their cultural modes and form their "Weltanschauung," i.e., their entire outlook to the world and life itself.

Although it may be considered as an already worn-out statement, we affirm that culture is dynamic. It progresses with human history, and if men were to have to live a second life, none would ever live in exactly the same cultural circumstantial impacts the second time as he would have experienced in the first society in which he first lived. What therefore is presented in the following paragraphs will be best seen in the light of what anthropologists call "the ethnographic present," i.e., past or anachronistic events described in the present with all the vigour they did have in the past; and which we may also in other terms call "trans-historical moment".

Therefore, before we delve into the task of examining the values of solidarity and co-responsibility inherent in Ghanaian culture in general, and the Dagara culture in particular, and how they may be relevant to the Christian Message of Salvation, this study deems it necessary to devote here the following few paragraphs to situate geographically the Dagara as a people, and to give some anthropological insights into them. These are conditions and factors which, in spite of their contingency, have created and continue to influence their cultural modes.

An Apercu of the 'Dagara People'

Geographical Description

In his three-volume ethnographical material gathered on the people of what was formerly French West Africa, Maurice Delafosse describes the **Dagaati People** (A variant of the **Dagara***) as a number of closely related "tribes" living in settled agricultural communities within the Great Niger Bend.[3] Down to the Southern part of the Sudanese zone of low trees and tall grasses, they inhabit either side of the Volta River (The Black Volta) which, in its mid-northern course, forms the natural border between Ghana and the former French colony, now the Republic of Burkina Faso. To the south of them in Ghana, are the Gonja, the Ashanti and the other Akan tribes lying from around the ninth parallel down to the Gulf of Guinea. The territory thus inhabited by the Dagaati (or Dagara) lies between the 9th and the 12th parallels. The greatest bulk of them, nevertheless, are settled in the North-Western corner of Ghana, and they extend into that part of the former French West Africa colony, The Republic of Burkina Faso.

This Sudanese zone inhabited by the Dagaati People is characterised by a well-marked division of the year into wet or rainy season and dry season.4 The wet season which begins towards the end of April and ends in October is immediately followed by a rather severe dry season, also of about six months' duration. During the rains, the savanna-land which for the previous six months have been suffering from the penetrating dry wind coming from the Sahara,5 and later, the scorching heat of the sun, particularly in the month of March, is quickly covered with green grasses. This is the time during which the people cultivate their fields and plant their cereals: guinea-corn, millet, maize, beans, rice, ground-nuts, etc., and on which they will have to feed themselves for the whole of the year. By the end of the month of November, practically all the crops are harvested and brought in, and this brings an end to the principal activity, by far the heaviest work to be done in the twelve months of the year.

This cyclic occurrence of the seasons of the year, beside the habitual and the set mode of life that it imposes on the people within the course of time, has also created a pheno-menon which has grown within time, and in more recent times has become, together with the fact of formal educa-tion,6 a major factor in the continual shaping of the Dagara Culture and mode of living. As the gathering in of the crops brings an end to what we have described as the major, and by far the heaviest working period within the year, the younger part of the population which is still full of energy and vitality, migrate in great numbers to the tropical forest in the south of the country in search of remunerative work in the farms and gold-mines lying there. They remain there for about four to five months after which they would then return to their own lands in the north only towards the beginning of April, to prepare their own farms in readiness for the rains which are due soon then.[7]

This seasonal going-and-coming has its effects on the population as a whole; for, through it the Dagaati people come into contact with other people in the region, nevertheless, different from themselves in a number of varied ways, and so other cultural modes of living, and ethical patterns different from their own.[8] Also, the unfavourable climatic conditions together with the 'primitive' techniques of agriculture have very often left the people of the north of Ghana in general and further up, victims to famine because of the repeated failure of their crops on which all their livelyhood depends so much. Faced with such constant threats and uncertainties, the Dagara "struggle" for subsistence becomes, not only an individual responsibility, nor is it perceived on a merely material level, but also turns into a "struggle for the survival of entire families, clans and even the whole people.

It becomes a struggle which touches the moral values and even the religious structures of the people; and with the passage of time enters into their traditions and takes on cultural forms. Thus, as we shall have occasion to examine more closely, the threat to survival becomes not only a threat to the existence of the individual but assumes a more embracing character: it becomes a threat to the existence of a whole family, clan or even people. The combat against this threat can therefore not remain only an individual responsibility, nor can it be won insofar as it remains fought only on the material level. It is not sufficient that the individual seeks to assure and preserve (save) his own personal and individual existence alone, but must also concern himself with that of the other members of at least the immediate group to which he belongs: the family.[9]

One obvious result from this common strife is not only that the bonds of fraternity and common concern are kept alive, but also that these ties are continually nurtured and strengthened throughout history among these people who are so heavily geographically conditioned. Other ideologies, systems or economies of human survival, liberation, security or "SALVATION" as it is called in Christianity, cannot be perceived and appreciated in their full light and value outside of these conditions to which these concepts are tied. They constitute in some way the background, the point of reference, and terms in which the people concerned will be able to conceive, appreciate and evaluate the various systems of "Salvation" that will have been proposed to them and preached by men in the course of human history.

Some Anthropological Insights

A purely anthropological consideration of the Dagara is not what these paragraphs regrouped under this title of our study want to undertake.[10] That would mean entering into the complexities of ethnological classifications, intricate linguistic problems and comparative studies; and would equally raise the uncalled-for difficulties inherent in the examination of ethnographical material. The fact that there have been no documented studies on the Dagara until rather recently renders these approaches and the discussion on them in any case unnecessary. The following short paragraphs therefore intend to give only some further description of, and insights into the Dagara People.

1. *Ethnological Belonging*

In his comprehensive ethnological survey of the West Sudan, Maurice Delafosse distinguished what he termed "the *cinq familles de race noire*". Speaking of the inhabitants in this part of the Sudan he writes: "*Ils appartiennent a deux races et se repartissent en sept familles don't deux de race blanche plus au moins mélangee... et cinq de race noire.*"[11] Delafosse enumerated the five families of the black race as: Tukulor, the Songhai, the Mande, the Senufo and the Voltaic. Later, Westermann, a German linguist, in his account of the Sudanic languages[12] admitted in general the classification made by Delafosse, even if there was what we may call minor differences between them.[13]

Following therefore the classification of Delafosse, the Dagara belong to one of the five families in the West Sudan. They belong to the Voltaic Family which spreads out within the Great Niger Bend from the 15th parallel in the north to below the 9th parallel, just before the thick tropical forest. According to Delafosse, this Family is subdivided into seven groups.[14]The Dagara form one of the six 'People' that make up what he calls the Mossi Group.

2. *A Short Historical Observation*

From the outset, the present study has taken, and considered the Dagara as a People already settled in their actual territory. It has already been indicated that the Dagara occupy either side of the Volta River which, from about the 12th parallel forms a natural border between Ghana and what is now known as Burkina Faso, and also of the Cote d'Ivoire. Oral tradition alone is not sufficient to state with certitude when and from where they came to have possession of their present territory.

There seem to be two preponderant opinions among the people themselves, which opinions, in fact, do not exclude one another. One holds that the Dagaaba came from the east of their actual territory. This would make them come either from the Nankam, which, from all evidence, is a "cousin tribe," still occupying the north-eastern part of Ghana together with other related tribes: the Kusasi, the Tallinsi and others; or from the Dagomba who are to the south of these latter tribes. All these peoples, in fact, belong to the Mossi Group and are actually very closely related to the Dagara/Dagaaba particularly in language.

The second opinion holds that the Dagaaba came from the north. This would make them come directly from the Mossi People. The argument used to support this other opinion is the fact that the Dagaaba and the Mossi consider each other as "brothers". The Mossi term 'Yo' or 'Yao' which means "brother" or "younger brother" respectively, are in fact very close to the Dagara term 'Yoo' or 'Yeb,' both of which mean "brother". In any case, the general argument is again the close similarity of the two languages.

That these two opinions do not necessarily exclude each other can be, in addition, maintained from the fact that the holders of either of them all agree that both the Nankam and the Dagomba, like the Dagaaba, also come from the Mossi. In this case, the question will be reduced to only one of time: i.e., to establish correctly the sequence of events and the exact detours that the Dagara would have made to eventually arrive at, and to occupy their actual territory on either side of the Black Volta. They came from the Mossi in the north either directly, or they did so indirectly, after having first descended with the Dagomba or the Nankam, and from whom they would then have separated at a later date and gone west to the area which they now occupy.

It is interesting to note that Delafosse, who situates the various migrations and mixtures of the populations on the eastern bank of the Volta in this area at the time of the 17th century, dismisses the migration of the Dagaaba onto the other side of the river as a result of a direct Dagomba invasion. He calls it the result of a *Ghanaian*[15] migration which as in fact, result of the Dagomba conquests at the time. However, according to him, the actual territorial occupation of the Dagaaba/Dagara was complete only by the beginning of the 19th century.[16]

3. *The Sociological Group Designated "Dagaaba/ Dagara"*

So far, we have continually used alternatively the 'Dagaaba/Dagara' to designate the people with whom we are here concerned. At this point of our gradually deepening insight into them, it will certainly be helpful to say a word in regard to this designation. It will further help define the area of our research undertaken here. At the same time, it will also dismiss, if not entirely, at least, in part the ambiguities that could arise from the use of the term itself, especially when found in other contexts or areas of co-related studies.

In his book entitled "The Social Organisation of the LoWiili," Jack Goody writes: "I went to West Africa looking for a tribe called the 'Lobi' … In fact I never found a group of people who replied to my question, 'We are Lobi'".[17] It took him some time to realise, as he later asserted, that although the terms "Lobi" and its derivatives are well known in the area in question, it is really difficult to meet someone who will say: "I am a Loba".[18] As Goody subsequently explains, the difficulty in finding someone who would say "I am a Loba" comes from the differences in the dialects spoken by the people. The term among the people themselves is always used in reference to the same people, but living in the next settlement and thus other than the speaker himself. Goody gradually came to understand that 'Lo-' and 'Dagaa-' are a pair of words used throughout the area by categories of people to refer to their neighbours and occasionally to themselves.[19]

This led him to the conclusion that there are no tribal names, and that there are no tribes in the accepted sense of the word. The scattered settlements are one 'People' with minor differences in linguistic expressions which Goody reckons vary even less than the English dialects spoken within the British Isles. These differences, nevertheless, increase as one goes from east to west.[20] The variants 'Dagaa' and 'Lo' used to describe reciprocally the south-east settlers and the north-west settlers reciprocally are clear examples of the use of the terms in the sense described above. In the settlements in the upper north-west corner of Ghana, and the adjacent area in the Republic of Burkina Faso, it is there that the people call themselves Degara or Dagara, but are called 'Lobr' by the settlements south-east of them.[21]

In any case, it would be a futile effort and unrealistic to try to dismiss all differences, be they linguistic or otherwise, among the people. The comparative anthropologist and the linguist in the evaluation of their ethnographical material may search precisely for the differences that exist between the individual settlements of such a people scattered in agricultural communities. However, this investigation which has its own defined hypothesis, bases itself on the whatever scanty ethnological studies and cultural anthropological findings already available, and assumes the Dagara as a "people," with a common history, institutions and a moral tradition. It is in this circumspection that the terms "Dagaaba/Dagara"[22] are simultaneously employed here.

It is not just a shelving of the discussion that can actually arise and be pursued in regards to the use of the designation as such; nor is it an ignorance of the actual existence of such discussions; but they are simply not the objective of this study, and we therefore prefer to leave them for other studies, or to the expertise of the linguists and the social anthropologists. Here our hypothesis of research is well served if we have succeeded in establishing the Dagara ethnologically as a "People," with their common history, institutions, beliefs and moral traditions; and who in their existential conditions have been looking for security from all the uncertainties of life which surround them. In a few words, liberation from the human conditions of misery in which they find themselves like all other human beings; a SALVATION from an otherwise DOOMED DESTINY. This is what we hope to have done in the last paragraphs above; and shall now go on to study how they endeavour to achieve this salvation, and obtain in COMMON this salvation which is not a task of the individual, but in SOLIDARITY with other Dagara.

Clan, Totems and the Building of Solidarity

The Clan

In African tradition, the more widely important re-groupment of people within which solidarity already passes from a mere conceptual status to an effectively operative level is "the clan". In the Ghanaian social system, the clan can be conceived paternally – "The Patriclan," or maternally – "The Matriclan". Every person thus belongs to two clans simultaneously.[23] In the Dagara Society, however, the Patri-clan (Yiiru)[24] unlike in some of the other tribes, even in Ghana,[25] is considered the more important of the two, since the "nuclear family," as we shall point out later, is patrilineal, and marriage is "viro-loco". Thus, what is usually considered "the Clan" among the Dagara is any of the groups of the tribe (the people) whose members are said to descend from the **same male line**.

For the lay observer, the difference between the Patriclan and what we shall later call "*the extended family*" is not always easy to make. Though the '*extended family*' is always part of the 'clan,' this latter – the clan – is not limited just to one *extended family*. The extended family, like the *clan*, enlarges and perpetuates by descent on the father's side, (although immediate kin on one's mother's side can be countered, in some way, among members of an individual's 'extended family'). So, the *extended family* takes the form of a "*patrilineage*" (Doru); and as long as individuals can trace their generations back to a common definite male ancestor, they form what is called the **extended family**. However, the living members of a lineage are not usually always capable of tracing their ancestral line definitely back to beyond five generations; for at this point the links are quite often already lost, and this is especially the case when part of the people have migrated to some other place, and have not been able to keep connections with the original family, or people.

But despite this inability to keep the lineage linked up to a great common ancestor beyond five or even less generations, several lineages may still claim a common ancestral heritage from which they are all supposed to have descended.[26] They thus consider themselves as descendants, coming from the same '*patriarch;*' and so, are said to belong to the same CLAN, calling each other brothers, despite the fact that the continuation of the ancestral line linking them all back to this common **patriarch** is not, nor can be, established with a "scientific certitude".

How the Clan members can come to recognise each other as belonging to that source of their common brotherhood on the basis of an unknown ancestor; how the different lineages come to identify themselves as being of one and the same clan is, nevertheless left to chance. It is not just by an arbitrary decision that two individuals call themselves brothers in that profound sense, nor that two lineages just decide that they are linked. There must be something profound to explain that the link is real and has a demonstrable basis. J. Goody gives one of these demonstrable explanations which may, in fact, be the only aspect of the more global and the same explanation. In his study of The Organisation of the LoWiili he affirms: "The patrilineal descent of the clan members is recognised not by specific genealogical ties but through a name and prohibition held in common".[27] Here we shall consider an element which, in our view, plays a rather very important role in the overall explanation.

The Totem and Its Role in Solidarity Building

Evaluating the notion of totemism in regard to Ghanaian culture in his book, subtitled: *Some Aspects of Ghanaian Culture*, Peter Sarpong writes:

Totemism is probably one of the most difficult religious phenomena to explain intelligently. No hypothesis is likely to serve adequately as an explanation of all the institutions which have been labelled totemism as these institutions are very varied. In fact, there appears to be no single criterion by which totemism might be defined that is not lacking in what is called totemism in some society. The beliefs and practices which are called totemism fall under the borderline between the notion of power in objects, or magic, and the idea of a personalized spirit in things or religion.[28]

This nuanced description of totemism by Sarpong which admits that "no hypothesis is likely to serve adequately as an explanation of all the institutions which have been labelled totemism," gives support by that fact to the hypothesis that we shall encounter here in our explanation of clanic totemism.

The institution of clannism, or still better, the regroupment of a people into clans, is surely one of those realities which draws its explanation mostly from totemism. It is not always the totemic object which is at the origin and constitutes the clan as some ethnographic material suggest. Among most clans in Ghana, where there is always a totem as the point of unity of all the members of the clan, the clan is held together and regards itself as being one, and the individuals responsible for one another and for the well-being of the clan because of the belief that they have a common ancestor who, though not the totem himself, is nevertheless the origin of this continual recognition of the unity of his clan members through the totem.

In his study of the West Indies societies, Sir James G. Frazer came forward with the proposition that clanic grouping is the creation of totemism. He asserts that totemism is characterised by the belief in a kinship relationship between a group of people and a species, either of animals, of vegetables, or a class of objects or even another category of human beings. This belief, he goes on to say, expresses itself through negative rites – taboos; and also, positive rites – ceremonies of initiation; and by matrimonial regulations – example: exogamy.[29]

As the inadequacy of any given hypothesis to explain all institutions of totemism satisfactorily is already remarked by

P. Sarpong, the conclusion which Frazer arrives at in the case of the West Indies seems to be inadequate in explaining totemism among the Dagara. This criterion of kinship relationship appears to be unnecessary for explaining the true origin of what is labelled totemism among the Dagara. The Dagara does not attach himself to totemic religion as Frazer seems to suggest in the case of the West Indies. Although people may come to be recognised as belonging to the same clan by the fact that they observe the same taboo, practise the same rites of initiation, and even belong to the same exogamous group, it is not all this that has originally constituted them into a clanic unity.

Chronologically speaking, all this is perceptible only because of an already existing ground of unity in origin, of which all these practices are only the external manifestations. For the Dagara, the object of the taboo as described by Frazer is not considered as the ancestor of the clan. The characteristics of the Dagara Clanic Groups presuppose the existence of the clan already duly constituted and in place; and the common belief, together with the other practices only serve to point out that this group or that group or people has a common origin at one point of time in their existence and its history although, due once more to the lack of written traditions, it is difficult to establish this fact with modern scientific certitude.

The practices characterising a clan have therefore come about in that, originally, an ancestor finding himself in some difficult circumstances in which he needed some rescue, salvation, some redemption, was fortuitously helped in one way or other by some animal or some creature.[30] For this unsolicited and unexpected deliverance, a redemption from his difficulty which, in other terms may be called "a miraculous" deliverance, the ancestor decided, for gratuitous recognition of such a miraculous deliverance, that this animal or this particular type of creature would be considered "sacred" to him and to all his progeny after him.

So, in remembrance of the deliverance of their ancestor by this being, and in obedience to the ordinance of their ancestor, who was thus rescued, together with his entire lineage to come after him, all the members coming from the various nuclear and extended families coming from him are obliged always to regard and treat this animal or creature whatsoever with respect and gratitude. Thus, they would always avoid as much as possible to do any harm to it. They would in no circumstance whatsoever eat its meat – if that is an animal. It is a TOTEM to them and so, has become '*sacred*' and, in this way, merits their deep reverence.

This animal or totemic object is not regarded as ancestor of the clan; for, the Dagara if asked about his relationship to such an object or animal will say: "This is the animal or object, which SAVED MY ANCESTOR'S LIFE, AND SO, MY OWN when my ancestor's life was in peril. This act of saving my ancestor is the reason why my ancestor has made it a TABOO, for himself, and for us his '*Yirdem,*' descendants". This hypothesis of considering the **totem** as **sacred** or **object of ritual attitude** is demonstrated by Radcliff-Brown in his attempt to define **totemism**,[31] and it is echoed by Sarpong who, through his personal ethnographic experience, supported by Fortes and Beattie, holds that people usually adapt an attitude of reverence towards their totems.[32] As Radcliff-Brown affirms in his study of the institution of taboos, especially among the Aborigines of Australia, "It is clear that the very diverse forms of totemism that exist all over the world must have had very diverse origins".[33] Carrying his point further, Radcliff-Brown shows his disagreement with Emile Durkheim's theory that the totem is sacred to the members of the group to which it is the totem. In his own attempt to explain he reformulates Durkheim's theory of totemism, and says:

> A social group such as a clan only possesses SOLIDARITY and permanence if it is the object of sentiments of attachment in the minds of its members. For such sentiments to be maintained in existence they must be given occasional COLLECTIVE EXPRESSION. By a law that can be, I think, readily verified, all regular collective expressions of social sentiments tend to take a ritual form. And in ritual, again by a necessary law, some more or less CONCRETE OBJECT is required which can act as the representative of the group. So, it is normal procedure that the sentiment of attachment to a group should be expressed in some formalised collective behaviour having reference to an object that represents the group.34

This may surely be regarded as a general hypothesis which can have its objections, as we shall point out later. But it is one which does not contradict, if not in fact, even supportive of the practice found in clanic institutions in Ghana, in general, and in that of the Dagara, in particular.

For the Dagara, therefore, clannism can be seen as the immediate larger extension of the "family" which is the privileged place of solidarity and co-responsibility of all, as we shall see in another chapter ahead. Taboos and other uniform practices within the clan are, as can be said, accidental means by which one can assert with a moral certitude that such a group or people come from a common ancestor. The fact that the clan, (Patriclan) falls under the same nomenclature, "Yir," as the 'extended family' (Patrilineage), gives support to this evidence. The taboo injunctions inherent in the clan therefore tell or remind the members of their common ancestral origin.

Although they may not be able to trace their lineages definitively back in reality to this one common ancestor, the fact that members who claim that they are of the same lineage do observe the same injunctions in connection with to the same totemic being which is said to have saved their ancestor is enough testimony for them that it must have been the same person; and so, the same ancestor. Hence it must have been the same person as ancestor who enjoined on them all the same ordinances of allegiance and gratitude towards the same totem. This reality that they belong together is therefore arrived at as a moral certitude. And so is sufficient to impose on them a common responsibility in many and varied areas of their daily activities, including well-being in life itself.

The importance of the clan institution among the Dagara, just as that of the family, cannot never be over-emphasised. Because the role that it plays is the very basic condition and constituent of solidarity, and consequently, is the reason for the sense of mutual co-responsibility in every aspect the life of the members of the clan. The sense of belonging together binds the clan's members together and makes every individual member see the destiny each of the other members as his own destiny, and vice-versa.

In discussing the clan and totemism, and the role these play at the origin of the building of the ties of common belonging and solidarity itself, the central place of the ancestor stands out most conspicuously. So, the investigation concerning our hypothesis now intends to devote the next paragraphs to this basic role accorded to the common ancestor as the ***Originator*** of the clan and the principal author of the totem, and hence the cornerstone of the institution of solidarity that binds together and ordains the members of the clan, tribe, and people in their DESTINY.

The Ancestor:
Norm of Morality and Mainstay of Solidarity

Introduction

Under the caption: "God in the Ancestor World," G.E. Kpiebaya asserts that of the great varieties of socio-religious activities that exist among the different tribes of Africa, there is one that seems to be common to all, namely: reverence for their dead. He goes on to underline the fact that though similar practices of reverence to the dead are found in all human societies, they go by other names, while the African *veneration* of his dead has been branded "Ancestral Worship".[35] Peter Sarpong who also observes the universality of this socio-religious conception, asserts that the belief in the spirits of the dead and their influence over the living is found among all peoples.[36] This leads him to conclude that belief in ancestors and their veneration is not peculiar to any age, religion or society, and that the difference only lies in the terminology used to express what is the same idea. So, he writes:

> When Christians call their dead, *saints* and refer to those of pagans as *ancestor*, they are not expressing different ideas. Both words express ideas about people who once belonged to their religious group, and are now dead, and are supposed to be in a position of influence over the living.[37]

Thus, Sarpong refuses to accept that reverence paid to the African dead in general, and this same reverence as it is practised in Ghana in particular, is "ancestral worship". He therefore prefers, and rightly so, the expression "ancestor veneration".[38] Who exactly is the "ancestor," then, that he would so deserve to be worshipped or venerated?

The Ancestor

It must be made clear from the outset that it is not everybody and anybody who can be considered an ancestor after death. Certain conditions must be verified in the life of someone who has died before one can be considered to have "gone to the land of the ancestors," and can so be recognised as an *ancestor* himself. It should also be clear by now that ancestors are considered ancestors, not just in general and for everybody, but are considered so by the particular lineage, i.e. patrilineage, to whom they belonged during their life time. They are considered ancestors of the clan, or tribe (People).

Among the Dagara, a prerequisite condition is that one must have had children; male children in particular, as the actual congregation of the ancestral cult is limited to the patrilineage. This means that the person who would be recognised as ancestor must have been a married man or woman. Hence a person who dies at an old age, but without issue, or has left behind only female children, cannot have an ancestral shrine erected to his or her honour.[39] A second condition is that he or she must have died a good death. If he or she dies a "kuufaa," that is, "evil death," he or she will not even have a complete burial rite for him or her, which complete burial rite is, in fact, only the first step, but a necessary one, towards the as-it-were "canonisation" of the deceased as ancestor.[40] Thus a tragic death, death through unclean diseases for example, leprosy, excludes the diseased from any ancestral investiture. Murderers, sorcerers, in fact, all those who will not be considered as having lived a morally edifying life in their respective communities, cannot be "canonized" as ancestors.[41]

The conditions that must be realised together before someone can be invested and declared an ancestor may therefore be summed up as follows: i) It must be someone who lived to adulthood,[42] since offspring, particularly male ones, are necessary for the erection of the shrine. ii) The person must have been already dead, as no living person can be venerated as an ancestor. iii) and thirdly, the cause of death must have been a 'natural' one.

In the light of the above reflection on the ancestor, many questions could be raised, and different pistes of co-related investigations undertaken at this point. This opens up to us, for example, the field of Ghanaian, or, more precisely, Dagaran, eschatology, indeed, a field which is central to most African, if not all African morality and the theology accompanying it. Because, the ancestor who is thus venerated is not only the relaying point of all his descendants whom he or she continues to influence morally and otherwise in their daily lives, but is also the contact point through which the deceased's living members can be said to have a true and real relation with the "World of the Ancestors," and thus, ultimately with the "Supreme Being" self, (Naangmen), which term translated into western-concept, is "God".

The intercessory role of the ancestors, the type of "veneration" that they receive, and other relational issues with them, could all be subjects of investigation, each in its own right. [43] However, our own objective here is a modest one: it seeks only to verify our hypothesis that the ancestor is the centre of unity of the family, the clan and the tribe; and that he is the actual living norm of morality for his clansmen.

The Ancestor as Centre of Unity, Solidarity and the Actual Norm of Morality

Our study on the clan and totemism led us to discover how the ancestor of the clan, or for that matter, of a tribe (people), becomes the point of convergence of all his clan members and of the several lineages that make up the clan.[44] He is considered as someone who held a responsible place among his people and therefore remains with them even after his death, and is continually involved in matters in their midst – perpetuated through the ritual veneration – as the bond of union among them all as they observe in common the various injunctions he left them. Through the shrines of veneration in his honour, and ultimately through the ancestor self, sacrifice is offered to the "Supreme Being".[45] Quoting Meyer Fortes, Sarpong writes:

> The ancestor cult, the supreme sanction of *kinship ties*, is a great establishing force counteracting the centrifugal tendencies inherent in the lineage system. However widely the lineage may be dispersed, its members can never escape the mystical jurisdiction of their founding ancestor.[46]

The central place thus accorded to the ancestor in all aspects of life makes him or her invariably the force behind the solidarity inherent in the clan. And at the same time, the norm of their moral acts. We have earlier remarked how the combat against the hazards of nature is thought of in terms beyond the individual and beyond purely material levels.[47] The solidarity action for survival and eventual "salvation" can only bear its fruits, with security and prosperity guaranteed, if every member of the clan or of the group in question has been upright before the eyes of the ancestor who continues to live among his people after the material death. As we shall have occasion to remark later, a deliberate, and even in some cases, non-deliberate infidelity to an ancestor can bring calamity to oneself and the clan.

The fact, therefore, that the ancestor is the centre of unity of his "descendants" imposes on each one, and all those who claim this descendance from him a "brotherhood tie". This "brotherhood tie" binds them together in solidarity, and makes them share a common destiny so that they become responsible for, and to, one another in the achievement of this common destiny. As Sarpong sums up this common tie of solidarity imposed on the members of the clan by the ancestor:

> Members of one clan are held to be related to one another and so, are bound together by a common tie. The tie is the belief that all members of the clan descend from one ancestor or ancestress. Hence members of one clan are held to be relatives – brothers, sisters, mothers, fathers, etc.[48]

This relationship and nomenclature are irrespective of time and space,[49] and can therefore be said to have a 'transcendental value,' that is neither limited to a particular generation, nor to a particular historical era, nor material space.

Individual Morality and the Solidarity Tie

Evaluating the Individual and his Responsibility

The kinship ties supremely sanctioned by the unique place given to the ancestor and the great stabilizing force that he is, counteracting all centrifugal tendencies within the clan system, would seem to suggest that the individual in such a system is left without identity nor any powers of self-determination; and that he is lost in a group in which any attempts at self-assertion would be futile and repressed by the mechanism inherent in the system itself.

It may be true that the forceful presentation of clanic solidarity would make one see this as the weak point of a system that would tend to forget, or have very little place for individual autonomy and the individual as such. However, one would think that such a view would be completely incorrect and, in fact, manifest a certain ignorance of the internal mechanism of the system that induces such ties of solidarity among members of the group. At best, one could say that the role of the individual seen through such a spectrum, would be a judgement of the individual within the background of a social set-up foreign to the one with which we are here concerned.

If 'individual' self-assertion would be conceived only in terms of the politico-economic theories of INDIVIDUALISM AND LIBERALISM which, in Europe, reached its culminating point in the 19th century, then there would perhaps be some truth in asserting that such a clanic system would leave the individual without self-identity, personal initiative and any self-determination. But such an interpretation of the 'ethnographic present,' which we have been investigating, would be an anticlimactic conclusion to arrive at.

In our attempt to put into clear perspective the origins of the Dagara Solidarity, much more than intended for our objective might have been said on the nature of the unity within the clan or tribe, and the ties of solidarity obtained among members of the particular group. But there is nothing that can be gainsaid; for indeed, on the contrary, there is much more that could be delved into on the subject than the limits of our study here have permitted. But after all is said, the position of the individual person on the other hand, together with the peculiarity of his acts in this bond of solidarity which he is bound to and is responsible before the other members, though not so complicated, seems to remain ambiguous and so, demands some clarification.

In this attempt to shed some light on this seemingly ambiguous position in which the individual is placed in this group of solidarity, and to see how far 'individual' his acts can really be said to be, we shall, in a first reflection, examine in brief the concept of evil[50] in his society, then subsequently the repercussion of the individual's acts. This should permit us to see the proper relation of the individual to his group of belonging, and what influence his acts can actually have in the realm of the transcendent.

Evil: Sin in Dagara "Theology"

1. *The Dagara Concept of Evil*

Just as among all people – primitive or developed – evil, and ultimately sin, is not something entirely foreign to the Dagara though. On the contrary, evil is a daily reality with which the ordinary Dagara has to contend. It is not just an idea which he has to sit down and make a theory upon; it is a daily experience to which he has to try at every turn to find an answer or explanation. As we have remarked earlier, the threats to life and the insecurity cannot be seen in any light other than as an evil from which he has to seek protection, and to liberate himself and others of his group. For the genuine Dagara, what may be called in other systems of thought – particularly scholastic – 'physical evil,' cannot be seen in isolation of the moral one which is indeed its cause. That is precisely the reason why, in the Dagara thought, the battle against these apparently physical evils cannot just be fought on the physical level alone. The physical evil that suffers, for example, being bitten by a venomous snake while working on the farm, will be seen not just as a physical mishap, or even a coincidence in itself; but will be considered the result of and only an indication of a moral evil that "must have been committed".

So, if we would want to attempt a definition of what "evil" is for the Dagara, we will have to start by way of the "cause," and therefore say that the physical evil which is observable, such as physical pain, and also spiritual anguish suffered, is the result, or rather the observable manifestation of an infraction in the moral order; that is to say, the transgression of some moral injunction imposed by one of the culprit's ancestors, and for which reason the ancestors refuse to give their effective protection and care.[51] Sarpong brings some light to our attempt at defining "evil" when he writes:

> Ghanaians do not consider the spirits of the dead to be gods, although in venerating them they may easily give the impression that the ancestors are thought to be in possession of absolute power which is autocratic and is used without reference to God. Ancestors are most powerful. They may be benevolent towards the living; they may be malevolent. In strict justice, they deal with people according to their deserves. Their concern is especially for the keeping of the law which custom has established.[52]

We have also made reference, in a footnote above, to G.E. Kpiebaya who, in one of his illuminating paragraphs he calls "Conclusions," agrees that since evil and misfortunes are caused by fellow humans or angered spirits, and God does nothing about it, it is to these sources of the evil that recourse must be had, to solve the problems of the evil.[53]

So, while other systems of thought, particularly classical Christian thought as we shall point out, in their notion of evil distinguish neatly between ***physical evil:*** the absence of some perfection required by the nature of a being or of an act, and ***moral evil***: a free shortcoming in man's proper perfection which is love in all its dimensions,54 ***physical*** and ***moral evils*** are seen by the Dagara as ***one single process***; the physical being the effect, or best still, the *incarnation* of the *moral evil*.

Analogies are not always the best for illustrating one's point of view, and they are, indeed, the last that one would like to make use of here. This, for several reasons. But here, for the reason that in too many a number of studies where comparisons are used, more often than less, the investigator's purpose is prejudicial. It is either to confirm his hypothesis of the nefariousness of the "Weltanschauung" of the particular people he or she is studying, and hence to show their inferiority in relation to his/her own or others;' or if his/her study is one of a religion towards which he/she is sympathetic, let us say Christianity, he or she simply searches for traits and elements that would permit him or her to affirm his foregone conclusion; for example, that the Christian message does not have anything new, or at least, spectacular to offer the particular culture and tradition into which the investigation is being made.55

Nevertheless, one cannot fail to remark how closely the Dagara concept of evil approaches in some way the notion that the Old Testament (O.T.) writers had of the moral evil as described by Robert Koch in the sense of 'sin,'56 as we shall see in an instant. The Dagara do not have an abstract notion of evil. They see in what we may call physical evil, the observable demonstration of some moral evil in the contingencies of their existential situation; and so, for them, moral evil and physical evil may be best distinguished as "cause and effect" respectively.

2. *Evil in Christian Theology*

While for the Dagara moral evil and physical evil are considered as a single reality, and best distinguished as "cause and effect," today, Christian theology makes a neat difference between what is simply called '***evil,***' and what is termed '***sin***'. Every sin, for instance, is evil; but not every evil is necessarily considered as a sin. The distinction between the two realities expressed by the two terms became most absolute and clear in the 13th century with Saint Thomas Aquinas who did not only uphold the neat distinction between *evil* and *sin*,[57] but also distinguished between various types of evils.[58]

Asserting that sin is evil, but that there is other evil beside sin, Piet Schoonenberg, using the terminology of scholastic philosophy, employs the terms "moral evil" ***(malum morale)***, and "physical evil".[59] The difference between the two, he says, does not consist only in their origins, but also in their **direction**. Whereas physical evil is the absence of some perfection required by the nature of a being or of an activity, "moral evil is a free shortcoming in a man's proper perfection which is love in all its dimensions".[60] Still more practical for us, he further makes more precise his distinction between the two by repeating the saying of Saint Anselm that sin possesses some kind of infinity because it offends ***Infinite God*** and robs Him of His honour; and that if one wishes to attribute some infinity to sin, it might be more solidly based upon the fact that man refuses his fulfilment in loving communion with an Infinite God.[61] From this, we can conclude that we speak of 'sin' most especially and perhaps only when 'moral evil' is in some way directed against God.

This is, in fact, the true sense of 'moral evil,' 'sin,' expressed by the so many and varied terms in the O.T., where most of the time they express in one way or another the non-observance of the Alliance which Israel the Chosen People entered into with Yahweh their God. Bernhard Häring studying sin, the 'moral evil,' in his book: *Faith and Morality in a Secular Age*,[62] uses Holy Scripture to bring out in a very concrete way, how this moral evil consists precisely in the fact that it is directed against God. Sin in its 'direction' becomes IDOLATORY; a fundamental attitude in man by which he, in the morality of his acts, alienates himself from God his creator, and searches for his ultimate end outside of God,[63] which, as Schoonenberg says, is love in all its dimensions. Describing sin, the moral evil in this secular age in terms of the 'Finite' and the 'Infinite,' Häring writes:

> When man no longer wholeheartedly entrusts himself to Go in an adoring spirit, he is involved in setting up and using the world as an idol. He pairs terrestrial realities and earthly values as absolutes before which and for which he will sacrifice his true self and his neighbour. The man who no longer adores God loses authentic sense and value of things including his own being; he becomes enslaved by lust, by his own realisations and earthly structures.[64]

The logical conclusion that can be deduced from all this is that 'moral evil' or 'sin' has indeed God as its object; and that is precisely why secularism and atheism for Häring, are "The Sin," and so we can say, "The Moral Evil" par excellence,[65] since they are directed against the Infinite.

So, while 'physical evil' remains only the lack of some good required by the nature of a being, hence directed towards the being itself as 'finite,' 'moral evil' is a voluntarily willed absence of some good – man's proper perfection – directed towards another being, 'The Infinite Being,' God. The distinction between 'moral evil' and 'physical evil' in this case would therefore be based on the "finitude" or "infinitude" of the being affected by this privation or lack of the good due to it.

However, this clear scholastic distinction between physical evil and moral evil does not seem to have been made in the O.T. In fact, Schoonenberg expresses the opinion that until quite recently, the theologian might have considered a deeper study of the relation existing between the two conceptions only as a philosophical theme that did not provide any direct insights or problems to his own specialty.[66] The fact of the absence of this clear distinction between physical and moral evil in the O.T. seems, in our view, to be corroborated by the semantic study made by R. Koch on the terms used to designate "SIN" in the O.T.[67] Commenting on the many and varied terms used in the O.T. to designate what Christian Theology now calls '*sin,*' he says:

> "This variety itself of the terms used enables us to ascertain that the O.T. authors did not have a completely elaborate theory or a systematic notion of sin, and thus had not given it a clear and distinct definition." And he goes on to explain: "As genuine Semites, they did not reflect on the essence of sin, but rather demonstrated concretely its malice and its dimensions throughout their millenary history as the Elected People".[68]

To bring his hypothesis completely home, Koch puts the limits to the semantic part of his investigation saying: "The Hebrew terms that we shall be analysing do not express as abstract notion of sin, or a notional, conceptualistic biblical morals, but they rather describe concrete situations in the framework of the ALLIANCE."[69]

In speaking about the Dagara concept of evil, we have been rather very sparing with our use of the term "sin". In the classical and scholastic discussion of evil, moral evil is equated with sin; for, it is seen as a free shortcoming in man's proper perfection which is love in all its dimensions. And in this capacity, it possesses some kind of infinity, because it offends God who is infinite, and so, robs Him of His honour.[70] From this, one goes to the assertion that if one wishes to attribute some infinite nature to sin, it might be more solidly based on the fact that man refuses his fulfilment of loving communion with an INFINITE GOD. In the O.T. discussion on sin, which describes rather concrete situations, these same concrete situations are nevertheless described in relation to, and within the framework of the ALLIANCE.[71] Thus in the ultimate analysis, 'moral evil,' 'sin' in both Christian Theology and the O.T. writings on sin, is seen in man's actions in relation to God as their "terminus ad quem". It is God the Infinite, Yahweh who has chosen for Himself a People, that is attained by man's moral acts.

This is where the Dagara notion of "sin" differs from both the Christian theological notion of sin as we have it, and also the O.T. concept of sin, at least, after the Alliance concluded with Yahweh, the God of Israel. While in both Christian theology and in the O.T. notion of sin, the morality of the act is considered in its relation to God; that is to say, either in "setting up and using the world as an idol"[72] and hence "a free shortcoming in his proper perfection which is love in all its dimensions,"[73] or a failure to the Alliance into which he has entered with God; the Dagara considers the moral evil, 'sin,' as not attaining the All Powerful God (Naangmen), but as an evil which attains directly one or the other of the ancestors.[74] They are the 'spirits' which are angered by man's act, and therefore are the ones to be appeased, and not God. Hence the fundamental difference lies in the *terminus ad quem*, the **direction** of the moral act. In the light of this fundamental difference, we can therefore come to the logical conclusion that, in "Dagara theology," sin is a transgression of one injunction or other imposed by the ancestors. The physical evil that may be experienced becomes a revelation of the moral evil committed, and thus serves to warn the guilty person or community to do expiation for the wrong done. It is this expiation which is done through ritual imploration of the ancestor or ancestors concerned.

But as no ancestor is ancestor to only an individual, but is centre of a whole system of 'nerves,' we shall now examine briefly in our next paragraphs the repercussions that the individual's moral acts can have in this network of 'nerves' of which he is a part.

The Repercussions of the Individual's Moral Acts: An Interpretation

Within the Dagara clanic system, the place of each member of the group, and hence of the individual person, is defined we may say even at birth. Thus, for example, the eldest son in the 'nuclear family,' is invariably the *"suosob,"* i.e., the one having the priestly powers to perform sacrificial rites. He will take up the responsibility of offering sacrifices in the family, in the absence or incapacity of the "pater-familias".[25] Also, an 'uncle' or 'grandfather' may be someone who is so by birth. He may even be 40 years younger than the one for whom he is 'uncle' or 'grandfather'. And so, according to tradition, must be regarded as such, and be given his due place that the system has accorded him in all customary affairs. Nobody is without his or her defined place accorded him or her by the system, through birth, be it in the extended family, lineage or the clan. Hence the responsibilities which go with the position that the individual occupies in the interior of the clanic grouping are his or her own, and no one else can assume them as long as he or she is available and not otherwise relieved of them in accordance with the system and the tradition.

So, it would be false to assume that in virtue of the ties that bind all members of a group together in such a solidary bond and manner, the individual would not have any personal responsibility, nor be held responsible as an individual for his actions. This again, will be using a yardstick of measurement which makes abstraction of and does not consider seriously the working of the rest of the system which has its auto-regulatory mechanism.

However, affirming the inalienability of the place of the individual person and the role that he has within the group, does not in any way enfeeble, nor even jeopardise the working of the solidarity machine, which is the mainstay of the system and of the group (society). In fact, the contrary would rather be the reality; for, in virtue of this type of working of the solidarity machine, the act of the individual, even performed in his capacity as individual, never fails to affect, either immediately or remotely, the other members of his group of belonging.

Writing on taboos and sin in Africa, Peter Sarpong states that the 'adverse consequences' of breaking a taboo may fall on the whole society both 'mystically' and 'physically'. He illustrates the reality of his assertion with an example of how one fool who commits fornication with a girl under the age of puberty can, by such an act (which is a taboo), brings famine upon an entire community, unless the community cleanses itself ritually of the abomination.[76]

We are not doing any semantic study here; but we think it justifiable to assume that what Sarpong refers to above by the use of the phrase and terms: 'adverse consequences,' and 'mystical' and 'physical' in this particular context of taboos, is what we have systematically referred to in previous paragraphs with the terms 'evil' and 'moral,' and the phrases 'physical evil' and 'moral evil,' respectively. In this respect, we shall do well to remember that by definition, taboo is a ritual avoidance or ritual prohibition: hence of a 'supernatural order'.[77] Again, as Sarpong sees it in the case of the one fool who commits the fornication with the girl under the age of puberty, "the spirits (the ancestors, in accordance with the ties within the clan system) are punishing the community for the crime of an individual".[78]

In this perspective, the repercussions of the act of a single individual on the entire group of which he is a member is evident and beyond any doubt. The physical evil, bodily suffering or material loss that a member endures, is caused by a moral evil: an infringement of an ancestral prohibition, or injunction broken by another member of the group, and for which reason this other member becomes victim and suffers. This is from the logical fact that the injured ancestor of the clan or group holds all members of his clan or group solidarily responsible for the wrong done, and may therefore choose any member of the solidarity group to manifest his anger or displeasure, and thus demand reparation for the wrong done. Goody expresses communal responsibility in the solidarity of the clan in this respect when he writes: "The death of any clansman concerns all the other members for it weakens the descent group as a whole." He supports this with the following eye-witness report:

The force of this attitude is vividly expressed in listening to the mourning songs to the *dagaa-xylophone* (*dagagyil*) during the three days of the burial ceremony. I have seen tears well up to the eyes of youth and elders when the singer cries that 'the clan has come to an end as all its members are dying one by one'.[79]

The study which Kpiebaya made on 'God in Divination or Soothsaying' among the Dagara is also quite illuminating for our present area of study.[80] Investigating the practice of divination among the Dagara (he uses the variant "Dagaaba"), he points out the reason why they practise divination, or soothsaying as it is sometimes called. It is precisely to find out the cause of an event – evil or good – and the connection between it and its involvement of people. He therefore subsequently defines divination among the Dagara as, "The technique by which can be known the hidden meanings or causes of events that happen in the lives of people".[81] Thus the head of the family, for example, would consult a diviner if ever something wrong, some physical evil, would present itself in the family. This can be sickness of one member of the family; an unexpected death in particular in the family; a miscarriage suffered by one of the 'wives' of the family; the failure of the crops this year, etc.

The purpose of the divination will therefore be to find out the underlying reason, the moral evil, which is the cause of this misfortune or even calamity, this physical evil which now affects directly a particular member, hence the whole group indirectly, as in the case of sickness; or which affects the whole group, family, or clan directly, as in the case of famine or other social evils. The victim of the physical evil suffered may even be completely innocent of the moral evil act, the result of which he is now the victim. The divination may show that he is suffering, not for any moral evil committed by himself, but by someone else of the group, family or clan, as the case may be, and for which he is the victim.

In his analysis, Kpiebaya did not bring out the implication of the results of the divination on the level of the group solidarity, as that was obviously not the main hypothesis he wanted to verify in his investigation. Nevertheless, this point comes out of itself at the conclusion of his dissertation of the 'Divining Séance' in which someone went to consult the diviner about a sick person in his family. The ancestors of the client were not pleased with the way the family's commonly own cattle were being misused by the one who had the responsibility of looking after them for the interest of the whole family. They (the ancestors) wanted him to stop his selfish behaviour. It was to remind him of this irresponsible behaviour that the ancestors allowed illness to come into the house. As a sign that the guilty one has recognised his faults and was ready to put an end to all the morally evil practices that were angering the ancestors, he had to make the appropriate sacrifices indicated by the ancestors themselves through the diviner.[82]

In all this, the repercussion of the individual's moral acts on the rest of his or her group of belonging becomes evident. In his comment after describing the ritual of divination, Kpiebaya writes: "Divination gives us a deep insight into the ethics of the Dagaaba. In other words, it helps us to know what the people consider morally bad". And he counts among the morally bad actions for the Dagara any action which "offends the family or the community, in other words, traditions". Such offences he says, are against the ancestors, since they are the custodians of the welfare of the family.[83] In any case, the fact that the Supreme Being is considered paradoxically so far away and aloof from human affairs, and so leaves the affairs of man to His intermediaries among whom are the ancestors, can be taken as a general argument why the Dagara does not consider that his moral acts would attain God, at least, directly.[84]

Taking the practice of divination as an instance, one can say that it does not only give a deep insight Dagara ethics, but reveals also the extent of the individual moral actions and responsibility. The moral evil committed by a member of a group of solidarity is revealed through divination to affect not only the guilty party, but all the other members as well. All become, as we can say, co-responsible and solidary in the action of the one, even if unconsciously. So, in this respect, the ties of solidarity cannot be more evident and urgent than this.

The aspect we have chosen with which to illustrate the value of solidarity among the Dagara can correctly be said to be a negative one. Schoonenberg may call it "the sin of the community, ultimately the sin of the world;"[85] or what B. Häring may term "solidarity in perdition".[86] However, this choice made it possible and easier for us, I believe, to interpret as clearly as possible the meaning and the implications of solidarity among the Dagara. This should allow the more positive and surely desirable value of solidarity to come out with greater clarity when we come to consider how the value of Dagara solidarity should be an asset in the context of Christian Salvation, and hence lead to "SOLIDARITY IN SALVATION," or to a "SOLIDARITY OF SALVATION".

But before we come to this hopeful aspect of our investigations, however, we shall attempt to make a short appreciation of solidarity. This appreciation should lead us to a more profound examination of solidarity as a true cultural value in the Ghanaian society in general, and in the Dagara social system in particular.

Co-Responsibility in Solidarity,
The Law of Society: Appreciation

Our investigation into African or Ghanaian solidarity in general, and Dagara solidarity in particular, and the evaluation that we have tried to give to it, have put into perspective, we hope, the concept of solidarity among the Dagara and the extent of the ties that it imposes. It is evident that not all what may, or may not still be considered as anomalies or illogical presentations within the system can be rationalised here, nor may they ever be; neither are all the ambiguities which lurk in the practice of such a 'value' all completely disposed of. Nevertheless, for the sake of minimizing as much as possible these ambiguities within the framework of our investigation, we consider it at least valuable, if not altogether important, to make what we may describe as a contra-distinction in regard to the appreciation of solidarity, either as a co-responsibility which is induced by a fundamental human value, or simply as a law of convenience imposed on the different groups by the fact of society.

Insofar as we are concerned, there is a clear-cut distinction between these two positions. 'A fundamental human value' cannot be considered on the same level as a 'law of convenience' even when this latter is imposed by the fact of 'society' itself. If a value is truly fundamental to man, it cannot be so easily disposed of without grave and adverse consequences; whereas a law of convenience imposed even by society at a given historical time remains contingent and appreciated for the reasons that brought it into being, but can easily disappear with successive generations of even the same people when these reasons seem to obtain no more.

In disagreeing in part with Emile Durkheim's conception that totem is sacred to the members of the group to which it is a totem, Radcliff-Brown, attempting to explain the origin of the totem, reformulates Durkheim's theory of totemism, as we have already alluded to above in another context, and which I repeat here:

> A social group such as a clan only possesses solidarity and permanence if it is the object of sentiments of attachment in the minds of its members. For such sentiments to be maintained in existence, they must be given occasional collective expression. By a law that can be, I think, readily verified, all regular collective expressions of a social sentiment tend to take on a ritual form. And in ritual, again by a necessary law, some more or less concrete object is required which can act as the representative of the group. So, it is a normal procedure that the sentiment of attachment to a group should be expressed in some collective behaviour having reference to an object that represents the group itself.[87]

Another instance will help to make our contra-distinction much clearer; Goody, in his study of the social structures of the Dagara, asserts at one point, the following: "The clan can be viewed as a linked series of effective areas of co-operation or neighbourhood groupings". And further on, he writes: "The clan constitutes a political community, in that, definite sanctions operate against the killing of another member irrespective of the ritual community to which he belongs".[88]

Now, one thing which seems to be strongly brought out by both of these assertions is the **social** and **communitarian** aspects of the clan. This is obvious and does not in any way conflict with the nature of the clanic solidarity that we have been discussing when one considers clanic solidarity in itself without reference to its origins; for, this solidarity truly finds its practical expression in a social system and in community. But if, as Goody says, the clan can be viewed as a "linked series of effective areas of co-operation or neighbourhood groupings," a question will be left open here. i) Will it be these linked series of effective areas of co-operation or neighbourhood groupings that would have induced the clanic solidarity through the laws that they must have demanded; or ii) is it the clanic solidarity through the urge of co-responsibility that would have given rise to these linked series of effective areas of co-operation or neighbourhood groupings?

The answer to this question, which is left open by this assertion, is quite important. It is not only a question of chronological succession between 'the necessity of co-operation in society which results in solidarity' on one hand, and the fact of solidarity itself on the other, but it concerns a fundamental aspect of clanic solidarity itself; that is to say, its origin.

In the assertion made by Radcliff-Brown in his reformlation of Durkheim's theory, and which reformulated assertion seeks first and foremost to explain the origin of totemism, with which explanation we agree in as much as he himself admits that the very diverse forms of totemism existing in the world-over must have diverse origins.[89] In this view, clanic solidarity seems to gather its operative force from an already existing, or rather, a constituted society which wants to perpetuate itself. Thus, it gets an object, the totem, to which the society's members are attached by sentiments, and which sentiments are in turn occasionally given collective expression, thus gradually taking on a 'ritual form'.

We shall not go into the intricate distinctions of the different kinds of laws which Radcliff-Brown himself discusses in the last chapter of his book under the heading "Primitive Law". Nevertheless, if one considers carefully the depth of the passage that we shall quote fully here below, discussing the origin of the law, one cannot but be led to what seems a quite logical conclusion, that the ritual form which is gradually adopted through the occasional expression of the sentiments of the members of the society fall under one form or another of law. Radcliff-Brown writes:

> The distinction between public delicts and private delicts illustrates the fact that the law has no single origin. A deed committed by a member of the community which offends the moral sense of the community may be subject to three sanctions, the general or diffuse **moral sanction**, which makes the guilty person subject to the reprobation of his fellows; the **ritual sanction** which reproduces in the guilty person a condition of ritual uncleanness that constitutes a danger to himself and to those with whom he is in contact – in such cases custom may require him to undergo ritual purification or expiation or it may be believed that as a result of his sin he will fall ill and die; the **penal sanction** whereby the community through certain persons acting as its constituted juridical authorities inflict punishment on the guilty person, which may be regarded either as a collective expression of the moral indignation aroused by the deed or as a means of removing the ritual pollution resulting from the deed by imposing an expiation upon the guilty person or as both.[90]

From this description, distinguishing the various delicts that the individual can incur, all seem to be left to the society and its laws. And the solidarity which is operative here seems to come solely from the society as such, and in this perspective, the moral acts (guilty acts) of the individual assume their guilt only vis-à-vis the particular society and its laws which ensure its perpetuation. Hence punishing in one manner or another those who through acts categorised by the society as offensive to it, pose a threat to the very perpetuation of the society as such.

If this solidarity would have only the society and its law as its 'raison d'etre' and mainstay, what would happen if the society would lose its original motivations that brought such solidarity into being? A society for example, where individualism would reign as we remarked earlier to have been the case during the period of Liberalism, Individualism and the Laissez-faire in the 19th century Europe, then the solidarity as we conceive it would easily be obnubilated and lose all its force in such a society. Piet Schoonenberg so well illustrates this reality; the ease with which even the most precious human values and norms protecting them can be obscured in society for so many reasons;[91] and this is the more so especially in modern society which is so transient.[92] This will thus justifiably demand a continuous revision, and even obliteration of obsolete laws which would be considered as no longer meaning anything, in the way of service for the society. If then solidarity would have as its ground of being just 'a linked series of effective areas of co-operation or neighbourhood groupings,' it would be hard to see how it could, at least in theory, maintain its ties and force in a society that has basically changed. The profundity of the argument here takes into consideration, not just the modification of a value to fit a given time and an evolved society, but the possibility of its complete obliteration.

Indeed, the discussion can be pursued on other grounds and on different levels. But the fact, as we have earlier been led to by our investigation, that co-responsibility among the Dagara is based on a *supernatural reality,* makes this solidarity a much more fundamental and perennial human value than one that would simply have been induced by some particular contingent social conditions. The ancestor who is the originator of the bond of solidarity among the members of the clan continues to live among his descendants, and thus is 'the perennial guarantor' and the one responsible for the continual observance of the injunctions which he ensures, becomes a solidarity responsibility of all the members; and would bring 'peace' and 'blessings,' in other terminology, SALVATION to the entire clan.

In this light, therefore, it becomes difficult to accept, in the Dagara context, what Radcliff-Brown seems to suggest as the autogenesis of totemism when he says that it arises from, or is a special development of a general ritual between man and natural species in society,[93] although we recognise fully that his issue was more specifically on totemism and not on the question of the origins of solidarity. But we think it is also evident that the two questions are in one way or another co-related and cannot be entirely divorced one from the other.

As we admitted from the outset, it would be an impossible task to fill all the lacunae that may be considered existing in the system, and to justify every individual practice in it, particularly in the face of other systems which have altogether their own autoregulatory mechanisms and therefore a different "Weltanschauung". Nevertheless, we think it remains a fact that the value of solidarity as we conceive it in the Ghanaian context which could well be called African, and particularly in Dagara context, is truly a fundamental human moral value, one that could be used most plausibly to the great advantage of the **Christian Message of Universal Salvation** of all men. This, indeed, is our hopeful objective here and which we shall, in our own modest way, reflect more seriously upon, especially in the last part of the study.

Chapter Three Endnotes

<u>1</u> Gaudium et Spes, art. 58.

<u>2</u> The term "conditions" here wishes to express the particular entire set-up in which man may be found. This includes the physical surroundings as well as social. The German term "Umwelt" expresses most accurately what is intended here.

<u>3</u> Maurice Delafosse, *Haut-Senegal-Niger*, 3 vols., Emile Larose, Paris, 1912, vol. 1, pp. 111-13. Delafosse calls a "tribe" a subdivision of a "people," and describes "a people" as an ethnic groupment, characterized by a common origin and history, and speaking generally a common idiom which differs sufficiently from neighbouring idioms. It is to be noted, however, that others use the term "tribe" in the same sense as what Delafosse calls "people". Thus, Nadel equates "tribe" with "people" and defines a "tribe" or "people" as "a group, the members of which claim unity on grounds of their conception of a specific culture". Cfr. S.F. Nadel, *Black Byzantium*, Oxford University Press, London, 1942, p. 17. At the instigation of Clozel, then Governor of the whole of French West-Africa below the Sahara, Maurice Delafosse, a French Ethnologist, began in May, 1908 a survey of the different groups of people living in the territory. This survey was to give to the Governor a more precise knowledge of the people he was governing, or at least, some information on them.

<u>4</u> The rainfall varies between 25 and 50 inches per the year, and is heavier as one leaves the savanna land in the north and approaches the tropical forest which lies from about the 8th parallel going down south to the coastal plains.

<u>5</u> This is the Harmattan which sweeps down from the Sahara Desert which during the period from the end of December till mid-March. The sand particles paints everything white, and are severe for the human body.

<u>6</u> A.A, Kuuire, *The Christian Faith in the Dagarti Culture*, Unpublished License (Master's) Thesis, Institute of *"Lumen Vitae,"* University of Louvain, Brussels, 1972, pp. 104-7.

<u>7</u> More and more, many take up more permanent jobs, and so, no longer return seasonally to their homes in the north. Some, in

fact, settle and take wives from other tribe or get married to people of other tribes with whom they have come into contact down there, and raise families.

8 A.A. Kuuire, op. cit., Part Two, Chapter III, "Western Culture and the Christianisation of the Dagarti," pp. 111-23.

9 The term "Family" here is not just limited to the parents, brothers and sisters, as it is conceived in the western sense; cfr. Chapter IV below. One of the reasons for which many used to travel South for work during the dry season was to earn money so that they Can subsidise the poor harvest brought in from the family farm.

10 Among others who have made reference to this particular field, confer Delafosse, *op. cit.*; St. J. Eyre-Smith, *Comments on the Interim Reports on the Peoples of the Nandom and Lambussie Division of the Lawra District*, Unpublished MS., 1933; L. Girault, Essai sur la Religion des Dagara, in "Bulletin de *l'I.F.A.N,*" Dakar, 1959; J. Goody, The Social Organisation of the LoWilli, London, i967; Death, Property and the Ancestors, London, 1962.

11 M. Delafosse, op. cit., vol. 1, p. 113.

12 D. Westermann, *Die Westlichen Sudansprachen und ihre Beziehungen sum Bantu*, Berlin, 1927; also D. Westermann and M.A. Bryan, *Languages of West-Africa*, London, 1952.

13 In their book, *Languages of West Africa*, Westermann and Bryan called the Tukulor of Delafosse, 'The West Atlantic'. Another linguist-anthropologist, J.H. Greenberg, excludes the Songhai altogether from the West Sudanic languages of the Central Niger Valley, giving it its own status. His hypothesis was to make of the West-Sudanic People and the Bantu one large family which he proposed to call "The Niger-Congo Family". Cfr. Greenberg, *Studies of African Linguistic Classification*. New Haven, The Compass Publication, 1955, p. 7.

14 M. Delafosse, op. cit., Vol. 1, p. 115.

15 The *"Ghana"* are one of the six People of the Mossi group, and are probably the people who are today known as the Gonja, lying between the Dagaaba and the Ashanti in the south. They extend eastward in the interior of Ghana to be adjacent to the Dagomba.

16 M. Delafosse, op. cit., *loc. Cit.*

17 J. Goody, The Social Organisation of the LoWiili, London, Oxford University Press, 1967, p. 16.

18 "Loba" is the singular for "lobr," the plural, of the "Lobi". The use depends very much on the dialect to which one belongs.

19 J. Goody, *op. cit.*, p. 17.

20 Cfr. R.S. Rattery, The Tribes of the Ashanti Hinterland, London, Oxford University Press, 1932.

21 L. Girault, "Essai sur la Religion des Dagara," in *IFAN*, Dakar, T. XXI (1959).

22 Delafosse, Goody and Girault have all remarked the use of the designation "Dagara" or alternatively "Dagaaba" or especially "Dagaati" by the English administrators to refer to the people we are discussing here. The French call them "Les Dagari". Even the way it is rendered in writing by writers among the people themselves may vary; for example, Gregory E. Kpiebaya in his research on "God in the 'Dagaaba' Religion and the Christian Faith," Unpublished Master's Thesis, Louvain, writes "Dagaaba" with a 'ba' at the end. Others use 'r' instead of the second 'a' (See for example A.A. Kuuire, op. cit.). Here we have decided to use alternatively, "Dagara" or "Dagaaba" except in quotations where it is written otherwise.

23 J. Goody, op. cit., p. 64; See also Deogratias Bukenya, Chapter One: "The Interlacustine Bantu and Their Social Structure," Bantu Mukago and Christian Fraternal Solidarity, Unpublished Doctoral Dissertation, Alfonsiana, Lateran University, Rome, 1971.

24 "Yiiru" which is a derivative of the term "yir," also means the patriclan. Therefore, "Yirdem" which would literally mean "people of the same house," also signifies "people of the same patriclan".

25 The Akan in the South of Ghana, for example, predominantly, consider the matriclan to be the principal one; hence they are matrilineal. Cfr. Peter Sarpong, Ghana in Retrospect, Ghana Publishing Corporation, Accra-Tema, 1974, pp. 36, 60.

26 J. Goody, op. cit., pp. 71, 75.

27 Ibid., pp. 75; also, in p. 74.

28 Peter Sarpong, *Ghana in Retrospect: Some Aspects of Ghanaian Culture,* op. cit., p. 59; Cfr, also Radcliff-Brown, *Structure and Function in Primitive Society*, Cohen and West Ltd., London, 1952, (latest reprint, 1971). See also, Émile Durkheim, On Morality and Society, Robert N. Bellah (Editor), The University of Chicago Press, 1973, Chapter Eleven: "Origin of the Idea of the Totemic Principle or Mana".

29 James G. Frazer, *Totemism*, Dawson Pall Mall, London, 1910; Cfr. also A. Van Gennep, *Le Totemisme*, translated from the English, Paris Librairie C. Rein Wald, pp. 5-72; see also, P. Sarpong, op. cit., p. 59.

30 A.A. Kuuire, op. cit., p. 28; Peter Sarpong confirms this hypothesis: cfr. P. Sarpong, op. cit., p. 59.

31 A.R. Radcliff-Brown, *op. cit.*, pp. 124-32; See also, Meyer Fortes, The Dynamics of Clanship Among the Tallinsi, London, Oxford University Press, 1945, p. 125.

32 P. Sarpong, op. cit., pp. 59, 60.

33 A. R. Radcliff-Brown, op. cit., p. 122; See also M. Delafosse who makes similar claim, op. cit., vol III, p. 101.

34 A.R. Radcliff-Brown, op. cit., pp. 123-4 (emphasis added).

35 G.E. Kpiebaya, God in the Dagaaba Religion and in the Christian Faith, *op. cit.*, p. 52; See also, M. Fortes, *African Systems of Thought,* Oxford University Press, 1949, p. 129; P. Sarpong, op. cit., p. 33; Callixte Kalisa, *Le culte, et la Croyance aux Ancetres au Rwanda Confrontes avec le Message Chretien*, Unpublished Doctoral dissertation in Theology, Academia Alfonsiana, Lateran University, Rome, 1972.

36 P. Sarpong, op. cit., p. 33.

37 Ibid., p. 33; emphasis added.

38 Ibid., loc. Cit., footnote 1

39 J. Goody, *Death, Property and the Ancestors: A Study of the Mortuary Customs of the Lodadaa of West Africa*, Tavistock Publications, London 1962, pp. 223, 238; See also C. Kalisa, op. cit., p. 81. Here the author describes the ancestor in the strict sense in Rwanda.

40 A fairly detailed description of the Dagara funeral rites and Ancestral Investiture is given by G.E. Kpiebaya in his book, *op. cit.*, pp. 53-65.

41 A.A. Kuuire, op. cit., p. 63; J. Goody, Death, Property and the Ancestors, op. cit., p. 223.

42 Sarpong remarks precisely that adulthood n some tribes is not determined by age, but by marital status. See op. cit., p. 34. See also G.E. Kpiebaya, op. cit., pp.56-7.

43 Cfr. J. Goody, *Death, Property and the Ancestors*, Chapter XVII; *The Social Organisation of the LoWiili*; also G.E. Kpiebaya, *op. cit.*, pp. 52-65; and P. Sarpong, op. cit., Chapter V.

44 Cfr. above, under the caption "The Clan".

45 In the mind of the Dagara, the Supreme Being, called "God," is so far away , and so great, that man himself cannot approach HIM to offer HIM direct worship. Thus, worship is offered to HIM through intermediaries. Cfr. A.A. Kuuire, *op. cit.*, pp. 65, 69. This is further explained by G.E. Kpiebaya, *op. cit.*, p. 62.

46 P. Sarpong, *op. cit.*, p. 43; Cfr. also M. Fortes, "The Political System of the Tallensi of the Northern Territories of Ghana," in *African Political Systems*, London, 1940, pp. 253-4.

47 Cfr. above, conclusions to "Geographical Description".

48 P. Sarpong, op. cit., p. 36; See also A.A. Kuuire, op. cit., p. 35

49 A.A. Kuuire, Ibid., p. 30.

50 The choice of the concept of 'evil acts' in the attempt to define the individual in relation to his group of solidarity is not just arbitrary. This is because we believe that in our case here, any moral act which is not conformed to the norms of the group, hence a 'deviation' from the norm, has more catalyzing powers than the moral acts which are already conformed to the norms of the group and so considered as good acts. Also, the fact that most norms in such a society are seen mainly from the prohibitive side, makes the breaking of the evil acts easier to isolate as 'evil acts'. As Sarpong has rightly stated, "it must be admitted that the taboos are an ingenious device by which 'primitive people keep life in their society free from neurotics". Cfr. *Ghana in Retrospect*, p. 58

51 The ancestors are not the only agents involved in whatever may befall someone; but their role in protecting their clan members, or allowing them to suffer some physical 'evil,' stands out conspicuously. Cfr. A.A. Kuuire, op. cit., p. 58; See also G.E. Kpiebaya, op. cit., pp. 109-14; And Jack Goody in chapter X of *Death, Property and the Ancestors*: "The Causes of Death," also makes this point clearly.

52 P. Sarpong, *Ghana in Retrospect*, p. 40.

53 G.E. Kpiebaya, op. cit., p. 114; see also Jack Goody, *The Social Organisation of the LoWiili*, pp. 49, 53.

54 Piet Schoonenberg, *Man and Sin*, Sheed and Ward, London, 1965, pp. 42-3.

55 See, *The Voice of Africa*, Vol. 1; material utilised by G.E. Kpiebaya in op. cit., with acknowledgement to E. Bolaji who quoted the original in his work: Pour une Theologie Africaine, p. 8.

56 Robert Koch, Il Peccato nel Vecchio Testamento, Edizioni Paulini, Roma, 1973.

57 Thomas Aquinas, Summa Theologiae, 1-2, q. 21, 1c and 2.

58 For the difference between '***Malum***' and other terms, cfr. ibid., I q 48 6c; I-II q 79, 1 ad 4. There is no intention here of going into all the distinctions and correlated terms used by St. Thomas in this field, and also by others; infrahuman acts: ***Malum humanum***, which derive from ***actus humanus***, and hence **moral evil**, which is based on a human passion, etc. For our purpose, to point out the general distinction between **physical evil** and **moral evil** is sufficient.

59 Piet Schoonenberg, op. cit., p. 40.

60 Ibid., p. 43.

61 Ibid., loc. Cit. (p. 43).

62 Bernhard Häring, *Faith and Morality in a Secular Age*, St. Paul Publications, Slough SL3 6BT England, 1973; translated from the original in Italian, *Etica Cristiana*, Editioni Paulini, Rome, 1973.

63 B. Häring, Faith and Morality in a Secular Age, op. cit., p. 31.

64 Ibid., p. 30.

65 Ibid., Chapter I: "Secularisation Today"

66 Piet Schoonenberg, op. cit., p. 40.

67 Robert Koch, op. cit., chapter I. In fact, the bibliography on this issue is abundant. See among others, E. Beaucamp, "Peche dans l'Ancien Testament" in *DBS VII*, Paris, 1962; J. Guillet, *Themes Bibliques*, Paris, 1954; A. Gelin, "Le Peche dans l'Ancien Testament," in *Theologie du Peche*, Tournai, 1950(28); S. Lyonnet, "Peche," in VThB, Paris, 2e ed., 1970; G. Quell, in *ThWNT* I, Stuttgart, 1957; L. Kohler, *Theologie des Altes Testament*, Tubingen, 1936.

68 R. Koch, op. cit., p. 11 (translation from the original Italian, my own).

69 Ibid., p. 12.

70 P. Schoonenberg, op. cit., p. 43.

71 L. Kohler, *Theologie des Altes Testament*, Tubingen, 1936, p. 158; G. Quell, in *ThWNT I*, Stuttgart, 1957; B. Häring, *Faith and Morality in a Secular Age*, pp. 30ff.

72 B. Häring, *op. cit.*, p. 30.

73 P. Schoonenberg, *op. cit.*, p. 43.

74 This comes from the fact of the conception the Dagara in particular and the Ghanaian in general has of God. Although they believe in the omnipotence of God who sees and knows all things, and is "the final explanation of all things," they also consider Him to be so great and so, far above all trivialities that He leaves the day-to-day affairs of men to the "Kpime" (the ancestors) and the "Ngmime" (the minor deities). This is what Sarpong calls the "Divine Paradox," cfr. op. cit., p. 10. See also G.E. Kpiebaya, op. cit., p. 6.

75 Cfr. A.A. Kuuire, op. cit., pp.71-2. The "pater-familias" is the head of the respective division of the 'family,' be it of the nuclear family, the extended family or the clan.

76 P. Sarpong, *op. cit.*, p. 53.

77 A.R. Radcliff-Brown, *Structure and Function in Primitive Society*, Cohen and West Ltd., London, 1971, Chapter VII: see in particular p. 134; Cfr. also, H.D. Schmidt, "Taboo," in Volume 3, p. 300 of *Encyclopedia of Psychology*, H.J. Eysenck (Editor), Search Press, London, 1972; See also P. Sarpong, op. cit., p. 52. The "supernatural" origin of the taboo evokes the concept of sin or

moral evil, as we have seen above. Radcliff-Brown is unequivocal about this when he calls the breaking of a prohibition in a religious context "sin," see op. cit., p. 135. It is to be noted that the term "supernatural," is used in this research to mean what is beyond the ordinary experience of the senses; and as adjective, it qualifies a reality that is over and above the ordinary perception of man. It does not necessarily imply "the divine".

78 P. Sarpong, *op. cit.*, p. 53.

79 J. Goody, *The Social Organisation of the LoWiili, op. cit.*, p. 75.

80 G.E. Kpiebaya, *op. cit.*, pp. 37-44.

81 *Ibid., p.* 38.

82 *Ibid* ., p. 44; For a more detailed description of a divination séance see pp. 41-6; Cfr. also J. Goody, Death, Property and the Ancestors, pp. 208-19; The Social Organisation of the LoWiili, pp. 80, 92, 97,99.

83 G.E. Kpiebaya, *op. cit.*, p. 50.

84 A.A. Kuuire, *The Christian Faith in the Dagarti Culture*, Unpublished License (Master's) Thesis, Lumen Vitae, Catholic University of Louvain, Belgium, 1972, pp. 57, 58-9.

85 P. Schoonenberg, *Man and Sin*, p. 103.

86 B. Häring, *Sin in the Secular Age*, Doubleday and Company, Inc., Garden City, New York, 1974, pp. 106-34.

87 A.R. Radcliff-Brown, *op. cit.*, pp. 123-4.

88 J. Goody, *The Social Organisation of the LoWiili, op. cit.*, pp. 74-5.

89 A.R Radcliff-Brown, *op. cit.*, p. 122; cfr. also M. Delafosse, *op. cit.*, Vol III, p. 101.

90 A.R. Radcliff-Brown, Structure and Function in Primitive Society, *op. cit.*, pp. 214-5.

91 Piet Schoonenberg, *op. cit.*, p. 115.

92 Alvin Toffler, *Future Shock*, Pan Books Ltd., London, 1970; see in particular part II of the same book.

93 A.R. Radcliffe-Brown, *op. cit.*, p. 126.

CHAPTER FOUR

SOLIDARITY AS A CULTURAL AND RELIGIOUS VALUE IN THE DAGARA SOCIAL SYSTEM

Introduction

THE VALUE OF HUMAN SOLIDARITY certainly has its place in modern moral theological thinking. After drawing attention to the importance of moral theology today, under-scored in the Decree on *Priestly Formation* (*optatam Totius*) of Vatican II,[1] and also after asserting the principal and central place of Christ in the exalted vocation of man and of the faithful in particular,[2] Josef Fuchs takes a realistic view of the Christian morality as envisaged by Vat. II. Observing that the Christian morality of the Council does not want to be just a morality of private relationship of the individual with Christ, he remarks how, on the contrary, the PCCMW of Vat. II takes the "world" seriously and considers it of great relevance to Christian Morality.[3]

Here, as he asserts:

The term 'world' is in its most essential sense man him-self, or humanity, in any case, with all that belongs to it. That means, above all, human relations but also all the realities and possibilities of earth and space. So, the for-mation and the organisation of the world certainly speci-fies a creation of culture and the human relations, as well as the exploration and right exploitation of the earth and the whole universe. Viewed at a deeper level, however, the formation and organisation of the world is concerned more than anything else with the formation and structure of man in the whole of reality which is related to him.[4]

Further on, speaking about the Christian living in the world, Fuchs considers the whole reality of creation, and once more, points out the necessity of this whole reality of creation to include the personal existence of man, human society and its various forms: culture, politics and technology. The grace of salvation, he asserts, does not make absent the seriousness of man's corruptibility in this total reality.[5]

In our last chapter above, we examined the value of solidarity, which is intimately linked with co-responsibility, in a particular cultural context of this 'world' which Vat. II takes so seriously in the PCCMW, and which Fuchs reasserts in his interpretation of the term to which we have drawn attention above. We discussed the origin of solidarity in the Ghanaian context with particular reference to that of the Dagara, and we arrived at the conclusion that such a human value in the Dagara culture is fundamental because of its "supranatural" basis.[6] We shall come back to what we provisionally call here "supranatural aspect of solidarity" later in this same chapter.

However, the first part of this chapter intends to continue on other grounds our examination of the "value of solidarity" in practice among the Dagara; an examination which should lead to a broader and deeper understanding of other aspects of the value of solidarity, and which will thus attempt to show its openness to, and possible application in, a wider circle, and so, eventually leading the Dagara from within his own "Weltanschauung" to a perception of the entire community of men as bound together in this brotherhood of solidarity, be it to "salvation" or to "perdition".

The Family:
Privileged Place for the Expression of Solidarity

The concept of 'family' exists in all human societies, be they western or eastern, European, Asian or African. However, this concept, or more precisely, the extension of what is expressed by the term 'family,' varies in our modern societies. In modern western conception, for instance, 'family' is defined as that social unit consisting of father, mother and children; whereas in most African societies, the concept expressed by the term 'family' has still the wider extension than just parents and their biological sons and daughters. Among the Dagara, the distinction between what we can call the 'restricted family' or the 'nuclear family' which, in the actual western usage, is the 'family' properly speaking, and the 'extended family,' which is a living and operative reality in most African societies, exists. This extended family among the Dagara takes the form of what anthropologists call the 'patrilineage'.

In the Dagara social system, nevertheless, it is within both the nuclear family and the patrilineage, as we shall respectively call them, that solidarity and co-responsibility find their full and candid expression. We shall therefore examine, as briefly as we can, each of these groups which form the basis of their society, but nevertheless, sufficiently enough so as to permit us to see in which way and how far the family is truly the privileged sector of the Dagara society in which solidarity finds its most concrete expression.

The Nuclear Family

In the Dagara society like in all other societies, every individual can be traced back to a cellular unit with which he or she has more intimate and more profound ties than with

the rest of the society around him or her. From this immediate community, the individual expects more for his or her
'continual being' than from the rest of the society around.
These we may call the rights of the individual vis-à-vis this
immediate community to which he or she belongs. On the
other hand, he owes it certain responsibilities: the demands
of the other members of this immediate community on him.
These we can call his duties towards it. Those who therefore
belong to the same cellular community enjoy and share reciprocally rights and duties among themselves; rights and
duties which they do not share, to a certain extent, with
others who are outside of their immediate group of belonging.

The family which is the nucleus of the society therefore
gives to its members a privileged relationship which they
enjoy between and among themselves in virtue of their close
kinship. Each enjoys certain rights which are due to him or
her from others, and in his or her turn assumes certain
responsibilities in their regard.

In reality, this privileged relationship applies to the
notion of the 'family' as a whole as we shall observe later. But
if this applies to the 'family' in all its forms, the fact of it
should still be more evident in the nuclear family of the
father, mother and children who live together. In this
'nucleus of a family,' among the Dagara, the husband has his
responsibilities toward his wife (wives)[8] and children. He has
the duty to provide them with food and shelter. This he does
by hunting and practically by farming; and by constructing
appropriate accommodations for his wife (wives), and re-
pairing them when they need to be repaired. While they
enjoy their provision of food and shelter from husband and
father as their right, wives and children also have their reciprocal duties: the wife (wives): mainly to prepare the food
and do their appropriate work on the farm;[9] and the children:

mainly to help in looking after the life-stock of the family, and when they are sufficiently grown up, also to help on the farm for boys, or in the kitchen for girls.[10]

However, for the Dagara, the notion of 'family' as conceived in this restricted form, although the distinction does not exist and it is a recognized part of his social structure, it remains of secondary importance, and has no characteristic marks of its own. Even though, for example, to express it in the English language we call it 'family' and may further precise it as 'the restricted family,' it does not have a term proper to itself. The Dagara term which is used to express this concept is "yir". But as we already pointed out, the term 'yir' has several connotations. At first instance, 'yir' refers to a building which provides shelter for a number of people, and of which the equivalent in English will be "house". In fact, it refers to any construction that serves as a shelter. This is the first meaning which comes to mind when the term is used.

With regard to human beings for whom it serves as a shelter, however, the term's significance goes beyond the material building or construction. It includes most especially the social unit of people who live in the building, the house. The number of people in this social unit can well be restricted to father, mother and children, hence the family in the restricted sense as we have described above. But more often still, when it is used in the sense of the social unit, it refers to a group larger than the restricted or nuclear family. This larger social unit, also called 'yir,' which extends so far as to cover the whole patrilineage, is the one that has more importance as a family, and as the first social groupment well characterized, often also the only political unity really existing.[11] It is where the expression of solidarity in the interior of the society can be more evident. We therefore propose in our next paragraphs to inquire into the 'patrilineage' the extended family: its extent, solidarity within it, and some practical difficulties.

The Patrilineage

1. *The Extent of the Patrilineage*

If the term "yir" in Dagara is also used to denote a group of belonging of people larger than what call the restricted family, it is not just by accident that the term, 'yir,' applies to it. This larger group of belonging is truly and properly the **'family'** in the mind of the Dagara, in the sense that all the members of this group, who originally lived in the same house-building, continue to enjoy and share mutually the rights and responsibilities that obtained in the family in the more restricted sense. Their same kinship relations remain always a reality, and so, the vitality of their peculiar relationship is maintained in operation.

Although this concept comes from the fact originally a man and his wife or wives lived in the same 'house-building' together with their sons and the wives of their sons also with their own children,[12] the concept of this vivid and operative reality of the family is not limited to only those actually living within just the same 'house-building'. For, even when a member leaves the original house-building to construct his own habitation, be it near or far away from the original one where he was born and where he lived, he is still considered as an integral member of his original "yir" in every sense of it. In virtue of this therefore, he still has exactly the same rights and duties towards the individual members of his original 'house' (yir), whether these have also left the original house or still dwell in it with their own children.[13]

This is what, in the actual western way of thinking and designation, we have described as the 'extended family'. This extended family is, for the Dagara, the 'family' in the true sense, and so, he calls it 'yir,' just as he calls the nuclear one living in the same building.[14] It is indeed the first social groupment with its own particular characteristics, and is often also the only political unity existing. It is therefore on this extended family that can be properly based the Dagara thinking of solidarity. Living together under the same family head who does truly have responsibilities towards everyone and everyone also having certain responsibilities towards him and towards one another, all become actively co-responsible towards their common ancestors, and also the same privileges under their care and protection.

In summarizing therefore, we can say that the Dagara term, 'yir,' which signifies in the first place, a habitation, a house-building, also denotes those who dwell in it. These inhabitants of the 'yir' do not only include the restricted or nuclear family: father, mother and children, but also include a "paterfamilias," his brothers and their cousins, their children and even the grandchildren of their children to whatever degree,[15] be they still living in or outside the original 'house-building'. In this latter sense, "yir" assumes a much wider dimension: the lineage (YIIRU), which is usually determined by descent from the male side – '***Doolung***'.

2. *Solidarity in the Extended Family*

It can be said to be therefore, the extended family which constitutes the recognizable nucleus of the Dagara Society considered as the social unit capable of being the basis of a political organism. The most elderly man[16] who assumes the role of the 'paterfamilias' exercises authority over the entire extended family.[17] Maurice Delafosse describes the rights and obligations of the paterfamilias of the extended family in this manner:

*Il a les memes droits qu'un pere sur ses enfants non-emancipes, mais il n'a pas vis-à-vis d'eux exactement les memes obligations.... Toutefois, si un membre meme adulte de la famille se trouve, par suite de circonstances independates de sa volonte, dans l'impossibilite de sub-venir a ses besoins et a ceux de sa famille reduite (the nuclear family), exemple dans un cas d'infirmite, le chef de la famille globale (extended family), est tenu de l'entretenir ainsi que ses femmes et enfants. De meme si un mariage agree par le chef ne peut etre conclu par suite de l'impossibilite ou se trouvent le future epoux et son pere ₁₈ de realiser la somme necessaire, le chef de famille globale **est tenu d'intervenir** pecunierement. Il est encore responsable de dettes et obligations contractees par les membres de la famille.₁₉*

The members of the same extended family owe one another mutual help and support. It can be in question of material goods, activities or moral support. This reciprocal help and support among the members of the family is what fosters and sustains the ***family solidarity*** in practice. Each member has the right to the goods of the other, and each one is also co-responsible with the others even respon-sible for the goods, actions and obligations of the other members. Each one is "a keeper of his brother," and they are all interdependent one on the other. Again, commenting on this solidarity of the Dagara, Delafosse vividly underscores it in practice when he writes:

L'acceptance de cette solidarite familiale du 'si ce n'est pas toi, c'est donc ton frère' est profondement ancree dans les coutumes de tous les peoples d'Afrique occident-tale, quelle que soit leur race ou leur religion. La famille

globale est certainement chez eux le groupement social
ayant le plus de cohesion et de vitalite.[20]

If there is therefore any specific characteristic that marks most peculiarly the extended family it is the active solidarity that exists among its members. It makes them actively live responsibly for one another, sharing their obligations and also the rights that are due to each at the interior of the family. This living solidarity among the members of the extended family manifests itself in practically every field of their life, and both the physical and moral consequences of it cannot go by unobserved.

3. *Some Practical Difficulties*

There is no doubt that such a solidarity, in the practice, would present some difficulties for the Dagara, and the more so in a world which is moving fast away from the one it used to be. A solidarity which identifies one member of the group of belonging, one member of the family with another, is more and more difficult to practise in a society which is becoming more technological and in which everyone seeks for more comfort; and most especially in a society into which individualism is gradually infiltrating. All this has come about through the cross-cultural influences which surely have their very good aspects and which, in some areas, even outweigh any harm that they could have had. Yet it remains true that these cross-cultural influences on the Dagara cultural value of solidarity are by no means slight, and one still has to see up to what point this solidarity in its practice can be kept in all its primitive vigour.

The technology of the modern world in general, and society in particular, has not failed to make its influence felt in this domain. To benefit from modern technology, especially when the technological know-how has its origin from outside one's cultural society, a whole process of adaptation in view of accommodation of it is necessary. This adaptation in a sector of a culture affects, not only just that particular sector, but practically the entire living system of a people; since all of culture is a single unit worked out from a long experience in history, tradition and life itself.

An example will well demonstrate what we are speaking about here at this point: Let us take a member of such a group of solidarity who becomes the possessor of a bicycle, a product of technological know-how, which makes travelling easier and faster for him in a society where the common means of transport for most is the foot. Such a one will no longer travel in the company of his peers, his group of belonging and so, of solidarity, be it to the market or to funerals as before. He will always go on his bicycle, and alone, as the bicycle can carry only one person, at most two. Hence, he will be deprived of the opportunity of the bonding he would have when traveling in the company of his kin to a funeral or the market.

This may only be a small example and may even seem insignificant. But it shows clearly how much technological development can introduce new patterns of living into a culture and hence transform the entire relationship within it. Little by little, the owner of the bicycle will separate himself practically from the usual group to which he belongs, and with the members of which he used to do such things, and would share certain responsibilities on such trips. Indeed, we could draw many more conclusions from this example, but we think that the point has been made, and what we intended to draw attention to here is sufficiently and clearly done.

Technology certainly brings some comfort to man. To continue with the same example of the bicycle; the one who owns it in the context of the Dagara society travels surely more comfortably and reaches places faster than most of his relations and friends. He is less tired covering long distances, and he at least covers them in a shorter time than those who have to make the same journey on foot. But this object of convenience and of comfort does not promote in the same way and nurture the sentiments of solidarity and its practice as the members of belonging have been used to. It is certain that the bases of the family solidarity are not immediately upset by such a reality; but when each member begins to seek his own technological object of comfort, there is less chance that the 'primitive' practice of solidarity can still remain the same and be maintained.

But the seeking of just one's own personal comfort is the result of individualism which makes the individual to concern himself with his own personal interests alone and to neglect the interest of his 'brother,' also those of interests of the group of belonging, no matter how legitimate they may be. As this privileged owner gets more individualistic, he forgets about the ties which bind his destiny to that of the other members of the family to which he belongs, and so, gradually, he neglects or even loses consciousness of the responsibilities that he has toward them and shares with them. He denies the right to exact this act of solidarity from him. In the family where the ancestors are still recognised and remain the point of unity, and hence of solidarity, and where they also continue to occupy the central place of morality, appeal can be made to them to correct the erroneous attitude.[21] But it becomes a different thing when the ancestors have also lost their place, and where, under the influence of other ideologies, such individualism pervades the society to such an extent that it becomes a detriment to the cultural value of solidarity in it.[22]

These are some realities in the modern cross-cultural society which could pose real threats to the 'primitive' practice of solidarity in the social set-up in which exists the extended family system and to which such a cultural value is still native. These difficulties are indeed bound to arise, taking into consideration the necessity of change. If we accept what Emile Durkheim says about the "progressive preponderance of organic solidarity," and that "mechanical solidarity" which first stood alone must gradually give way to the "organic one," [23] then inversely to this assertion that this modification brings about an inevitable change in the structure of society, we can say that the structure of society, being influenced from outside, also brings about this change of one type of solidarity to another; and the Dagara social system must be prepared for such a change.

Nevertheless, the difficulties that the modern society may pose to the 'primitive' practice of it, the type of solidarity described above still remains fundamentally a cultural value that is much alive and much cherished among the Dagara; and while it still exists, the presentation of the Christian Message to them cannot just ignore it. The practice of the family solidarity which holds that: *"si ce n'est pas toi, c'est donc ton Frere"* still obtains and is operative, not only among the Dagara in particular, nor among the people of Ghana in general, but in most parts of Africa and its people, who, certainly have not been excluded in any way from the Salvation which the Message of Christ brought for all of humanity.

In the next part of our investigation of the value of solidarity, we shall discuss how clanic solidarity is not enclosed in itself, but is actually the basis of tribal unity. That should lead us to discover what possibilities solidarity, as a value, has of going beyond the purely family, and even clanic, frontiers to a much wider horizon.

'Clanic' Solidarity as the Basis of Tribal Unity and Factor of Identification

In chapter three of our present study, we discussed the origin of **solidarity** in the clan, and the role that ***totemism*** plays in the building of this clanic solidarity.[24] In a consolidating effort, we have been examining in the last article the practice of solidarity in the 'family,' particularly in what is called the 'extended family,' but which, for the Dagara, is the family in the absolute sense. However, the Dagara People[25] does not consist of only one clan, just as the clan is not made up of only one patrilineage, but of several lineages.

Delafosse distinguishes the clan from the extended family, and from what is called the tribe, saying, and I quote:

Le clan, que l'on confond souvent a tort tantot avec la famille globale, tantot avec la sous-tribu, parait etre un cheminement de la premiere, qui est un groupement social, vers la seconde qui est une division ethnique. Mais ce qui est important et tout a fait digne de remarque, c'est que le meme peut comprendre des familles globales appartenant a des divisions ethniques tres differentes.[26]

Now, in the Dagara social set-up, what role does solidarity play among the people as a whole? In other words, what is the force family or clanic solidarity within the entire tribe, the people, and to what extent? This is what we shall try to assess in the paragraphs that follow.

The Basis of Tribal Unity

Among the Dagara, the solidarity which operates on the level of the clan is also operative on the level of the whole tribe. Just as clanic solidarity is a wider, nevertheless real and unmitigated form of family solidarity, so is clanic solidarity the basis for sentiments of solidarity that can exist in the tribe, and ultimately, be the basis for the unity itself of the tribe.

To explain the universal law of **incest** which prohibits marriage between certain categories of persons and within certain degrees of blood relationship, Levi-Strauss considers the law of prohibition to be first and foremost a "positive law" which, in its application to human societies, appears as a negative injunction. He drew much inspiration for this explanation from Marcel Mauss who considers 'a gift' in certain societies to be an exchange.[27] Thus in this perspective, Levi-Strauss sees the ground for his "principle of reciprocity," by which he goes no to describe marriage as an exchange. *"Le mariage,"* he affirms, *"n'est pas avant tout le lieu de sexuel genital mais un echange"*. Levi-Strauss thus reduces the institution of marriage, and the prohibition of incest connected with it, to a question of 'exchange'. As he is convinced,

> "Le caractere primitive et irreductible de l'element de parente tel que nous l'avons define resulte en effet, de facon immediate, de l'existence universelle de la prohibition de l'inceste. Celle-ci equivaut a dire que, dans la Société humaine un homme ne peut obtenir une femme que d'un Autre qui la lui cede sous forme de fille ou de soeur.[28]

So, the incest prohibition, translated into its positive aspect, marriage, makes a family not to close-in upon itself, but to let out the female members in it into other families from which it can also obtain wives in exchange, thus creating , sustaining and fortifying social links that involve a wider social spectrum than just those links already existing in the family itself which is only the least denominator of the society.

Now, if we accept at least the validity of the social aspect of the argument which, in our view, is empirically demonstrable and therefore acceptable, we can conclude that not only is the entire Dagara People united solidarily together on the grounds of 'a common specific culture,'[29] nor is it only 'an ethnic groupment characterized by a common origin and history,'[30] but we can also assert that through marriage the members of the entire tribe have become, in one way or another, interrelated one to another. The reality of this relationship is most perceptible in a pluralistic society where many different tribes live together. Therefore, under the same principle of family and clanic solidarity, the individual members of the tribe consider themselves as bound together in a common **destiny**. Hence, they share certain responsibilities as **one people**, and these include the common welfare of everyone since the tribe as a whole can find itself menaced in the misfortune of a single member. ALL ARE BOUND TOGETHER IN SOLIDARITY.

Yet, the simple fact of marriage alone does not explain all the force on which the tribal solidarity is based. Even though marriage, which allows an exchange between families, permits the creation and the sustaining of social ties which in turn create some solidarity between two families thus linked together, in our view, there seems to be yet a more profound basis for, and yet a deeper level of the solidarity than the social links that marriage alone can bring about.

In discussing the clan and the building of solidarity, we also pointed out the difference between the family and the clan. But at the same time we also remarked how both the clan and the family are patrilineal, originating from the same ancestor, with the only difference that the clan regroups in itself several patrilineages which, during the course of time, have lost a generational link between the families, and which link, had it been reestablished, would have maintained the entire clan as a much wider but nevertheless as only one and the same family.[31]

Now, the fact that both extended family and clan are patrilineal prohibits as a general principle any marriage whatsoever between members of the same clan. For, just as in the family where everyone is considered as either a grandfather, father, brother or son on the male side, and vice versa as grandmother, mother, or sister on the female side, there can never be marriage between any of these categories. In this case, they are all of them agnates who thus belong to the same exogamous group within which marriage between any of them is not possible. And so is marriage between similar categories of members in the same clan prohibited by the traditional custom.[32]

Considered in this light, therefore, marriage which has been practically only within the tribe is responsible not only for social links that would bring about "social solidarity," but it also creates more profound ties of kinship which makes the solidarity thus existing among the members of the clan to go beyond the purely social level to a more profound one of 'brotherhood'. And this, for the reason that the prohibition to marry within the clan obliges the members of the entire tribe to enter into this more profound and fundamental relation-ship of 'brotherhood' beyond the clan.

The fact of marriage outside the clan creates a network of kinship relations which thus impose on members so related this solidarity of brotherhood, and hence a mutual responsibility between them. Emile Durkheim's discussion on **the Progressive Preponderance of Organic Solidarity** has been alluded to above.[33] He states the fact of this level of relationship among clans when he said: "Not only has the clan consanguinity as its basis, but different classes of the same 'people' are often considered as kin to one another".[34] But this kinship between classes of the tribe is created precisely through marriage. For, as Roosens, in a general conclusion to a study he made in the Congo which applies well to our context here, he affirms: *"Le mariage en Afrique n'est pas simplement, et n'est pas meme avant tout l'affaire des partenaires; il concerne en premier lieu les clans, lineage".*[35] For the Dagara, in fact, for the majority of African people, the marriage to an individual is perceived, in a certain manner, as marriage to the whole lineage, and even clan. The members belonging to the two parties become regarded as "in-laws," and so, are bonded to one another respectively.

The light of these arguments therefore leads us conclude that the unity of the 'people,' hold them to a common destiny, the achievement of which they perceive in terms of solidarity and co-responsibility. And the basis of this is found in the extension of the clan and the solidarity obtained therein. In all, this in our view offers the possibilities for a wider horizon in which the solidarity and the co-responsibility that it imposes can operate beyond the limits of the restricted family, the extended family, and the clan to the entire tribe in the sense of PEOPLE.

Clanic Solidarity as Factor of Identification

However, not only is the value of solidarity clan a factor of unity of the people which now lives in more pluralistic society. It also by the same fact distinguishes and identifies them as one people with a devotion to, and practice of, the cultural heritage which are the accumulated and bequeathed means for achieving that destiny which is common to them all. It is to this cultural heritage that belongs the natural tendency of the individual member to solidarity with the other members of his tribe. Hence an inclination to greater sympathy towards them than ordinarily towards others.[36] This is a feeling of **belonging together** which can be translated into action when the need arises; and this is also a factor which distinguishes him in our modern societies becoming more pluralistic, and at the same time identifies him with every other member of his tribe, thus making him responsible for his 'brother'.

1. *Genuine and Positive Tribal Solidarity*

Such a tribal feeling, based on the family and clanic solidarity that we have discussed earlier, is genuine and positive. When tribal feelings are truly genuine, they become: a) the mainstay of solidary union among members of the tribe itself that would otherwise have long disintegrated for lack of any common point of interest – destiny, yet without making it close in upon itself. A phenomenon which is fairly well known in modern missionary circles in Africa, and which could serve as an example, is the conversion of the Dagara people itself to Christianity, and with which people we are here concerned. What is usually considered as the miraculous conversion of the Dagara in the years between the 1930s and 40s can be viewed, from the human aspect, as being due to a certain expectancy of a better 'future' and a high degree of solidarity among them, and a sense of co-responsibility in regard to their common destiny which were inspired and nourished by a long-standing tribal cultural aspiration.[37] b) This type of positive tribal solidarity could also be the chief preserver of the cultural heritage of the tribe itself within a pluralistic society. Otherwise, this cultural heritage would be lost as a result of ultra-individualism and subjectivism. And thirdly; c) when the cultural heritage and practice which unite the members of the tribe are sound, and the ideal of solidarity and brotherhood thus strongly emulated, genuine tribal solidarity could become a positive aid to personal formation of the individual in the society to a broader conception of solidarity and brotherly concern for all.

2. *False Tribal Solidarity*

It is fair to point out the danger which tribal solidarity in the practice could carry with it in a pluralistic society of the modern cities in particular which are more and more heterogeneous in their population.[38] The devotion to, and practice of what is the common cultural heritage, strengthened by the fact of their belonging together as one 'people,' can be exaggerated by the members of the tribe. Thus, for example, they could be led to consider only their tribe as being the best and, so, make them look upon all others as secondary to them, and from whom little can be learnt.

It is at this point that 'tribalism' takes on the pejorative sense in which it is often heard used in reference to a great number of social problems particularly in Africa. A member of a tribe who has a good position of responsibility in a pluralistic society can easily forget his obligation to the entire society for the service of which he acquired this responsible position, and turn to use it mostly to the advantage of what concerns his tribe, thus promoting and furthering its interests often to the detriment of some groups of the pluralistic society for which he is responsible. This type of tribalism, which we would qualify as exaggerated, is in fact not that genuine tribalism that has its basis on family and clanic solidarity. It rather closes the doors to a tribe upon itself, and is at best 'group individualism'. In the pluralistic society, it breeds nepotism and blocks the way to true justice and brotherly concern, which is indeed solidarity in action and leads to that wider brotherhood and 'belonging togetherness' of all men.

Exaggerated tribalism cannot therefore be truly said to be based on that genuine solidarity which springs from the family and clanic solidarity. On the contrary, it presents in a false manner what is true solidarity and offers little prospects, if any at all, for a wider brotherhood of men. In fact, it stifles the feelings of true solidarity within a larger circle of men – pluralistic society – that should lead them to the realisation of their common destiny. Furthermore, such exaggerated tribalism in the name of tribal solidarity would easily nurse and sustain in the members of the tribe prejudice against others and thus lead to perpetual unrest with other tribes or groups of solidarity in the pluralistic society of today.

It is therefore sure that the danger of derogation in the actual practice is always imminent and the more so in the modern societies of the newly growing cities where certain modifications are usually necessarily imposed upon the actual practice of the "primitive solidarity".

However, the principle of tribal solidarity, that solidarity which originates from the family and clanic communities, remains in itself a profound cultural value and heritage, the advantages of which cannot be diminished by whatsoever probable dangers there may be, in its practice, to the pluralistic society of today. On the contrary, it can and should be the basis on which the brotherhood of mankind could be modeled.

Take for instance, today's world of technology in which travelling has been very much facilitated, and more and more, people actually do travel. if someone is on a journey to a place where he knows he has people on whom he can count because of his profound bond of solidarity that exists between them, the preoccupations he will have in regard to the other end of his journey will not be centered so much on the material wellbeing at his arrival there, but on the 'persons' whom he will be meeting. He knows that he is going to his own who will receive him very well into their midst on account of what binds them together as 'brothers' and makes them responsible for one another. He belongs to them; is one of them and therefore, they will have to share with him whatever little they may have. Hence, the first preoccupation such a person would have on his journey would not be that of worrying about how much money he has to take along in order to pay for his hotel and meals, nor fear that he may suffer from cold and hunger for lack of these material means. Rather, his first attention will be on the persons he would be coming to.

This is certainly a very simple and daily example. Nevertheless, it demonstrates very well what an asset indeed what a valuable asset (tribal) solidarity can be, and how it could be tapped by the modern pluralistic society for its 'humanization,' and what an enrichment it would be for its own milieu.

From the Narrow Limits of Tribal Solidarity to a Broader Spirit of Belonging and Co-Responsibility

So far, we have discussed the nature of solidarity within the Dagara social system: solidarity within the family, clan, and the tribe as a whole. But this cultural value of the Dagara, the examination of which we have undertaken here, is not just being discussed for its own sake. As the theme of what we are researching announces, this study is in view of the salvation proclaimed by and through Christ. If then this cultural value is to be made relevant to, and become a true asset to, the message of Christian Salvation, the capacities it has of going beyond the narrow limits of the tribe must be explored in order to see in which way it can truly come to embrace all men since the Salvation of Christ is for all (Mk. 16:15-16). We have already alluded to this fact. However, before we discuss explicitly 'the transcendent,' or in other terms eschatological aspect of Dagara solidarity, we think it appropriate to explore briefly here this possibility itself that tribal solidarity has of going beyond its own narrow confines of the tribe.

The Instance of Nation Building

If we consider the actual situation in Africa, the struggle in which most of the countries are involved, reduced to its most common element, is that of the building of **one nation**. This means a national society in which all the various traditional social groups, tribes or otherwise, would come together, and each realizing that within the framework of a nation, they all share a common destiny, the achievement of which common destiny is the responsibility of all the citizens.[39]

Taking Ghana as an instance, the naked fact was that in that age of nation-building, a common phenomenon throughout Africa and other countries which obtained self-government and 'political freedom' from colonial rule in the middle of that century, one had to face the reality that one was trying to build one nation of many different tribes[40] each of which already had its established links of solidarity.

In this perspective the building of a nation, and hence a dream of nationalism, consists in trying to make the various and individual citizens to think always in terms of national interests. This we can call the common destiny that they have to achieve together as a nation, a 'people,' and so be co-responsible for the achievement of these interests which would lead to the common destiny. They therefore either have to stand 'solidarily' together for the realisation of this end, or they fall together.[41] Considered from this point of view, therefore, the effort of a nation-building draws basically from the same value of solidarity just as the links operating within the tribe are those of solidarity.

Nevertheless, there remains a difference. Whereas the common interest and the links of solidarity within the tribe, deriving from those of the clan, are more natural, those necessary for the building of the nation have to be emulated, created and sustained by the protagonists of the national ideal, who seek to make out of several tribes one people. In fact, this process of building people out of the several tribes does not seem to be an unprecedented phenomenon altogether. If we were to look for a similar fact in human history, the composition of the "People of Israel" that became the "People of God" would be a classical case in point. The twelve tribes are seen as a sacral "*amphictyony*" (a sacred league of neighbouring states for the common interest), based on their common allegiance to Yahweh,[42] and therefore was not a people bound together from the beginning by any close blood relationship, not even loosely as tribes.

Even if we would set aside any historical comparisons, tribal sentiments of solidarity as we have in particular depicted among the Dagara, remain a great asset to, and are indeed the basis on which national feelings of solidarity can be grounded. For, in the first place, nationalism in the situation we have in view, i.e. the effort to make of a larger society of one single nation the several and different tribes, as is the case in most African countries, one cannot ignore the fact that the riches of such a larger society, a nation and its coherence as "One Nation," "One People" come only from the individual tribal cultures since national culture at this point does not exist outside of that which comes from the individual tribes.

Thus in thinking of a wider society of belonging which is beyond the limits of the tribe, the native cultural value of solidarity which is already existing in the tribal group of belonging and of co-responsibility is not only to be emulated as a pattern and a model to be followed, but is indeed indispensable for what Peter Sarpong calls "National Pride".[43] But which nevertheless should have the capacity of going beyond the narrow limits of the tribe to bring into its sphere of operation the circle of brotherly belonging together, the national society.

The common destiny to which the nation-in-building sees all its members bound as 'a people in the making' can be said to be the sum-total of the various aspirations to which each of these groups of solidarity, the various tribes making up the nation, see themselves "called". This becomes their common bond which binds each and every one of such enlarged brotherhood together, and makes the achievement of their common destiny as a people a solidarity responsibility to which all of them are called under the task of building one nation.

The "Supranatural" Aspect of Solidarity in a Wider Human Society

Just as there is a possibility of building various and different tribes into one nation by emulating, elevating and broadening the value of solidarity which is only native to each tribe, so should there also exist the possibility of building a brotherhood of men, even wider than that of national belonging, based on the same values of solidarity and, so, co-responsibility as we have analyzed among the Dagara. In fact, this is not only an empty presumptuous wish; for, the so many groups of solidarity in our modern world, especially in the area of economic well-being and security, is a clear demonstration of this possibility.[44] Man has become more aware in the modern times that the only way to his individual survival and security, liberation and ultimately, "salvation," is the positive and active recognition that he shares the same destiny with other men and that unless he acts in solidarity with others, assuming his part of responsibility which falls to him through the bond of this solidarity with the others, his personal security, survival and, indeed, 'Salvation,' remains persistently threatened.

However, as we observed earlier, in the case of the Dagara solidarity, both solidarity and the co-responsibility which sprouts from it are based on a *'supranatural reality'*.[45] So the end of *such solidarity of a wider brotherhood of human society* should be looked for beyond the purely economic interests and gains that the co-responsibility in this solidarity for the sake of economic survival may bring. It goes beyond the material well-being to the dignity and destiny of the individual and everyone; in reality, from his liberation from the nefarious and menacing conditions in which he constantly finds himself to his **true survival** and **true security**.

This liberation and true security, **his true survival**, can only be assured when the individual realises that it is in co-responsible action with others, based on this 'supranatural reality' of the brotherhood of all men who share the same fundamental destiny, that he can reach his individual and personal liberation and security. He also has to realise that his own total survival, his security and 'salvation,' depends on, and is the responsibility of, those to whom he is bound in solidarity just as theirs depends on him and is his respon- sibility.[46] This is that 'native' and 'primitive' solidarity practised among the Dagara, particularly on the family and clan levels.

The possibility that in the national society sentiments of solidarity can go beyond the limits of the tribe, and that Christians, illumined by the brotherhood of Christ, can rise superior to the narrow barriers that tribal loyalties could impose, was affirmed by Peter Cardinal P. Dery.[47] He faced up to the reality that Ghana was still a young nation, with many and different tribes, still struggling to form herself as a nation. So, speaking precisely about tribalism and nation-building, the remarks which he made, and which are quite relevant to our point of discussion here, were presented in such realistic and penetrating terms, that they were applauded, as tribalism was presented and made to be seen in its most genuine and best form.[48] For fear of impoverishing his words in a paraphrase, I would prefer to let the prepared text he pronounced that day, speak for itself:

> "The complexity of the modern State with its large scale national organisations, and the multi-tribal nature of town and city life, demand that we as Christians rise superior to our legitimate differences, and work together as **one nation and one people.**
>
> "Modern conditions ... require new attitudes of mind, and a wider loyalty *(bonds of solidarity)* than tribal loyalty. The modern State demands **a loyalty which transcends tribal barriers,** and which seeks the good of the nation as a whole. However, it must be borne in mind that **it is from the tribes that the nation is born.**
>
> "Some people associate tribalism with backwardness and narrowness of outlook. Tribalism, in my view, is the sum-total of all that is good in a tribe. We must not asso-ciate tribalism with discrimination, selfishness, nepotism,

superiority, complexness, etc. ***These things are sins against even a tribe***. These characteristics are unworthy of a tribe and of a Christian.

"Tribalism is local patriotism. Local patriotism is the natural bond of love and loyalty which binds the individual to his home, his village, his culture, his customs, his tribe. ***It is the natural expression of family love*** and has its roots in ***religion***.[49] This natural bond of love and affection we have for our home, our village, our tribe, we should never relinquish.

"There is therefore nothing inconsistent between local patriotism and national patriotism. Indeed, ***the second is impossible without the first***. The wider loyalty of national patriotism can only exist when the smaller loyalty is strong and deep.

"A person without loyalty to his home, his village, his tribe, can have no loyalty to the larger unit of the State. He is a person without affection, without roots, an aimless drifter with ***no fixed point from which he may adjust himself to the wider world around him***.

"Local patriotism is an essential ingredient for the development of wider interests, and for the cultivation of the sense of *involvement* in, and *responsibility* for, matters of national importance.

"Viewed in this perspective, differences of tribal affiliation are a strengthening and unifying factor in the life of a nation. When men are ***bound together by a common loyalty to God and to the State***, however much they differ as regards tribal allegiance, ***they can be united in One Spirit*** (in solidarity), and come together and work together unreservedly in all that pertains to the common good'"[50]

A Recapitulation

Within the framework of our research, there is much that one could say on these remarks. However, it is sufficient to observe, in conclusion to this present section, three salient points which come from these remarks, and which are quite relevant to, and in a way, sums up the various aspects discussed in the chapter.

1. *The Value of Tribal Sentiments of Solidarity*

The first of these three points, which is made in no ambiguous terms, is ***the identity of the tribe and the fundamental value that tribal sentiments of solidarity have***. Peter Dery calls them "tribal loyalty," and further describes these sentiments of solidarity in the tribe – which he also calls "local patriotism" – as the natural bond of love which bind the individual to his culture, custom and tribe. It is the same reality Sarpong seems to describe when he asserts that "tribes see themselves as unique communities and their cultures as unique."[51] These are fundamental values native to, and spouting from the tribal solidarity, thus identifying the tribe and at the same time unifying the members into a brotherhood that imposes on them mutual responsibility.

But tribal solidarity, particularly among the Dagara, as the first part of the chapter attempted to demonstrate, has its foundation in the 'family' brotherhood – solidarity in co-responsibility – by and in which the individual finds his dignity as a person, and perceives his destiny as bound to every other member of the group of belonging. Thus, genuine tribal sentiments find their true value in the light of, and are based on that natural bond (of love). It is this which binds the individual in the tribe to all the other members, and makes him see himself responsible for their good, just as he expects, as a right, the same thing from them in his regard.

2. *The Possibility of a Wider Brotherhood*

Yet this bond which, in the tribe, is perceived as local patriotism and loyalty to one's tribe and culture, should not be an element that would cause the tribe to close in upon itself. Rather, it should be "an essential ingredient for the development of wider interests" and therefore of a brotherhood that would urge the individual to assume responsibilities as those deriving from the family, clan and tribal solidarity, but responsibilities reaching out to a wider extent than the limits of the family, clan and even the tribe. This openness to a wider brotherhood is indeed when tribal sentiments are not falsely associated with backwardness and narrowness of outlook, nor with discrimination and selfishness which are all practices foreign to true tribal sentiments.

In this perspective, therefore, true and genuine tribal sentiments have the potentiality of reaching out to a broader brotherhood in society, a brotherhood which makes it possible for one to see every other individual in the society as having the same destiny that one has, and the achievement of which can be made only through that solidarity which makes all mutually responsible for one another.

3. *The "Supranatural" Foundation of the Wider Brotherhood of Solidarity*

If tribal solidarity sentiments, or "local patriotism" as Dery calls it, is an essential ingredient and basis for any wider brotherhood, then this wider brotherhood of solidarity is also founded on that 'supranatural' basis, since tribal solidarity which ultimately comes from the co-responsibility expressed in the family – family love as Dery calls it – has its roots in "religion".[52]

Certainly, it could be argued that in this wider brotherhood of solidarity, the influential force of the ancestors as the supreme sanction of kinship ties, the supranatural force counteracting all centrifugal tendencies that could be inherent in the family, would have diminished. However, from our discussion, the argument can still be maintained that this supranatural foundation, this force that would be the reason for which the individual would perceive the other as bound to him in brotherhood, remains a true and forceful reality in such a wider bond. This is the point that we have endeavoured to demonstrate above.[53] As we remarked in the case of the clan, one generational link or other demonstrating true genealogical descent from the same ancestor, may be missing. Yet the clan not the least less solidarily united on that account. Each individual, once it is established that he belongs to a particular clan, he is truly an integral member of the group of belonging, and, so, has his responsibilities vis-à-vis every other member of the group.

Therefore, looking at it in this light, the enlarged solidarity group of brotherhood and co-responsibility that would be based ultimately on this clanic and family mode of belonging together would have in it this 'supranatural' foundation whereby the individuals in the society see themselves as bound together and responsible for one another. This is the reality even if, in the context of our modern society with its complexity, what is immediately perceptible as the foundation of this solidarity and co-responsibility is expressed mainly in the economic area, where the moral attitude and mutual co-responsibility to act in solidarity, is seen as necessary for economic survival.

In our research, therefore for the ground of solidarity, seen from the light of the cultural value which binds the

Dagara to other members of his family, clan and tribe, and which has in it the capacity of opening up to a wider brother-hood of all men, the 'supranatural reality' that has always been considered as the ground and foundation of this bond of solidarity, has to be looked for in a broader perspective. This is where the Message of Christ and the Salvation that it proclaims to and for all men – the 'call' of man to his original destiny shared with all other men – finds its perfect lodg-ment, and would be perceived by the Dagara in this light and context as quite relevant to him.

As it is asserted by the PCCMW, and pointed out in the second chapter of this research, Christ – the WORD OF GOD – by becoming man for all men, has bound all men together in a solidarity of brotherhood, one which is deeper and truly more profound than all the brotherhood ties that can result from tribe, clan, even from family relations.[54] For, as "the eldest among a large family of brothers" (Rom. 8: 29), he who is "the image of the invisible God" (Col. 1: 15) has become the foundation and the centre of unity, and having taken flesh, has made it a visible reality, coming "to dwell among us" Jn. 1: 14). Thus, he has made it possible, not only for a few, but for **all men to call God their Father** (Rom. 8: 15) and are truly God's children (Rom. 8: 16), because of the fact that all men have attained **the kinship of brotherhood in and through Christ** who has become brother to each and every one.

The common destiny – the eschatological call of all men by Christ – and most especially the "fact of Christ" himself[55] thus binds all into one single family, clan or tribe of soli-darity – "the family, clan or tribe of Christ" – which remains open to embrace all, and so imposes on the individual in this bond of solidarity the duty of co-responsibility with the others by which the common destiny – call – will be achieved. Christ and "his reality" become in this light the foundation, the binding force and total security, liberation and ULTIMATE SALVATION IN THE LIGHT OF THE MESSAGE that he proclaimed, the *"fact of him"* becoming the norm of their life and action.

Dagara Solidarity as a 'Transcendent Reality'

"Dapar," The Land of the Ancestors

In the last chapter, and also in what is discussed above in the present chapter, we have made an attempt to examine the traditional and cultural value of solidarity which leads to brotherly co-responsibility, particularly among the Dagara People, in the light of the "ethnographic present". As is obvious, it would be impossible to examine all the inferences and implications that could be deduced from it, even those that could be considered as quite relevant, given the scope of our theme of study here. Nevertheless, we would not regard this chapter, which puts into greater light the value of Dagara solidarity, as complete without giving due consideration to what we shall call the "transcendent reality" of the Dagara People.

So far, the accent of our analysis has been on the level of the existential, the environmental, the contingent and the circumstantial situation in which the Dagara has found himself in this actual life and in his daily experiences. But as the belief in the ancestors' world[56] and in their continuous but supranatural presence among the members of their group of belonging[57] would intimate, the Dagara does not regard his actual existential situation and this mode of existence as the only one. The ancestors who, after their death and installation as ancestors, remain present in their family, clan and tribe, and are the foundation and point of union of their group of belonging, have also assumed, and precisely through this death, a form of existence different from that of their earthly living members. They live in a 'land' of their own: "The Land of the Dead," the "Land of the Ancestral Spirits" (Kpime Teng), the "Country of God" (Dapar).₅₈

Speaking about the "terre des ancetres" (Dapar) of the Dagara, Louis Girault states the fact of how little the question of the exact location of this Land of the Ancestors preoccupy the ordinary Dagara. For the Dagara, as Girault interprets it, "c'est une conception d'un ciel materiel, lieu ou l'on est plus heureux que sur la terre, et ou ne manqué ni la nourriture, ni la boisson, ni les femmes".₅₉ The interpretation of the concept of the ancestors' abode given here by Girault is only a partial description of that reality which the Dagara calls "Dapar," the land of the ancestors. Nevertheless, partial as it may be of the whole reality, it portrays an existence which the Dagara believes to be already that of his ancestors, and the term towards which he himself, in his actual terrestrial existence, is aspiring to have after his death. This is, and properly so, the Dagara "eschatology," a reality which **transcends** his actual conditioned existence, but in the fact of which reality he believes.

A number of questions can be raised in regard to this "transcendent reality". Since this "Land of the Ancestors" is also the "Country of God,"₆₀ one could in effect inquire into the reality of God himself as he is conceived by the Dagara?₆₁ who else are dwelling in this Land? What work do they do? Etc. One could also ask about the type of relationship between God and the ancestors there, in their common abode; and also, the relationship God has with the other beings there beside the ancestors. And not least of all, what is the relationship between the "Country of God" and the actual present world of men?

These are all questions that, in one way or another, are connected with the concept of "Dapar". However, the question which interests us most is: 'What is the relationship between the members of a group of belonging here in this actual life – let us say, the clan – and their ancestors who live in "Dapar"? Does their new mode of existing, and their land, have influence in any particular way in their relations with the members of the group that they once belonged to in this life? To help us provide an answer to this last question, we shall consider in greater depths the Dagara belief regarding the "After-this-Life" as the reality to which death opens the door.

The Significance of Death: "Dagara Eschatology"

For the Dagara, sickness and the eventual death of a young person, or even middle-aged person is a catastrophe. It is an evil event, and the cause of which must be found out,[62] and if precautionary measures can be taken, then to do so. As Goody gives us the common reason for joining "Bagre," or more precisely, for allowing oneself to be 'caught' by "Bagre," the major motivation for doing so is that of health. He writes: "From the actors' standpoint, what counts is their success or failure in promoting and maintaining health (in the widest sense)".[63] While, on the other hand, the death of one who has lived to see his grandchildren and even, great-grandchildren, can be looked at altogether differently. The death of such a one is seen as an accomplishment, and this explains why there is often such gaiety surrounding his funeral celebrations.

However, putting aside this aspect of death, either as a catastrophe or as an accomplishment, all death is seen as a *journey* back to the "Land of the Ancestors" (Kpime Teng). Thus, the Dagara will speak of the dead person as having "gone home" (O kulla), or in the case of newly born children, they speak of them as having "gone back;" in the case of one such newly born child who has died, "he or she has gone back (home)," (O leb'na). Whether the one undertaking this journey to the "Kpime Teng" arrives immediately (after death), or only sometime after the occurrence of death, is another matter that can be undertaken in a study.[64] One important thing to remark here is the belief that it is the ancestors of the lineage and the other "kpiikore" (those members also of the lineage already inhabiting "Dapar" with the ancestors and God), who will either receive the newly dead (Kpiipaala) – "the newcomer" – into their company. And this will be on the grounds that he, or she, 'resembles' or does not 'resemble'[65] them (O be yitaa ni ti'e).

This belief that it is the ancestors who accept into their company the "Kpiipaala" who belongs to their group, clan or family, is based in its turn on the firm belief that the "After-this-Life" is the continuation of the group of belonging, particularly the family and the clan, but only in another mode of existence in which the one who has attained the goal is more certainly secure in the midst of his ancestors and will lack nothing.[66] The members of the ancestral lineage, therefore, the present life, go to join their ancestors and all those that had preceded them, and in this way the whole family, clan, and indeed the tribe and beyond, come together again to form what we call here, ***The Transcendent, Eschatological congregation of solidarity.***

Viewed in this light, two realities come in sight: 1) the continuity of the group of solidarity in the "After-this-Life;" and 2) the powerful influence that this "***Eschatological Congregation***" of ancestors can have on the actions of their clan here in this life, in virtue of the belief that it is they who will accept him or reject him according to how his actions in this life were in conformity or not in conformity with their norms.

1. *The Eschatological Congregation of Solidarity*

The individual who leaves this actual life therefore goes to join his ancestors and all those who belonged to that group which share responsibilities, and considered themselves bound together in this life.[67] This *Eschatological Congregation* in which the members of the lineage and the clan are reunited becomes that goal, the **destiny** to which the individual members had been aspiring in solidarity with others, to attain. It is in this Eschatological Congregation that one finds definitively the **"pieno zie"** (the place of the rest) that he lived here on earth for. He has no longer the fears, the worries, nor the insecurities by which he was constantly beset in this life. He has "REACHED HOME," "ou l'on est *plus heureux* que sur la terre et ou ne manqué ni la nourriture ni la boisson"[68] In this Eschatological Congregation of brotherhood, the individual member is out of the reach of the evil spirits and evil men who might have always sought to harm him in his earthly existence.[69]

But the individual can only get acceptance into this congregation because of the fact that he is a member of the same lineage or group that was **solidary and shared responsibilities** in this existence on earth. It is on this title that he can be admitted into the "Eschatological Congregation" which is thus, indeed, another form of existence of the actual bond of solidarity, and hence a true continuation of the group of belonging and of solidarity of the present life in the land of the Ancestors – in the country "After-this-Life".

2. *The Influence of the "Eschatological Congregation of Solidarity" on its Members in this Actual Existence*

Seen in relation to this Eschatological Congregation, which transcends the present family or clanic group of solidarity, the entire actual life of the Dagara is lived in perpetual reference to this eschatological congregation – the reunited members of the present group of solidarity in the After-this-Life. The individual member of the present group of solidarity therefore lives his life in a permanent awareness of this eschatological congregation, which is the continuous existence of the group of solidarity to which he belongs here in this life. He knows that he must one or the other, make this journey to the: Land of the Ancestors, to join in the perpetual joy of his family and clan. But he also knows that he will be accorded a joyous welcome or he will be refused entry into their midst, depending on how he lives his life here; and he himself will become an ancestor or not in this congregation, all the other conditions being fulfilled. His being made an ancestor depends on the type of life he lived here – whether in conformity with the norms set down by ancestors or not. G.E. Kpiebaya asserts it in this way: "We see then that (the) judgement starts already here on earth. When a person puts right strained relationship by a public confession, the ancestors will receive him in Dapare".[70]

The belief of the existence of such an "After-this-Life" therefore becomes a hefty inspiration, which influences in no mean terms, and ordains the entire ***moral life*** of the Dagara. But this eschatological congregation which is a transcendent reality would have no meaning for him were he not destined to it in a ***bond of union with others*** through the ties of solidarity in this existence. For, it is the members of the actual group of the solidarity here on earth who go to form, by way of continuation, ***THIS ESCHATOLOGICAL CONGREGATION IN THE LAND OF THE ANCESTORS, WHICH IS ALSO THE COUNTRY OF GOD.***

CONCLUSION

With the consideration on the eschatological aspect of solidarity, we are persuaded to consider the necessary elements of our investigation of the cultural value of solidarity in the Dagara social system within the limits of our study, as being outlined and complete. It is not an overstatement to repeat that what is examined has been viewed within the scope of the *"ethnographic present"* only.[21] As Goody rightly says, "Religion is more dynamic as many analyses suggest. There is an ongoing process of continuous creation of religious concepts and behaviour".[22] This "ongoing process and continuous creation of religious concepts" could be an interesting study in itself, but that is not the objective of this study. It is necessary to put limits to the area of one's investigation. This we have done by limiting our matter to what the anthropologists call "the ethnographic present". We also recognize that most of the elements we have selected could be treated in various other ways, and at greater length and depths. However, here we have made a deliberate effort to avoid wandering too far away from our objective and have thus tried to examine them only in the measure that we consider them as necessary for shedding light on our subject of discussion.

As it is obvious, the second part of this research has been made from an anthropological, especially from ethnographic approach. This is motivated by the conviction that, for the present, it is the only valid approach by which the theological importance of what is examined here as a cultural value, the value of solidarity among the Dagara, can be rightly appreciated. Besides, the fact that for the Dagara, what is purely religious and theological, can hardly be separated from what is not,[23] makes any other approach unintelligible, and at best, unsatisfactory and not going to the real core of what makes their "Weltanschauung". For, what may be called the true theological concepts and beliefs of the Dagara, my people for that matter, cannot be approached and examined outside their anthropological setting, unless if one is decided a-priori to transplant into their "world," but which the trans-planter would, nevertheless, consider to be "The Theology," and therefore would naively think it to be convincing enough to determine the morality of their actions.

The message of salvation that Christ proclaimed was presented as the ***arrival of the Kingdom:*** "The time has come; the kingdom of God is upon you; repent and believe in the Gospel" (Mk. 1: 15). This Kingdom of God which is also "the Kingdom of Christ"[24] is already present. For, insofar as it is the "triumphant grace of God which has been vouchsafed to the world as a whole with eschatological irrevocability in Jesus Christ and his death, and has become manifest in him, the Kingdom of God has already come ... ".[25] It is "the eschatological kingship which has intervened in these very days.... It is salvation for men, not judgement".[26]

But though the Kingdom – salvation for men – is proclaimed as imminent and even already present (Mt. 4: 17; Mk1: 15), it remains basically an eschatological reality, "an object of hope" of which the Church is the primordial sacrament and its beginning.[27] As Peter Huenermann says in reference to the use of the expression "Kingdom of God" in the Johannine writings, "the message of Christ is characterised by an eschatology – of life, death, judgement, joy and peace – which has been made a present reality (Schneckenburger)".[28] So the imminence and even the actual presence of the Kingdom does not in any way take away the eschatological character and, indeed, reality of this Kingdom – the final and definitive salvation form men.

The Kingdom of God, Salvation for men, is therefore actual but also eschatological. As Bultmann says: "Christ belongs in the eschatological kerygma – nevertheless not only as the judge but in that very fact also as the Saviour for those who belong to the congregation of the faithful".[79] Huenermann again expresses very well this dual aspect of the message of Christ, the "Kingdom of God," when in reference to the Book of Revelation he says: "In Revelation the eschatological Kingdom of God is identical with the Kingdom of Christ (Rev. 11: 15), and through Christ the Church has become the Kingdom of God (Rev, 1: 6; 5: 10). History is the battle-field where the hostile powers fight against this Kingdom, which triumphs in the end".[80]

This message of Christ: "The Kingdom of God" which is "Salvation for all men," is the core of what we have undertaken as study here, although in a particular context. As men living in history, which is "the battle-field where hostile powers fight against the Kingdom," we are all taken up in it. But this reality, if it is to be perceived rightly and intelligently, can only be perceived within those limits, circumstances, concepts and categories which are defined for the particular individual and people taken up in this global historical movement.

This reality of "The Kingdom of God," the Kingdom of Christ, man's total liberation and salvation, is both an existential reality and a transcendent, eschatological reality. It is a reality which is relevant to man in his actual existential situation, but at the same time transcends this existential situation and finds it fulness and totality in the eschatological. This is the reason why in examining the value of solidarity in view of the salvation in Christ, in what is the existential reality, we considered it necessary to investigate its transcendent aspect, to see in what way such a fundamental value can be an asset even on this level. In this way, it will bring home to the people concerned a better understanding of the salvation that Christ proclaimed and continues to proclaim. It will also help the people concerned to see how best this salvation can be conceived in their own categories and "Weltanschauung," so that it may truly say something to them. For, as experience has shown, if the categories, concepts and indeed, the entire "Weltanschauung" of the existential situation in which the people for whom the message if Christ's Salvation is destined are not taken into serious consideration in the continual proclamation of this message, they will turn out to be the greatest impediment to the understanding of the message. They will also be stumbling blocks to the practice of Christian charity itself; and they will obscure and make impossible the true vision of the message of Christ, meant for ***all of humankind***, as indeed universal.

Chapter Four Endnotes

1 Josef Fuchs, *Human Values and Christian Morality*, Gill and Macmillan Ltd., Dublin, 1970, p. 1.

2 *Ibid.*, pp. 3-15.

3 *Ibid.*, p. 70.

4 *Ibid.*, pp. 70-1.

5 *Ibid., p.* 71. See chapter one above, art. III, last two paragraphs of subdivision 'F': "The Fourth Session and the Emergence of Text V". (The amendment introduced by the German theologians).

6 Cfr. chapter three above, art. V: "Co-responsibility in Solidarity or A Law of Society".

7 In earlier western concept, the term 'family' also had a wider connotation than just the biological parents and children. Thus, for example in the 16th century, it included also the servants of the household. *See the Shorter Oxford English Dictionary on Historical Principles,* C.T. Onions (Editor-Reviser), Oxford University Press, Oxford, 1972; cfr. also, *Petit Robert*, Dictionnaire de la Langue Française, Paris, 1972.

8 The use of the plural, wives, here simply indicates the fact of polygamy, which subject, however, is not part of the research.

9 This is, in fact, part of the formula used in the formal request made to the 'parents,' (father and uncles, of the bride to be), for their daughter as a wife. At the end of courtship, representatives of the bridegroom-to-be are sent to ask the "parents" of the bride-to-be for their daughter's hand in marriage in this way: "so that she may come and be drawing water for him (the bridegroom)". For more details on marriage and courtship, confer A.A. Kuuire, *The Christian Faith in the Dagarti Culture*, op. cit., pp. 33-42. See also, J. Goody, The Social Organisation of the LoWiili, *op. cit.*, pp. 48-53.

10 Jack Goody gives a comprehensive description in the above *op. cit.*, pp. 38ff.

11 Robert N. Bellah (Editor), Emile Durkheim on Morality and Society, *op. cit.*, pp. 65, 66.

12 A.A. Kuuire, *op. cit.*, p. 12; See also J. Goody, The Social Organisation of the LoWiili, op. cit., pp. 41-3.

13 "Children" here refer more to the male descendants, since female ones get married and leave their patrilineage to build the lineages of their husbands. Cfr. J. Goody, op. cit., 52.

14 The expression "extended family" is used by anthropologists to refer to the concept of the family which goes beyond the social cellular of father, mother and children, most especially in reference to African societies. Among others, see Jack Goody and Maurice Delafosse whose works have often been referred to here.

15 A.A. Kuuire, *op. cit.*, p. 24.

16 Such a person becomes what we may describe as the intermediary between the ancestors and the living members of the family.

17 A.A. Kuuire, *op. cit.,* footnote 6, p. 22.

18 The "pere" referred to her is the biological father of the bridegroom-to-be. However, it can also refer to the one who takes immediate care of the groom-to-be in the case of the death of the latter's biological father. The responsibility of providing the dowry for the first wife of a man falls first to his biological father, or in case of his absence, to the one to whom such responsibility falls according to the tradition.

19 M. Delafosse, *Haut-Senegal-Niger*, Emile Larose, Paris, 1912, vol. 3, p. 95. Emphasis in highlight added.

20 Ibid., *loc cit.*

21 Confer chapter three above, Art. V, under the heading C; 'The Repercussion of the Individual's Moral Acts'.

22 Ibid., art. VI: 'Co-responsibility in Society, or a Law of Society, An Appreciation'.

23 Robert N. Bellah (Editor), *op. cit.*, p. 63.

24 Cfr. Chapter three above, art. III: Clan, Totemism and Solidarity Building.

25 The term 'People' is used here in the sense of "Tribe," Cfr. S.F. Nadel, *Black Byzantium*, London, Oxford University Press, 1041, p. 17; See also chapter three above, footnote 3.

26 M. Delafosse, *op. cit.*, vol. 3, p. 98.

<u>27</u> Marcel Mauss, *The Gift*; original: *"Essai sur le Don,"* Paris, 1950; trans. by Ian Gunnison; Cohen and West Ltd., London, 1970, pp. 6=16.

<u>28</u> Levi-Strauss, *Anthropologie Structurale*, Plon, Paris, 1958, p. 56.

<u>29</u> Cfr. footnote 20 above.

<u>30</u> Ibid.

<u>31</u> Cfr. chapter three above, art. III, A., "The Clan".

<u>32</u> A.A. Kuuire, *op. cit.*, p. 35; P. Sarpong, op. cit. When the patriclan is so large that it has been sub-divided, marriage between members of the individual sub-clans may be tolerated. But such marriages are still not viewed with much respect.

<u>33</u> See footnote 23 above.

<u>34</u> Robert N. Bellah (Editor*), op. cit.*, p. 65.

<u>35</u> E. Roosens, *Anthropologie Culturelle*, Unpublished MS, Lumen Vitae, Universite de Louvain, Belgique. 1970-71, pp. IV-2

<u>36</u> In his chapter on "Ghanaian values," under the sub-heading, 'National Pride,' Peter Sarpong sees in 'tribal pride' a value which, though could be a potential threat to national unity, nevertheless, could be channeled to the creation of national solidarity and reconstruction; *op. cit.*, pp. 67-8.

<u>37</u> Cfr. Andre Prost, *Les Mission des Peres Blancs en Afrique Occidentale Avant 1939*, Paris, 1970. See also A.A. Kuuire, op. cit., Part II, "Traditional Culture and Christianity at Cross-roads'"

<u>38</u> The city of Accra, for example, and the industrial area around it has groups of practically all the tribes in the country and others from outside living there. More and more, people, especially the young school-leavers from the rural areas, flock to the cities in search of employment. This phenomenon raises its multi-pastoral difficulties and questions, especially those of coping with the numbers and of facing up to the challenges sometimes presented by exaggerated tribal feelings.

<u>39</u> The Charter of the National Redemption Council (NRC), the Military government at the time in Ghana – 13th of January 1972 – had as the first of its seven basic goals of action: "One Nation, One People, One Destiny". In reality, all the "Seven Goals of Action" aimed to instill in all the citizens, despite their many

tribal differences, the sentiments of ONE PEOPLE. Thus Colonel I.K. Acheampong at the time, Head of State and Chairman of the NRC, saw the revolution by which the NRC had taken over power of government, as a chance for the country as a whole, to redirect herself towards "her God-given destiny". *The Charter of the National Redemption Council*, was published in December 1972.

40 The various number of languages, which correspond to the number of tribes in the country, is estimated between 50 and 80. Thus Sarpong says in "Vivant Univers," that "Le Ghana est un example de creation politique artificielle: 108 Etats indigenes' ont ete, vaille que vaille, mis ensemble par le colonisateur anglais et coexistent donc dans la republique independante nes de la Cote-de-l'Or ... Ils parlent 50 a 80 langues ... Leurs structures tribales sont restees tres vivaces, de meme que leurs croyances ancestrales. See "Reportage Special sur le Ghana," Vivant Univers, 269 (Juillet-Aout, 1970).

41 The most obvious expression of such national solidarity in our modern times is manifested particularly in the area of economy.

42 Raymond Brown, Joseph Fitzmayer and Roland Murphy (Editors), *The Jerome Biblical Commentary*, Geoffrey Chapman, London, 1970, vol. 1, p.30 (Jacob's Children); On the composition of the People of Israel cfr. M. North, *History of Israel*, revised transl. by P.R. Ackroyd, New York, 1960, pp85-108; also, John Bright, *A History of Israel*, SCM Press Ltd., London, 1972, particularly pp. 130-9.

43 P. Sarpong, *op. cit.*, pp 67-8

44 In most nations, workers come together in order to defend themselves against the daily economic threats to their survival. Their perceptible common destiny is that of survival, and to achieve it they must defend themselves against oppression and exploitation, but only if they are united together in solidarity. This is the very (economic) motive which brings together several nations producing the same raw material; for example, the cocoa producing countries (of which Ghana, my country is one); The OPEC countries who come together to take solidary stand (in pricing) after having felt themselves exploited long enough by the

buying countries. The European (Economic) Community is also an obvious example of such a struggle for survival through solidarity action.

45 Cfr. Chapter three above, towards the end of section VI, "Co-responsibility in Solidarity or a Law of Society: An Appreciation".

46 Ibid., Section V, c: "The Repercussion of the Individual's Moral Acts;" see also above, under Section I, B, number 2: "Solidarity in the Extended Family".

47 This was in a sermon delivered at the occasion of his Installation as the first Ghanaian Archbishop of Tamale on March 23, 1975. Present at the ceremony was the Head of State himself at the time, I.K. Acheampong, and many other members of the Government of the day, and also prominent Ghanaian personalities.

48 Cfr. above, under Section II, Subdivision B, under no.1, "Genuine and Positive Tribal Solidarity".

49 The term 'religion' here can loosely be taken to extend to what, in our anthropological approach, we have preferred to express by the term "supranatural;" cfr., chapter three.

50 Peter Cardinal P.P. Dery, "Installation Homily," Tamale, March 23, 1974. The emphases are added, and so are the texts in brackets.

51 Peter Sarpong, *op. cit.*, p. 68.

52 Cfr. Chapter Three above, Section V, B: "Evil, 'Sin' in Dagara 'Theology,'" last two paragraphs of number 2; also, Section VI of the same Chapter. And cfr. also footnote 49 above.

53 See chapter three, section III: "Clan, Totemism and the Building of Solidarity". Cfr. also, above, the discussion of true and genuine tribal sentiments. CALLIXTE KALISA consider that the cult of the ancestors. (Bazimu), is all that which put the Rwandan in constant contact with the dead members of his family. These include the honour he renders to them, the invocations and requests he makes to them for their intervention, offerings, libations and immolations made in their honour. Nevertheless, he is convinced that "through the immolations, the libations, offerings, the Rwandans has absolutely no intention whatsoever of rendering the 'Bazimu' as creatures of their level, to the

subalternate beings of which they acknowledge some defects and some weakness, but of which they also acknowledge great power" *(translation from the original French, mine)*. The cult therefore, with which the ancestors are honoured is a means by which contact with them is closely kept, and which in its turn fosters and maintains that brotherhood between members of a particular family.

54 GSp, art. 22; see also chapter two above, section V, subdivision B: "Other Values Reaffirmed by the Incarnation". John Macquarie, a noted Anglican theologian, in his discussion on Christian Unity and Christian Diversity considers the reality of Christ as the core of Christian Unity. As he writes: "Jesus Christ himself is the foundation of that Unity". Cfr. his book; *Christian Unity and Christian Diversity*, SCM Press Ltd., London, 1975, p. 4.

55 This expression, "fact of Christ," is used here to mean all what Christ **is** and **stands** for.

56 J. Goody, Death, Property and the Ancestors, pp. 371-8.

57 Cfr. chapter three, section IV: "The Ancestor: Norm of Morality and Mainstay of Solidarity".

58 J. Goody, *op. cit.*, p. 371; See also, A.A. Kuuire, *op. cit.*, pp. 52-4.

59 Louis Girault, *"Essai sur la Religion des Dagara,"* in *L'IFAN*, Dakar, 21(1959), p. 352.

60 J. Goody, *op. cit.*, p. 371.

61 J. Goody, *The Myth of the Bagre*, Oxford University Press, London, 1972, p. 22, footnote 2.

62 J. Goody, *Death, Property and the Ancestors*, pp. 208-219; Cfr. also, G.E. Kpiebaya, *op. cit.*, p. 38.

63 J Goody, *The Myth of Bagre*, op. cit., p. 39. G.E. Kpiebaya devotes a whole section of his second chapter to what he entitles, "God in Divination or Soothsaying," and in this section, discusses how the cause of every mishap is looked for. Cfr. *op. cit.*, pp. 37-52.

64 A.A. Kuuire, *op. cit.*, pp. 61-3; *J. Goody, Death Property and the Ancestors*, pp. 236, 374 ff; G.E. Kpiebaya, op. cit., p. 105.

65 The resemblance or non-resemblance, on the grounds of which the "Kpiipaala" is admitted, or not admitted into the

company of his ancestors, is not that of a physical resemblance, but a moral one. He resembles his ancestors or not, through what he has done in his actual life here on earth; whether he has been loyal to the customs and traditions of the lineage, established by the ancestors, or clan; and has faithfully carried out his part of the responsibilities that fell to him as member of such a group of belonging. If he has done some wrong, and has not purified himself of it through ritual sacrifice by which he becomes reconciled again to his ancestors, then, he will have lost that "resemblance" of them, and therefore, cannot be deemed worthy to be admitted into their company. (For, the offense which has been committed in the group of belonging, and has not been expiated remains in him until he has been purified and so returns him to his status as a faithful member). This explains the so many and complicated ceremonies of divination, and subsequent rites of purification that must take place at and after the death of a person. Cfr. *Jack Goody, Death, Property and the Ancestors,* especially pp. 49-269.

66 G.E. Kpiebaya, *op. cit.,* p. 106.

67 In the "Dagara Eschatology," the idea of a state of permanent separation, by which one would never be reunited with the ancestors and the Eschatological Congregation, does not obtain. The "journey" may last longer for those who have been bad and therefore have not been recognized as having the resemblance of the ancestors in this eschatological congregation – Dapar – and so, are rejected at first by the ancestors,' may take even as long as "one thousand years," with many hard trials such as in the "dazuge vuu," before they may eventually get admission to '*Dapar*'. But the final arrival in Dapar is never put into question. See J. Goody, op. cit., pp. 374-8; also, A.A. Kuuire, op. cit., pp. 61-3.

68 Food and drink are what keeps man in being and alive. So, the abundance of it in the "Land of the Ancestors" symbolizes the totality of security and so, endless joy.

69 A.A. Kuuire, *op. cit.,* pp. 58-9.

70 G. E. Kpiebaya, *op. cit.,* p. 107.

71 Confer chapter three above, in Introduction.

72 J. Goody, *The Myth of the Bagre,* p. 15.

73 A.A. Kuuire, op. cit., p. 78. This fact is what led Louis-Vincent Thomas to write of Africa in general in this way: "La conduite religieuse africaine frappe son caractere de globalite et le sacre n'y apparait que rarement a l'état pur. Il est meme loisiblede se demander si les dichotomies occidantales: profane-sacre, religion-magie, conservent quelque semblant de verité dans une optique negro-africaine traditionelle". In a footnote, he further quotes G. Dieterlan, who holds the following: "Dans les croyances et les systems de pensée d'Afrique noire, aucune reelle n'est faite a ce que nous nommons le profane ... Chaque chose, meme la plus humble, a sa place, joue un role et ou le hazard n'a pointed part ... Rien de ce que Dieu a cree ne peut etre neglige." Louis-Vincent Thomas, *Les Religions d'Afrique Noire*, Fayard/Deneel, Paris, 1969, pp. 23-4.

74 Karl Rahner, Herbert Vorgrimler, *Concise Theological Dictionary*, Cornelius Ernst (Editor), English translation by Richard Strachan, Burns and Oates, London, 1965, p. 251.

75 Ibid., loc. Cit.

76 Peter Huenemann, "Reign of God: The Kingdom of God in the Message of Jesus," *in Sacramentum Mundi*, Karl Rahner (Editor), Engl. Trans. , Burns and Oates, London, 1970, vol.5, p. 235, emphasis supplied.

77 K. Rahner, H. Vorgrimler, *op. cit.*, loc. Cit.

78 P. Huenermann, *op. cit.*, p. 237

79 Rudolf Bultmann, *Theology of the New Testament*. SCM Press Ltd., London (Fourth Edition), vol.1, 1974, pp. 78-9.

80 P. Huenermann, op. cit., p. 237.

81 Peter Huenermann, "Reign of God," *Sacramentum Mundi*, Editor, K. Rahner, Burns and Oates, London, 1970 vol. 5, p. 236; cfr. also, Wolfhart Pannenberg, *Jesus – God and Man*, The Westminster Press, Philadelphia, 1974, Chapter 10, in particular pp. 365-97.

82 P. Huenermann, *op. cit*, pp. 236-7

83 Ibid., *loc. cit.*

84 GSp, Art. 32: see also, art. 30.

85 Ibid., Art. 24.

PART THREE

FROM POSSIBLE CONFRONTATION TO MUTUAL ENRICHMENT

AN INTRODUCTION

The Human Situation: Reception of the Salvation
Proffered by and in Christ

In the conclusion to our last chapter, we remarked the fact that the message proclaimed by Christ was one of the coming of "The Kingdom of God," Christ's own Kingdom. This message carries in it the good news, great hope for all men; hope of deliverance and of liberation. For, The Kingdom whose arrival is proclaimed "is salvation for men, not judgement". The 'fact of Christ' himself has become the reign of God, and, so, the salvation for men. As Peter Huenermann puts it: "Jesus' message of the reign of God at hand is absorbed in the Christ-event;"[81] i.e. the paschal mysteries, passion, death, and resurrection of Christ. Thus, he continues: "The post-paschal faith sees the passion and death of Jesus as a salvific event of the reign of God proclaimed by Jesus".[82]

This same Jesus is the one in whom the Kingdom was at hand,[83] and so, in Jesus himself is realised and made perceptible the Kingdom, this salvation for all men. This Kingdom of God, the message of Christ which is **salvation for all men**, is therefore the *"Evangelium"* which Christ asked his Apostles to proclaim in all parts of the world: "Go forth," he said, "to every part of the world, and proclaim the Good News to the whole of Creation. Those who believe it and receive baptism will find salvation" (Mk. 16: 15-16). In this perspective, it thus becomes obvious why Paul, who was not "ashamed of the Gospel" but rather considered it "the saving power of God for everyone who has faith" (Rom. 1:

16), preached Christ himself as the core of the *Evangelium*, this salvation for all. "He (Christ) it is whom we proclaim" (Col. 1: 28). Christ who died and was raised to life is the Gospel of salvation preached by Paul (1 Cor. 15: 1ff).

It is opportune to remark here how the same Paul who was not ashamed of this Gospel also considered himself under obligation to both Greek and non-Greek, to the learned and to the simple (Rom. 1: 14) in his task of proclaiming Christ; and this he puts forward as the reason for his eagerness to go to Rome where he could proclaim this Gospel also to the people there. Although himself a free man under no master, Paul has no illusions about his obligation of preaching the Gospel – Christ, the Kingdom of God that saves – to all without any prejudicial distinction of the different cultures of the people to whom he must preach. This he states unequivocally when he concedes: "To Jews I became like a Jew, to win the Jews ... To Gentiles ... I made myself like one of them ... To the weak, I became weak, to win the weak. Indeed, I have become everything in turn to men of every sort, so that in one way or another I may save some." And he reveals the reason for which he does that: "All this I do for the sake of the Gospel, to bear my part in proclaiming it" (1 Cor. 9: 20-23).

What is therefore imperative for Paul is that Christ, God's Kingdom and Men's Salvation, be preached to everyone irrespective of the cultural situation in which he may be, or finds himself, even of to the Jews this Gospel, Christ, is a stumbling-block, and to the Greeks, folly (1 Cor. 1:23). For, it is this *Evangelium*, this news of the "Christ-event" which is the saving power of God for everyone, Jews as well as Greeks (Rom. 1: 16).

This imperative, that salvation be preached to all without any prejudice to cultural differences, is what GSp reaffirms, as Has been discussed in chapter two of the present study.

But GSp, basing itself on Holy Scripture, also sees the attainment of this salvation not as a task of the individual alone, but one of solidarity.[84] For, the vocation of man to his ultimate destiny – thus to Salvation – is communitarian in nature, in which all men should form but one family and "treat one another in a spirit of brotherhood".[85]

It is under the inspiration of these affirmations reiterated by PCCMW that we undertook to examine the cultural value of solidarity in a given culture, that of the Dagara, so that we could see how far such a value could permit the and reign of Christ who is salvation for all men, in their midst. If the value of solidarity among them, as we have analysed it, is so fundamental, and pervades their whole moral stratum and, in fact, all spheres of their life, why should such a value be allowed to be thrown out together with everything traditional, which has been considered as "unchristian" and superstitious or smacking of superstition as many other cultural and traditional practices have been branded?

The important thing which is even sometimes, unfortunately, obscured by some particular circumstances is that "Christ be proclaimed" (1 Cor. 1: 22); Paul even argues that Christ did not send him to be administering baptism, "but to proclaim the Gospel; ... so that the fact of Christ on his cross might have its full weight" (1 Cor: 1: 17). In the light of this, therefore, it is logical that any cultural value that has been cultivated and cherished by a people, and which is not in any direct opposition to the coming of the Kingdom in their midst, should not only not be uncritically rejected, but rather, should be utilised to the maximum "so that the fact of Christ on his cross – the coming of his Kingdom which is salvation for men, and indeed, the thing that matters – may have its full weight". Such, after our close examination of it against the background of the affirmations of GSp, with particular reference to the Dagara, is the cultural value of solidarity. A sound cultural value, the concepts and categories of which could fully be utilised to bring out the full weight of the salvation in Christ in their midst.

In the task which remains to be done in this research, we shall reexamine the implications of human solidarity in salvation as it is affirmed in GSp, using a theological approach to the question of salvation as a task of solidarity. This will serve as a search-light with which we shall, in our last chapter, attempt to reappraise the value of solidarity in the Dagara context in the light of Christian salvation, after an evaluation of the Dagara concept of salvation.

CHAPTER FIVE

SALVATION AS A TASK OF HUMAN SOLIDARITY IN "GAUDIUM ET SPES" AND IN THE LIGHT OF CHRISTIAN THEOLOGY

The Theological Situation: An Assessment

Earlier in the research, we pointed out how the two constitutions of the Second Vatican Council: Lumen Gentium (LGen) and Gaudium et Spes (GSp) complete each other, and for which reason the latter must be read in conjunction with the former.[1] This remains a valid premise throughout our research.

Speaking on 'Moral Theology of Human Culture,' John O'Riordan pointed out that Vat. II, in dealing with the cultural realities of our times, especially in GSp, has solemnly proclaimed the Church to be accessible to all cultures; hence cultural pluralism in unity of the same faith. This, the author asserts after he has remarked how the Roman culture of the Western Church had continued her geographical expansion in the post-medieval era, but then gradually diminished to only an ideal culture in the face of the growing force of new cultures.[2] This is quite interesting for us, especially when it comes to discerning the message from some particular epochs with their cultural background that did not remain neutral to the message.

Now, as LGen has made it clear, the Church is "a society of fellowship with God, the sacrament of salvation the People of God established as the body of Christ".[3] But this Church, despite the tension that exists between it and the Kingdom, and which tension thus shows the non-complete identification of the two,[4] is nevertheless also the salvation for men. Seen as the "Mystery of Christ" (Eph. 3: 4), the effective sign (sacramentum) of Christ who himself is God's Kingdom, salvation for all men,[5] the Church is thus also "salvation for all men, "the universal sacrament (sign) of salvation, (of the presence of God's Kingdom (of Christ himself) among men".[6] Thus Peter Huenermann, basing himself on the Book of Revelation (Rev. 1: 6; 5: 10), says: "... through Christ the Church has become the Kingdom of God".[7]

But this Church also carries in it, as Christ himself did, the Good News which she has to proclaim. As Marie-Joseph le Guillou says: "The sacramental structure of the Church is also the foundation of the mission of the Church". [8] This Good News is none other than what Paul and the other Apostles proclaimed – Christ dead and risen (1 Cor. 1: 22-3; 15: 1-4, 12), the presence of the Kingdom of God, the Kingdom of Christ (Rev. 11: 15),[9] salvation for men.

It is therefore still this Gospel – the Kingdom of God, Christ dead and risen, the salvation for all men – which this Church has the mission to proclaim. But in so doing, the Church cannot forget that her fidelity to this mission lays at the same time also in her the obligation to both "Greeks and non-Greeks" who, in their existential conditions, differ from one another, and that she therefore has to "become everything in turn to men of every sort" in order that she may bring the Kingdom of God, Christ, salvation to the doors of every man in the circumstances that *is* the "*world*" for him and is, indeed, part and parcel of him. Becoming everything to everyone cannot be realised without entering into his "*world*" and its values through which he "can come to an authentic and full humanity".[10] The different forms of culture into which the Church has to go and to proclaim her message is therefore what J. O'Riordan points out as being clearly and solemnly proclaimed by Vat. II, especially by the Constitution, GSp, when it admitted the accessibility of the Church to all cultures.[11] This does not in any way destroy the unity in the same faith.

Indeed, this mission of the Church to proclaim the mission of salvation to all men in their particular *"Sitz-im-Leben"* so clearly restated by GSp is a fundamental premise in the preaching of Christ. When the PCCMW affirmed the role of faith in Christ in the context of human culture which has its importance in the total vocation of man, [12] and had previously recognised the historical, sociological and ethnological aspects which give culture its pluriform,[13] it thus recognised that same imperative which already obliged Paul to "become everything in turn to men of every sort," in order to make them perceive in the context of their own particular *"Sitz-im-Leben"* and so in their own mode of perceiving, and through their own categories the salvation that is contained for them in this message, Christ proclaimed. It is no wonder that Paul had to face Peter squarely, and blame him for what he was convinced was the wrong thing the latter was doing (Gal. 2: 11-2). And in fact, his own discourse to the Court of Areopagus shows Paul getting into the "world" of the Areopagites, with the message of salvation, so that from within their own "world" he could proclaim God's sovereignty to them in their own concepts (Acts 17: 22-34).

This recognition and restatement of the values inherent in culture, and of the pluriform of culture itself by GSp, is important for our whole argumentation here for presenting the Gospel of salvation to all men, but in the most fruitful manner to each. Although before the Council, some theologians and missionaries were already reawakened to the apostolic and patristic true concern that Christ's message of salvation reach man in and through whatever circumstances constitute his "world,"[14] nevertheless, remains, unfortunately, true that for the most part, Christ's message of salvation was perceived for centuries by many evangelisers to be mainly in confrontation with, and in opposition to, the very original cultures and traditions which claimed the Evangelium as if theirs only.

With this claim by those of the original cultures in which the message of Christ's salvation was preached, all the cultures and traditions of all other peoples could never be considered as ever being possible assets and vehicles, or even instruments by which and through which this **Good News** of salvation in Christ might ever find a valid and firm lodgment. And so, in addressing Christ's message of Salvation to the people in such other cultures and traditions, these cultures would have to be changed into the so-called Christian cultures before the adherents therein may be made ready of for the salvation Christ has proffered to all of mankind. The concrete example which G.E. Kpiebaya has given to demonstrate such an attitude; rejection of practically everything cultural and traditional to a particular previously non-Christian people by some missionaries, is typical of many other overt manifestations of the quasi complete rejection of a culture as being contrary to, and incompatible in every way with, 'Christianity'.[15] Gregory Kpiebaya writes thus, about a missionary:

> When he commenced his inquiries into the customs of the people, he wrote at the top of his note book the subject of his study: 'Concerning the useless things of the Dagaaba (Dagaaba Bonwiiri yele)'. Among these useless things, he went on to enumerate all the things the Dagaaba do at the most crucial moments of their live: All the 'Rites de passage,' i.e. pregnancy, birth, naming of the child, childhood, courtship, marriage and death. Then he included in the useless things all that they do during

sickness, the various cults and festivals. As a matter of fact, the entire culture of the people was branded: 'Useless Things'".

Kpiebaya, after enumerating all this, finished up with his personal comment of disgust at such an attitude, exclaiming, "What horror, to call the culture of a people 'Useless'!"[16]

In fact, not only had the message of Christ often been wrongly identified with one particular culture, with a 'system,'[17] by which fact others could be considered as opposed to and therefore not capable of offering their values as assets for the reception of the message of salvation, God's Reign in their midst, but salvation itself has often been from a single dimensional point of view and the attainment of it perceived as an individual task in which charity for the "neighbour" became at times just a means by which one would gain individually his heaven.

The One-Dimensional Approach to Salvation

In an article entitled "One-Dimensional Christianity?"[18], Jacques-Marie Pohier criticises the absence of the Supernatural in the writings of Herbert Marcuse for whom, not only is God dead (as for Marx and Freud), but religion itself is dead and so, no longer represents any danger for the modern western man on his way to liberation. However, for Pohier, the total absence of God and of the supernatural in the writings of Marcus who is also in quest of man's liberation just as Christianity, Marxism and psychoanalysis (associated with Freud), focuses his attention rather on another question tacitly raised by this lack of the supernatural in Marcuse does not confront him so much as a believer face to face with complete unbelief. It rather poses before him, as a Christian theologian, a more internal, personal and fundamental question which, in fact, every Christian should pose himself.

This question is other than a confrontation of the claims of Christianity, and Marcuse who criticises the western man as "one-dimensional," and prophesises the ultimate 'Great Refusal' of this one-dimensionality by which he (the western man) will obtain the liberation of himself. Pohier's question centers rather on "whether the Church does preach the liberation announced by Christ; and if what Jesus Christ announced really is a liberation". As he puts it, "I need to know if Christian man is one-dimensional man"[19].

In his quest for an answer to this question, Pohier is convinced that the point of departure and the area of interrogation should be in the *actual and historical attitudes* of Christianity, i.e., in the practice itself of Christianity, and not simply in ideological affirmations. He arrives at the conclusion that it is a question of confronting the prophets and Jesus, and the cries raised by men, children of God. Thus, he says: "Much rather than causing us to have recourse to more or less messianic, eschatological, or apocalyptic utopias, this causes us to consider the question of whether or not to believe that there has come to be, through God and in Jesus Christ, in the here-and-now of our history, that which, in man and his world, stands for the principle of this other 'dimension' and makes its realisation possible".[20]

Christian practice should never allow a 'one-dimensionalisation' of the relation of man to his world through a weakening of his relation with God; nor should it permit a 'one-dimensionalisation' of man's relation with God, in which the relationship to the world will simply be reduced and absorbed into the relation with God. For, as Pohier affirms with good reason, "the paradox of God's creative action is precisely that it gives man his human dimension and the world its worldly dimension;"[21] and he concludes by saying that it is a Christian's witness which must prove that the faith is not one-dimensional, just as the love of God for men is itself not one-dimensional but multi-dimensional.

This critical scrutiny of Christianity as 'one-dimensional' by Pohier is obviously inspired, in our view, by GSp, particularly chapter two of part one which concerned itself with the community of Mankind. In underscoring the divine plan which gives man's vocation a communitarian nature, GSp has clearly indicated that salvation to which man is "re-called" by God is not attained simply and only through one's direct and exclusive personal relationship with God alone. For, after affirming the brotherhood of all men in God's plan, GSp argues saying: "For this reason, love for God and neighbour is the first and greatest commandment".₂₂ Further on, recalling the prayer of Christ for unity (Jn. 17: 21-22), GSp considers that Jesus, in this prayer, "has opened up new horizons closed to human reason by implying that there is a certain parallel between the union existing among the divine persons and the union of the sons of God in truth and love".₂₃

The call of man therefore to his ultimate destiny, salvation, does not demand only the establishment of the one-dimensional relationship between man himself and God – the vertical dimension – but also and equally a relationship of love between man and his fellow men; a horizontal relationship in which men will be united to one another as "the sons of God in truth". Thus Semmelroth quite rightly remarks in his comment on article 24: "The remarkable fact is pointed out that love of God must not only not be separated from love of neighbour, but that in the N.T. both seemed to be so fused that the one almost seems to be identified with the other".₂₄ As he later asserts, "The third point of this article (i.e., the prayer of Jesus which opened up a certain parallelism between the union among the divine persons and union in the love that should obtain among men themselves) give the essentially Christian interpretation of the unity of love of God and the neighbour, and thereby explains how the vertical and horizontal dimensions are linked".[25] Thus it is indeed in the practical application of this horizontal dimension, "through his dealing with others, through reciprocal duties, and through fraternal dialogue develops all his gifts and is able to rise to his destiny".[26]

In fact, if we return to a certain point in the history of PCCMW, the discussion on the fourth Text of PCCMW in a meeting which took place between some German bishops and theologians on one side, and some French and Belgian bishops and theologians on the other side, on the 17th of September 1965, a certain concern to see that both man's relations with the supernatural and with his fellow men and the world around him are clearly presented in the totality of his vocation, was quite manifest.[27] This represents respectively the vertical and the horizontal dimensions in which man is taken up in his salvation history.

So GSp, in reasserting the brotherhood of all men (art. 24) and also in recognising the value of the activity of man himself (art. 34), has made it clearer than ever that the salvation to which man is called, or rather recalled, is not attained by way of a "one-dimensional Christianity," the vertical dimension alone, but that in the plan of God, the answer to this call to salvation must also embrace the horizontal dimension by which he, man, is united in truth and in love to his fellow men who are also sons and daughters of God, and have also the one and the same vocation.

Individualistic Morality Insufficient for Salvation

Considering that the horizontal dimension in man's vocation is put on practically the same level with the vertical, salvation can therefore not be an individual task; not even in that in which charity for the neighbour is said to be present but may turn out to be only a sort of relation by which the individual simply uses the neighbour as a means for gaining his heaven, rather than a sincere concern to reach salvation together.

In his magistral work, 'The Law of Christ,' Bernhard Häring, in a discourse on the salvation of others as a universal obligation, points out, on scriptural grounds, the obligation of everyone who has already heard of the Good News and believed, i.e., every Christian, to engage actively in the work of salvation of his neighbour. After asserting the particular task of those specially dedicated to the salvation of others by consecration, he states unequivocally the obligation of the others: "But nothing could be further from the truth, more hazardous to our spiritual welfare and more unchristian in its implications than to think that the obligation to care for the salvation of souls with active effort depended solely and utterly on a special or specified office. ... every Christian must be concerned with the salvation of his neighbour's soul. He must further the work of salvation by active engagement wherever and whenever he can".[28]

This is a theological perspective of Christian morality in regards to salvation that was stated before Vat. II.[29] Although the author does not go on here to relate this perspective explicitly to the motivations of the one who engaged actively in the salvation of the others, one thing which seems obvious is that such an engagement excludes from its motivations any selfish and individualistic objective by which the one engaged in it would, in so doing, simply seek to gain some "purchasing power" for "buying" his heaven, his own personal individual salvation. This is clear when the author, in explaining the meaning of dedication of oneself to the apostolate, says: "It is to yield to the impulse of love, and to strive that divine love which animates us, fulfill its mission;

that it become the bearer of glad tidings to others, assist them to discover the love of Christ and also, for their part, surrender to him in a consummation of divine love". [30] This demands nothing short of a moral attitude which is based on the conviction that the Kingdom is not something that the individual can "buy" the right to enter into, but that he can enter into it only through a dedication of himself to the others in the genuine desire that they may **together** answer their common vocation, the invitation of all men to come into this Kingdom, God's Kingdom for which they were destined – THEIR SALVATION.

The individualistic and self-centered conception in regards to salvation, by which the individual is so preoccupied with his personal salvation to such a degree that all charitable acts become for him mere 'buying power,' is surely included in what PCCMW considers as individualistic morality that needs to be transcended. After admitting a one-sided development towards individualism in morality,[31] article 30 of GSp goes on to affirm: "It grows increasingly true that the obligation of justice and love are fulfilled only if each person, contributing to the common good, according to his own abilities and the needs of the others, also promotes and assists the public and private institutions dedicated to bettering the conditions of human life".

It is certain that the Council was here concerned with the social domain in particular. But as Otto Semmelroth points out, this one-sided development towards an increasing individualism has its origin in a theology of salvation and piety that dates back to the latter Middle Ages.[32] As he says: "Individualistic preoccupation with salvation has adversely affected the Church's doctrine in the eyes of the public, and is also to some extent strongly opposed to Christian affirmation of the social domain;" and he continues:

A purely individualistic ethics is treated in the conciliar text as prevalent to a large extent, but as something to which we must not remain attached. This applies to the individual who has to overcome the indolence which imprisons him in his own ego. But, reading between the lines, we can see that it also applies to the general mentality of Christians, this cannot continue to be tied to the individualistic attitude which has dominated the life of faith and piety in the last few centuries.

By this, he concludes.[33] Bernhard Häring, speaking about what he calls "The Shift from a Generally Individualistic Determination of Sin to a Vision Determined by History of Salvation and Solidarity of Salvation," focuses precisely on this individualistic idea of salvation when he said:

In the Bible, the main decision of salvation is the choice between a saving solidarity in Christ, and a destructive solidarity in sin. ... An individualistic concept of sin that developed in the past centuries was culturally conditioned. ... We can see an example of this individualistic concept of salvation and sin in the otherwise beautiful book of Thomas a Kempis, 'The Imitation of Christ.'[34]

Further on, speaking on the concept of Original Sin, Häring says:

Revelation and authentic theology speak on sin, particularly on Original Sin, only in the essential context of the grace of the Covenant, the calling to live in co-responsibility for the salvation of the world, and thus be free from co-responsibility for corruption in the world. Therefore, the fundamental option of one's own life is not centered on the salvation of one's own soul – although surely each individual is called to salvation – but on the final choice for salvation in solidarity with the good, which is offered us by Christ and which alerts us to the horrifying slavery under the solidarity of perdition for those who do not choose Christ.[35]

Thimotheus Rast also confirms this individualistic attitude in theology in the last centuries. Writing on individual eschatology and universal eschatology, in 'Bilan de la Theologie du XXe Siècle he says:

Jusqu'il a peu – du moins inconsciemment, mais souvent cependant de facon fort reflechie – il se cachait derriere toutes les questions eschatologiques que l'on posait a la theologie, l'aspiration a obtenir la certitude concernant son propre salut, la securite touchant son propre sort, et donc individu et l'eschatologie individuelle. Aujourd'hui, l'eschatologie cherche a nouveau, de plus en plus, a inserer la question du sort individuel dans une eschatologie authentique, a fondement Biblique, de toute la creation, dans l'attente de salut de toute l'Eglise du Christ et de tout le cosmos.[36]

One can therefore validly see in the teaching of GSp a rejection of any 'human salvation' which would be self-centered and individualistic, and in which the ethic would be thus reduced to one of purchasing one's paradise, even if one would falsely and shrewdly use the term *'Christian charity,'* which, in its true meaning, is the all-embracing love of God[37] that makes the lover to give himself up for the beloved (Gal. 2: 20; Jn. 3: 15). The Christian who has the responsibility to work towards his salvation, "to rise to his destiny by spending himself for God and for others" (GSp art. 31), needs to go beyond all individualistic morality, and to answer to his invitation to salvation within the framework of a solidarity in which he is related to, and united with all other men who, because of their common dignity, share the one and the same destiny (art. 12).

Thus, the value of human solidarity as basic for salvation, both in the vertical and horizontal dimensions, the multi-dimensional aspect of salvation, has been re-asserted by GSp within the global context of the salvation that Christ proclaimed. This gives back to the strife for salvation its multi-dimensional Christianity of the past centuries, and also the solidarity aspect of salvation which became marginalised through the individualistic tendencies of the later Middle Ages that pervaded even the domain of theology.

Salvation in Christ Summit of the Reality of Human Solidarity

Jesus Christ and Human Solidarity

If 'Gaudium et Spes' considers individualistic morality as insufficient both for the bettering of man's conditions of life now, and, a fortiori, in view of his ultimate destiny, it did not just stop there. The document went on to point out explicitly how the ultimate destiny itself of man, salvation, is a communitarian task and therefore a task of solidarity. This characteristic of salvation, GSp further affirms, finds its perfect fulfillment in Christ and thus, in the salvation proclaimed in the 'Christ-event'.

After recalling that man was not created to live as an individual, but in social unity with others, GSp repeats what is already stated in LGen₃₈ saying: "So also 'it has pleased God to make men holy and save them not merely as individuals, without any mutual bonds, but by making them into a single people, ...' So, from the beginning of salvation history He has chosen men not just as individuals but as members of a certain community".[39] In this assertion, the reality that men are bound to work together in solidarity towards their salvation could not be more clearly stated. The fact that God created man, not an isolated individual but that he may form a unity with other men, is a clear indication that man will only attain that destiny for which God created him and to which he called him, not as isolated individual, but in a community of solidarity with others.

This communitarian character of the salvation to which God has destined men from creation reached, in human history, its supreme perfection, its summit, in the Incarnation of the Word of God who was with God from all eternity, and was himself, God (Jn. 1: 1). It is in Christ, the Incarnate Word of God, that the communitarian and solidarity character of salvation finds again its true foundation, and is further illuminated and perfected. As the PCCMW says: "This communitarian character is perfected and fulfilled in the work of Jesus Christ, for the Word made flesh willed to share in human fellowship" (art. 32).[40] Christ the Second Adam (Rom. 5: 14), who is God made visible (Col. 1: 15), by his Incarnation has not only revealed man's own mystery to him, but has also united himself with every man.[41] Thus, in his Incarnation in which he has become solidary with every man, "He revealed the love of his Father and the sublime vocation of man in terms of the most common of social realities. ... He sanctified those human ties, especially family ones, from which social relationships arise".[42]

It is certainly true that by the Incarnation, Christ has raised all the domains of human life to a sublime dignity; one by which not only the individual but the whole of humanity is divinised, or re-divinised, as we may say, and has thereby become capable of attaining the fullness to which God has destined it.[43] But another reality which the Incarnation of the

Word has brought to its greatest and total illumination is that, not only is human life and the whole of humanity raised "in Christ into living unity with God," but that Christ who has thus become solidary with all men, and given himself up for love of each and everyone (Jn. 15: 13), has become himself the foundation of a new brotherhood among men. He has become a bond of saving solidarity in which all the members become related and bound one to the other. As Häring puts it, "We find the chief manifestation of the solidarity of salvation on this earth in Jesus Christ, the Word Incarnate".[44]

It is this community of brotherhood, "this solidarity which must be constantly increased until that day on which it will be brought to perfection[45] - saved by grace – which will be able to offer glory to God as a family. Thus, the full perfection of the social solidarity of men, which Semmelroth says is confirmed and sacramentally represented on the plane of salvation,[46] can be perceived as such in the light of Christ, God's Incarnate Word, who has thus truly given back the dignity of man to him by becoming solidary with man in sharing his humanity. The Church therefore as a continuation of the historical Christ, and so, proclaimer of his salvation, can be perceived as the "sacrament" of that supreme perfection here of the bond of human solidarity. Thus, through his Incarnation, Christ has become the summit of the reality of human solidarity apart from the fact that through the same Incarnation, he has raised human life into a living unity with God through his own life – the ***"Christ-event"***.

Solidarity in Salvation, and Solidarity in Alienation and Perdition

One cannot speak about the salvation proffered by and in Christ, or any other salvation, without having to face also the reality of the situation in which man 'was' and still, in fact, is constituted – the situation of sin and alienation – and from which situation he needs to be saved, to be liberated, to be redeemed, to be freed and set on the way again to that destiny for which he was created, to which he has been recalled after sin.[47] As GSp reaffirms the revelation of Holy Scripture, man was created "in the image of God," with a dignity and a specific destiny. Neither was he created as a solitary being in his kind, but right from the start he was created in companionship and interpersonal communion, and for which reason "unless he relates himself to others, he can neither live nor develop his potential".[48]

However, through 'sin' the situation of security, the destiny for which man was created, has been disturbed, and man finds himself surrounded by insecurity and uncertainty. This is the fact asserted by GSp when it says: "Often refusing to acknowledge God as his beginning, man has disrupted also his proper relationship to his own ultimate goal;" and by so doing has become out of harmony with himself, with others, and with all created things at the same time.[49] This demonstrates once more, how though each person is and remains an individual, man cannot realise his fulfilment, his ultimate goal in creation as an isolated individual. Karl Rahner has reason therefore when describing man's personal nature, he calls him 'a community-building person' and further specifies him as "an incarnate, mundane person who realises himself in his ultimate core only in a spatio-temporal, pluralistic expansion, in concern for his bodily existence (economy) and within a community communicated in a tangible manner".[50]

So, human history, which is also the history of salvation, is truly the battlefield where the powers hostile to man are at war against the Kingdom,[51] that the Kingdom in which all uncertainties would be dispelled and man regain his original security to which he was destined at the dawn of creation. The communitarian nature which God gives man through his vocation (GSp art. 24), thereby creating the solidarity of men, makes man enter into this battlefield either in solidarity with others for the Kingdom and hence to salvation, or in a solidarity that is sinful and is dominated by the hostile dark powers, and hence leads to perdition. This teaching of GSp on human brotherhood – solidarity among men – and man's dignity and destiny, has been given further penetrating insights by contemporary theologians.

In quite a remarkable study based on Scripture, in which he discussed the nature of sin itself and its reality in the world today, Piet Schoonenberg came to focus precisely on the solidarity aspect of sin in what he calls "The Sin of the World".[52] After he had outlined sin and its consequences, Schoonenberg turned and drew attention to this particular concept of sin which, though found in Scripture, is a new characteristic in regard to traditional and scholastic hamartiology which has rather been preoccupied with the individual[53] to a certain oblivion of the social and communitarian dimension best known as 'corporate personality' in biblical language.

Without denying the personal responsibility of the individual, Schoonenberg makes quite apparent and brings to the fore the social dimension of sin; that solidarity aspect of sin which an individualistic approach to the history of salvation easily leaves in the background.[54] The idea of the "corporate personality" in the O.T., in particular, permits the conclusion that there is solidarity in the successive generations in evil as well as in good.[55] The "Corporate Personality," which is the collective concept of God's People, does not deny personal responsibility. The two exist alongside one another even if the latter is only a later development particularly with the Prophets (Example: Jeremiah, Ezekiel).

This solidarity in the case of sin, of the community which Schoonenberg ultimately calls "The Sin of the World," is something more than just the sum-total of the sins of the individuals of the considered without any inner connection.[56] On the other hand, the solidarity sin of the community cannot be said to the simple passing on of one person's guilt either – the classical doctrine of Original Sin – since that would conflict with the principle of personal responsibility which is equally upheld by Scripture. What connects the sins of one person with those of another is the situation. As Schoonenberg asserts; "All influence which pass from one free person to another free person as such, respecting the latter's freedom and (yet) appealing to it, may be lumped together under the term 'situation'".[57] So, besides the sinful action itself, the situation thus created by it, invites to sin and pervades the community of men in which the act has taken place. This situation Schoonenberg defines as the totality of the circumstances in which somebody or something stands at a certain moment, the totality of circumstances prevailing in a certain domain.[58]

If one would take this definition of the sinful situation as it is, one would find it difficult to see how far different this situation is from a scandal or bad example, and thus, how justified can one be in qualifying the evil act committed in such a situation as being done in solidarity with other members of the community. However, this fact receives more light when one takes what Schoonenberg considers as 'the innermost core of the sinful situation'. This he says "consists in opposing the whole reality of God and world, in conflicting with love, both natural and supernatural".[59] As he explains, the fact that humanity is a community of education and of companionship advancing towards complete development in love makes man in his communion with God through grace a mediator in some way for his fellow man.[60] This shows still better and more clearly the dependency of man on his fellow man, and therefore the dimension of human solidarity, be it to the full and perfect realisation of his destiny – the complete development in love – salvation, or be it to a failure in reaching this destiny – this complete development in love – hence perdition.

This position of man in which he is in communion with God through grace, and is solidarily related to his fellow men as their mediator, thus incorporating the others in himself, makes perceivable the role of "Adam," who is capable of influencing us for the better, or for the worse; and so, also for the same reason, makes the mediatory role of Christ, who is bound to us in solidarity by sharing our humanity through his Incarnation, an acceptable reality. In this light the rejection of Christ becomes a forefront event which causes such an existential situation of deprivation of Grace – sin.

It is in this that the catastrophic peak-character of the sinful situation which Schoonenberg calls 'the Sin of the World' is present. For, the rejection and killing of Christ with whom we share in solidarity a common brotherhood, and through who we become God's children and are in communion with, "has created between us and Him who is our life, the abyss of death."[61] In this catastrophic peak-character, therefore, can be recognised the "signs of the times" since it reveals the reality of a situation which is a continuous threat to our solidarity with Christ, that solidarity which truly leads to salvation. It thus manifests the presence of that Hateful alternative solidarity – a solidarity without Christ and which leads to perdition; that sinful situation, the summit of which is marked BY THE REJECTION OF CHRIST.

Human History as a Tension Between Two Poles

While GSp officially expresses the saving solidarity of love and brotherhood into which the Incarnate Word of God has entered into with all men, it has not failed to recognise that this saving solidarity remains to be accomplished at the end of "history". After having asserted how God "from the beginning of salvation history" has willed to save man as a **people**, and also having restated the role of Christ in the development and perfection of human solidarity, article 32 concludes that: "This solidarity must be constantly increased until that day on which it will be brought to perfection. Then saved by grace, men will offer flawless glory to God as a family beloved of God and of Christ their Brother". Semmelroth commenting on this last part of the article, admits that even in the Christian order of salvation, the solidarity of a freely accepted community is not assured once and for all, but that it has to grow and be preserved against perpetual threat until it reaches its fulfilment.[62] He therefore regards this conclusion to the article not just as a pious statement, but as a "renewed reminder that God is not glorified where solidarity with other human beings is neglected".

The gradual intensification of this solidarity till its full perfection takes place in human history. It is the gradual realisation of the Kingdom of God; God who "from the beginning of salvation history" has willed to save man as 'a people'. But human history which is also salvation history, is the battle-field where this realisation OF God's Kingdom is opposed by hostile powers,[63] making human history a place of tension between two poles.

That human history is one of tension between two poles – a solidarity with Christ to salvation and a solidarity without Christ leading to perdition – has received a renewed attention in recent times in the research of Bernard Häring.

In two of his recent studies in particular,[64] Häring studied closely the tension that is between these two solidarities. Examining the frustration that the world has suffered as the result of sin, he writes: "Through one man's sin, the original salvific plan uniting the cosmos and humanity is transformed into a desperate solidarity of sin and death."[65] It is therefore a noxious solidarity of iniquity that dominates men's hearts.[66] However, in Christ a new solidarity is formed, and indeed, a solidarity which offers the possibility of a return to the original salvific plan of God. It is this solidarity that Häring expresses in its more global sense as follows: "Having come to save man, Christ redeems him in his personal totality and in the fulness of his fraternal and cosmic interdependencies. In Christ, human brotherhood returns once again to the solidarity of salvation, and the world partakes of his victory over a sinful interdependency and death. A new solidarity is thus established."[67]

In this last observation, Häring touches upon the fraternal solidarity of men into which Christ has united all men by his incarnation, and in which brotherhood he leads with him all men who are willing to gain victory over sin and death, himself being solidary with all. Christ therefore occupies the central place in this solidarity that leads to salvation. Nevertheless, that other solidarity, of sin and death, continues to exist, and the tension between the two is always present[68] in the history of man.

This tension between the two solidarities is yet more strongly affirmed in contemporary moral theology as a reality in human history by Häring in his study which we have already referred to; "Sin in the Secular Age". After referring to the evidence that there has been lately a transition from the individualistic concept of sin to one characterised by solidarity,[69] he goes on to state in regard to situation ethics in general, the tension between the two poles in which man is the 'in-between'. "We are therefore caught in the vicious circle of discussion on legalism and situation ethics unless we break through the radical comprehension of man's life as a final choice between the solidarity of salvation and the solidarity of corruption".[20] This choice, either for the solidarity of salvation or for the one of corruption, can be made only in the contingencies of man's life, the existential situation which surrounds him. It is in this existential situation of the individual, that part of the global movement of history which is proper to him, that the individual faces the personal choice of solidarity in good which is that of salvation, or in evil and alienation which is opposed to the first, and leads to perdition.[21]

From all these considerations, therefore, we can say that the concept of the 'Sin of the World,' advanced by Schoonenberg as a "hypothetical alternative" for the 'Chronologically first Sin – Original Sin –,[22] presented by Häring as that solidarity of corruption and alienation in which the world finds itself,[23] offers not only a better understanding of man's co-responsibility in sin, the terrible solidarity which leads to perdition, but also and more especially a better understanding of, and a deeper insight to that human solidarity into which Christ has entered with all men, through his incarnation, in the historical process of salvation. Through creation of man in his own image, God has not created him as a solitary being but in companionship and interpersonal communion (GSp art. 12 and 32),and has also given him a total and ultimate vocation by which all men are called to the one and the same goal, not as individuals, but as a community (GSp art. 24 and 32).

But through sin, a noxious solidarity has come into existence in the history of man, and all of human life becomes "a dramatic struggle between good and evil" (art.13). Adam[24] who was created for *life* has, through sin, allowed the existence of another solidarity – that of **death** and perdition. Nevertheless, through his incarnation, the Word of God, the 'New Adam' has rallied man again, and proffered him the opportunity to re-enter into that solidarity of life for which he was created and destined right from the beginning (GSp art. 22). The Word Incarnate that has made this possible has become the Head,[25]Center and Perfection of this re-established solidarity which redeems man from death (GSp 32).

But as man continues to live in time and space, his history remains the battlefield in which the two solidarities, which are the two poles, are at a continuous tension. The victory is assured when the solidarity of salvation with Christ will reach its perfection and men give flawless glory to God (art. 32); but meanwhile, as the tension between the two continues, the choice for one solidarity or the other has to be made by man in his 'world' and within the conditions and circumstances of his own context of the global historical movement, and in the categories and concepts which the realities and the possibilities of heaven and earth[26] offer him in these conditions and circumstances particular to him.

The historical circumstances in which various people live, the different values which the particular and given time and space have permitted man to develop – call them cultural – do not detract from the values inherent in this common brotherhood and solidarity that leads to salvation, but, on the contrary, can rather enrich it and make it indeed an objective of their own. GSp says of the values in contemporary culture, that they can all provide some preparation for the acceptance of the message of the Gospel; a preparation which can be animated with divine love by He who came to save the world.[27] But not only is solidarity, as a practical value in the context in which we are examining it, a preparation for the acceptance of the message of the Gospel. It is a value that pertains intimately to the fulfilment of this message itself. As a value it does not only help man to reach the salvation that the message of the Gospel proclaims, but salvation itself is a task undertaken and the end attained in solidarity. Salvation has to be attained by man in a community with others; a community in which all are bound together in solidarity by their common destiny.[28] It is this community, this solidarity of brotherhood which imposes on everyone the moral responsibility of genuinely seeking the salvation of the neighbour.

This is where we see the Dagara cultural value of solidarity lodge itself. In the light of GSp this practical moral value which we have described as cultural to the Dagara is quite central to the presentation of the Christian message of salvation. The salvation proclaimed by Christ is not just a call of man as an individual to the Kingdom of Christ, the Kingdom of God, but a call of man as a community in a solidarity brotherhood with his fellow men; for, it has pleased God to make men holy and save them not merely as individuals, without any mutual bonds, but by making them into a single people which acknowledges Him in truth, and serves Him in holiness.[29]

This is our hypothesis; the central point of our proposition in the light of which we undertook to examine the cultural value of solidarity, with particular reference to the Dagara People, in this study on salvation. The question we ask ourselves in this regard is whether the Dagara concept and practice of solidarity could not be an asset, and therefore an enrichment to the true practice of that brotherhood which is part and parcel of the salvation proclaimed *in* and *by* Christ; that brotherhood which is feared to be forgotten.[30] This raised, of course, the question on a broader level than just the isolated value of cultural solidarity; it raises the question on culture as a whole; for, as we remarked above, culture is a whole, and not a single element can be considered in isolation without having to make some necessary accommodations in other areas of the particular culture. Nevertheless, facing even this prospect of necessary accommodation – which is however not our task here – is not illegitimate. In affirming the autonomy and plurality of various and different cultures, the PCCMW has recognised the values inherent in them.[81] Indeed, the values inherent in a culture, and the concepts and categories through which they are vehiculated, are the more suitable ways in which the salvation message of Christ could be better communicated and understood. Thus, instead of looking at them from the outset as being in confrontation with, and in opposition to the Christian Message of Salvation, we should ask whether they could rather not be an asset, and thus enrichment to its understanding, and at the very least, whether they could not provide the best approach possible for presenting the message to, at least, the people concerned.

Before we consider what our research set out to do within its defined limits as accomplished, we shall make a final attempt to restate, as briefly as possible in the light of Christian Salvation, the Dagara concept of salvation in terms of solidarity. It is our belief that this would lead us to our conclusion, which becomes the more and more evident.

Chapter Five Endnotes

1 See above, Chapter Two, Footnote 5.

2 John O'Riordan, "Theologia Moralis Culturae Humanae," *Theologia Moralis Systematica*, Unpublished MS of course (for the use of students), Academia Alfonsiana, Roma, 1967/68.

3 Marie-Joseph le Guillou, " the Theology of the Church," *Sacramentum Mundi*, Vol 1, p. 323.

4 Ibid., loc. Cit.

5 Cfr. Chapter Four above, in "Conclusion".

6 *LGen*, Art. 48; See also *GSp*, Art. 45, "The Church has a single intention: that God's Kingdom may come and that the salvation of the whole human race may come to pass". Text in brackets provided.

7 P. Huenermann, op. cit., p. 237.

8 M-J. le Guillou, op. cit., p. 325.

9 P. Huenermann, op. cit., 237'

10 GSp, Art. 53.

11 J. O'Riordan, op. Cit., p. 14.

12 GSp, Art. 57.

13 Ibid., Art. 53.

14 Cfr. Henri Crouzel, *"Patrologie et Renouveau Patristique, Bilan de la Theologie du XXe Siècle*, Robert Vander Gucht and Herbert Vorgrimler (Editors), Casterman, Tournai-Paris, 1970, vol. II., pp. 679-82. See also, B. Häring, Sin in the Secular Age, Doubleday and Company, Inc., Garden City, New York, 1074.

15 Perhaps "contrary to a 'Christianity'" which has been identified with a culture, but not with the message, the Kingdom of God – Christ who wants to come into their midst, to bring them salvation – and to reign over them where they are.

16 G.E. Kpiebaya, *op. cit.*, p. 3.

17 Henri Crouzel makes a distinction between "system" and "synthesis," in which distinction he describes 'System' as "une construction humaine a partir des principes don't on tire de consequences par voie de logique," and he goes on to say that since God does not allow himself to be limited by principles formulated by man, the system sacrifices the divine mystery, which it

desecrates, to the exigencies of the human logic. Cfr *op. cit.*, pp. 680-1.

18 Jacques-Marie Pohier, "One-Dimensional Christianity?" in *Concilium*, Burns and Oates, London, vol. 5. No. 7. May(1971), pp. 27-38.

19 Ibid., p. 31.

20 *Ibid.*, p. 34.

21 *Ibid.*, p. 37.

22 *GSp*, Art. 24.

23 *Ibid., loc. Cit.*; the quotation here is from the translation: *Vatican Council II, The Conciliar and Post Conciliar Documents*, by Austin Flannery (General Editor), Dominican Publications, Dublin, 1975.

24 Otto Semmelroth, "The Community of Mankind," *Commentary on the Documents of Vat. II*, H. Vorgrimler (Editor), vol. 5, pp. 166-7.

25 *Ibid.*, p. 167; the bracket provided.

26 *GSp*, Art. 25.

27 Cfr. Chapter One above, pp. 70-1.

28 B. Häring, *The Law of Christ*, The Mercier Press, Cork, 1963, vol. 2, pp. 407-8.

29 The Original work, which was in German, *"Das Gesetz Christi,"* was first published by Erich Wewel Veerlag. Freiburg im Breisgau.

30 B. Häring, *op. cit.*, p. 408. Cfr. also, "The Teaching of Collectivism," in *This Time of Salvation*, Herder and Herder, New York, 1966, pp. 201-213. Here Häring demonstrates the "Salvation Solidarity Teaching" inherent in Marxism as a theory of Collectivism.

31 Confer P. Schoonenberg, Man and Sin, *op. cit.*, p. 178. LGen, already stated the Will of God to save men "not merely as individuals without mutual bonds, but by making them into a single people," Art. 9.

32 Otto Semmelroth, *op. cit.*, pp. 176-7.

33 *Ibid.*, p. 177.

34 B. Häring, *Sin in the Secular Age*, p. 27

35 *Ibid.*, p. 110.

36 Thimotheus Rast, "L'Eschatologie," *Bilan de la Theologie du XXe Siècle*, vol. II, p. 516; also, W. Weber, "La Comunita degli Uomini," La Chiesa nel Mondo di Oggi, G. Barauna (Editore), Vallecchi, Firenze, 1967, edition, p. 294. See also Juan Arias, Give Christ Back to Us (Translation of 'Cristo da Riscoprire), The Mercier Press, Dublin, 1974, pp. 34-45, esp. p. 35.

37 Waldemar Molinski, "Love of Neighbour," *Sacramentum Mundi*, vol. 1. P. 293.

38 *LGen*, art. 9.

39 *GSp*, art. 32.

40 The quotations (from Flannery's translation) are provided.

41 *GSp*, art. 22.

42 *Ibid.*, art. 32.

43 O. Semmelroth, *op, cit.*, p. 180.

44 B. Häring, *Sin in the Secular Age*, op. cit., p. 113.

45 *GSp*, art. 32.

46 O. Semmelroth, *op. cit.*, 181. Confer also, W. Weber, "La Comunita degli Uomini: Il Contenuto Teologico-Sociale" *La Chiesa nel Mondo di Oggi*, Guilherme Barauna (Edittore), Vallecchi, Firenze, 1967, edition, p. 289.

47 It should be remarked here that in the pursuit of such a discussion, the terms used assume various nuances and even different meanings at times, and therefore require a number of distinctions. However, we are not undertaking here a study of the distinctions that may come in the discussion. The use of the terms here in connection with 'Salvation' is all meant to describe that global reality, that situation in which man feels he is 'realising' himself, and which will culminate in the perfect realisation of that destiny for which he has been created – salvation. Cfr. Y. Congar, *Un Peuple Messianique: Salut et Liberation*. Cogitatio Fidei (85), Les Editions du Cerf, Paris, 1975.

48 *GSp*, art. 12.

49 *Ibid.*, art. 13.

50 Karl Rahner, "Man in the Church," *Theological Investigations*, vol. !!, Darton and Todd, London, 1963, p. 239.

51 P. Huenermann, "Reign of God," in *Sacramentum Mundi*, vol. V, p. 237.

52 P. Schoonenberg, *op. cit.*, Man and Sin was originally published in Dutch: *De Macht der Zonde*, L. G. Malmberg 'S-Hertogenbosch, 1962

53 **B.** Häring, *Sin in the Secular Age*, pp. 23-24, 27.

54 P. Schoonenberg, *Man and Sin*, pp. 98, 99.

55 *Ibid.*, pp. 99, 101-2.

56 *Ibid.* , p. 103.

57 *Ibid.*, p. 104.

58 *Ibid.*, pp. 104-5.

59 *Ibid.*, p. 118.

60 *Ibid.*, p. 119.

61 *Ibid.*, p. 123.

62 O. Semmelroth, *op. cit.*, p. 181.

63 P. Huenermann, *loc. Cit.*

64 Bernard Häring, *Faith and Morality in a Secular Age*, St. Paul Publications, Slough, England, 1973. The original which is in Italian is entitled *Etica Cristiana in Un Epoca di Secolarizzazione*, Edizioni Paoline, Roma, 1973. *Sin in the Secular Age,* Doubleday and Company Inc., Garden City, New York, 1974.

65 B. Häring, *Faith and Morality in a Secular Age*, p. 25.

66 *Ibid.*, pp. 26-7.

67 *Ibid.*, p. 36.

68 *GSp* art. 13 concludes: "The call to grandeur and the depths of misery are both part of human experience. They find their ultimate and simultaneous explanation in the light of God's revelation".

69 Cfr. also, above, under "Individualistic Morality Insufficient for Salvation".

70 B, Häring, *Sin in the Secular Age*, p. 106.

71 *Ibid.*, p. 107.

72 Piet Schoonenberg, *Man and Sin*, pp. 179-80.

73 B. Häring , *op. cit.*, p. 114.

74 As Robert Koch explains, the name "Adam" in the use of the O.T. does not refer to only an individual, but also to the collective, thus referring to the biblical concept of "Corporate Personality". See Robert Koch, *Il Peccato nel Vecchio Testamento*, in especially pp. 82-99.

75 Wolfhart Pannenberg in interpreting Luke's conception of Salvation points out this unique place of Christ in the divine plan of salvation as he writes: Jesus is elected not just for himself, but to a very specific function in the whole of saving history and thus for the whole of humanity": W. Pannenberg, Jesus – God an Man, pp. 379, 386. See also pp. 380-1, Paul's conception of history and salvation.

76 Josef Fuchs, Human Values and Christian Morality, pp. 70-1.

77 GSp, art. 57.

78 Ibid., art. 32.

79 Ibid., loc. Cit.

80 Bernard Häring, *This Time of Salvation*, Herder and Herder, 1966, pp. 17-9.

81 "Gaudium et Spes," arts. 54, 59.

CHAPTER SIX

THE DAGARA AND THE QUESTION OF SALVATION: AN EVALUATION

Introduction

From our argumentation illuminated by the *Pastoral Constitution on the Church in the Modern World,* and corroborated by some theologically sound discussions, based on Sacred Scripture, on the question of salvation and of moral values, it has become quite evident that solidarity as a cultural value among the Dagara, in spite of all the limitations that it may seem to have, has the potentiality of enriching the practice of genuine Christian love, if not really fostering it, by which men form a community of salvation. Not only does it not detract from the fundamental Christian Message of Salvation – much less stand in opposition to it – but could indeed be the primordial value by which many concepts of the message of Christian Salvation could be made more meaningful. In fact, one could go further and affirm in the light of the whole of our argumentation that, in its practice, the Dagara cultural value of solidarity would not only enrich and make meaningful the whole of the Christian message in general and some hitherto abstractly presented concepts of it, but is in itself central, in its essential dimensions to the message of Christ – the Message of Salvation.

If, for instance, Dagara solidarity *in its practice* cannot be taken as, at least, a minimum of the expression of that "life in community" to which the whole of mankind has been *re-called*, and which life in community is an image – no doubt imperfect but nevertheless an image within the limits of created reality – of the divine community which is the uncreated reality of the Three Persons, then it will be difficult to find a more suitable substitute as an existential value which will apply genuinely and sincerely express the "Christ-event" and that message of the "Evangelium" which calls to salvation in unity, brotherly love and sharing. It is certainly not by means of abstract concepts and theories, which virtually simmer down to empty ideology, that the Dagara can come to grasp the 'salvation' presented in the Christian message as the fulness of what they have been aspiring to have in the life on the other side, in the supranatural world. As Pohier's discussion on the "One-Dimensional Christianity" makes clear,[2] what is affirmed in the name of ideology is of little account if practice is not in conformity with what is affirmed in the abstract.

In chapter three where we studied the origins and the role of solidarity and co-responsibility in the Dagara moral life, we discussed in broad terms, particularly in our appreciation of co-responsibility in solidarity, some aspects of salvation. In this last chapter in which we shall evaluate salvation within the Dagara 'world view' against the background of the Christian message and especially in the light of GSp, we shall attempt to reformulate in more explicit terms, what the Dagara understand by salvation in the "Sitz-im-leben" of existence proper to them.

The Dagara Concept of Salvation

Man's search for a situation better than whatever actual situation in which he may be, seems to be a universal aspiration. It may thus be called a quest for salvation, security or human maturity.[3] However, the universality of this aspiration is a reality, and is what Ignace Berten depicts in Christianity as a venture among many others, seeking an answer to this fundamental quest of all men, for which he uses the term, "salvation". After giving an etymological description of the term "salvation," he writes:

> *Si on remonte a l'origine la plus lointaine du mot (salut) et de l'idee de salut, on trouve donc l'aspiration a l'integrite. Il s'agit donc d'une aspiration se fondent sur l'experience que l'homme fait de n'etre pas integralement lui-meme, aspiration a combler cette distance douloureusement vecu par rapport a la 'vraie vie'. A ce niveau le plus primitif du concept, le salut est ce qui permet a l'homme d'etre vraiment et pleinement lui-meme.*[4]

From this, it can therefore be said that salvation is truly an aspiration towards self-fulfillment. It is indeed a quest which preoccupies all human religions, scientific theories such as Marxism, and even philosophical systems and histories. They are all concerned with the question of the salvation of man, even if they express this objective of man in different terminologies. It is in line with this universal quest that African traditional religions also search for salvation. In a search for pastoral theology today, an important factor that cannot left out is the phenomenon of change that has swept across all human societies and culture.[5] Yet the basic question at the bottom of all pastoral approach is that of salvation for which man searches. Any pastoral option could not be realistic nor genuine without raising this fundamental and universal question.[6] This explains why it is the very reason for any pastoral activity of the Church.

Relating this question to the Dagara, it can be affirmed from our discussions in chapters three and four,[7] that for the Dagara, salvation can be considered on two levels: i) the temporal salvation, which concerns his salvation in his mortal state;[a] and the transcendent or eschatological level which concerns his salvation in the "After-this-Life". But analysing salvation on both of these levels, a common element emerges as basic and fundamental to them. This common element is the quest and aspiration for what we shall call *SECURITY*.

For the Dagara, salvation in it most simple terms are that which consists in life guaranteed against all evil, physical as well as moral, and in the present life as well as in the life of the "After-this-Life," in the existence of which he believes. Salvation means for him then a life of security in its full sense – both in this life and in that of the transcendent; and thus the quest for salvation for him could be summed up as quest for, and an aspiration to that state of life in which he will have total security that guarantees peace and happiness, be it in this present life or in the life in the company of his ancestors to which he is looking forward.

Security as Salvation in the Temporal Order

In his temporal life, the quest for some security is what pervades everything that the Dagara does. If he is assiduous at his work-place, or in the cultivation of his farm, it is not because he is afraid that he will otherwise be laid off by his employer, nor that he will not have anything left over to sell. Rather, the motivating factor is that he wants to ensure that his family has something to eat and so, would not suffer from the 'insecurity' that the lack of grain or means for getting it. It is the quest for this security which also gives rise to the preoccupation of assuring the continuation of the family or clan, the members of which in solidarity, could procure security for the individual members.[9] This manifests a sal-vation which, though it does not exclude the personal interests of the individual members, is nevertheless seen as possible only within a group of belonging – a group of solidarity. And the fact that the final retribution is seen in terms of the rejection of the individual from, or his addition into, the congregation of his ancestors is a confirmation of such a concept of salvation even in this life.

However, as has already been pointed out somewhere else in a different context, the Dagara concept of salvation is in no way restricted to the "After-this-Life".[10] The first bearers of the Christian Message to the Dagara, for example, bettered their existing situation of life for them by the fact that they liberated them and their families to a certain degree, from a situation which was full of constant fear and of evil spirits and their spells, and delivered them from hunger and other material ailments. Although this amelioration of their actual existential situation became the principal factor for their mass-conversions to Christianity, it was, nevertheless, in itself a salvation for them to a certain extent in this life. They were being delivered from a situation of *insecurity* and were able to live a life of security even if this security was only temporal and therefore, limited. They were being saved; and in this sense, the bearers of the Christian message, and ultimately, the Christian message itself was already one of salvation for them in this temporal order. The temporal situation in which they lived was one which left something still to be desired, something that could be made better. It was a situation in which there was still room for more peace, for more health of body, for less hunger, for more harmony and greater happiness even if all these were only limited but were pointing to a more profound reality.[11]

Eschatological Salvation as the Fullness of Security

But the Dagara quest for security is not limited to the temporal order and his state of existence. It is certain that he relies on the ancestors even for the attainment of this temporal state of security. This is why he will do all he can in his moral life to remain in their favour and to keep united to them by not breaking in anyway the bonds of solidarity that binds them together. He believes that the solidarity into which he entered with his ancestors through the family relations is not terminated with the death of the ancestors. They are still bound together, and he can count on them to look after him and protect him from harm in this life; from sickness and hunger, and from the threats of witches, sorcerers and malevolent spirits who dominate the situation of his mortal existence, and may want to harm him.

Yet, nevertheless, he is aware that these other beings which play such an important role in his actual world prevent his existential life in its mortal state from even attaining the perfection and the fullness of that security to which he aspires so deep within himself.[12] The future state of life in the company of his ancestors which he therefore awaits, and towards which he prepares himself, is what will guarantee to him such a more complete and perfect security.

This state of full and perfect security is what we described in chapter four as a "Transcendent Reality" in 'Dapar,' the Land of the Ancestors. Conceived in material terms as it may seem, the fullness of happiness that belongs to the one who has attained it, and which fullness is expressed in the abundance of food and drink, is a translation of a by far superior degree of peace and happiness which the subject would not have enjoyed at any time in this mortal life. But what makes this peace and happiness possible is the fact that one is received into his ancestral congregation, which provides the state of complete security for which he has been longing, and to which he has been aspiring in all of his life here on earth. In this eschatological group of belonging, the ancestral congregation in this transcendent state is guaranteed the fullness of this security, guarded by the ancestors.

The one who attains this state of being, the one who has been admitted into the ancestral congregation has therefore attained salvation in its full sense. For, he is in the company – the group of solidarity – of his ancestors in which there can be no more cause for fear of any harm; neither dread of hunger nor of sickness, nor fear that he will ever again one day be the victim of some evil spell. He is fully safe, living now in the state of salvation with his ancestors in their land, which I also that of the Supreme Being – God. For the Dagara therefore, 'Dapar' is the place of salvation 'par excellence;' a situation of existence where the members of the clan reunite together with their ancestor in their *HOME* in which nothing good is wanting, and in which no evil spirits nor sickness can anymore bother them. It is the complete fulfillment of his desire for and aspiration to absolute perfect 'security': abundance, peace and happiness. It is the full realisation of that state of security of which the temporal security of material well-being can only a partial fulfillment and a sign.

The Dagara Value of Solidarity and Christian Salvation in the Light of "Gaudium et Spes": A Reappraisal

If we pose the fundamental pastoral question in its depths in the Dagara context; that is, the question of salvation in terms of pastoral action, it seems obvious that the main element which comes to the fore as creative of the reality of security – salvation for the Dagara, be it on the temporal or the eschatological plane – is solidarity. Neither the temporal salvation nor the fullness of it, on the eschatological level is conceivable outside that group of brotherly belonging, the group of solidarity.

Solidarity in "Gaudium et Spes"

This element – the dimension of solidarity – in salvation is what the Pastoral Constitution on the Church in the Modern World has underscored and made more evident in the terms of the world of today. GSp recognises this dimension as fundamental in the very mission of the Church, which is "to make men holy and save them not merely as individuals without any mutual bonds, but by making them into a single people,"[13] a people bound together in solidarity in Christ who founded this brotherhood of salvation. Most clearly, GSp points out the role that Christ plays as the centre of this solidarity of salvation, the saving brotherhood to which he "recalls" the whole of mankind. As the Constitution, basing itself on scripture asserts, man has been created in God's image, and "not as a solitary" but in companionship, and therefore, in interpersonal relationship and communion (art.12).

Thus, right from the beginning, man, in the dignity he possessed from creation, was solidary with the rest of mankind which shared the same dignity. In the eating of the forbidden fruit, for example, it was both Adam and Eve that ate the fruit, and not just either Eve alone or Adam alone. In man's dignity which he shared with all other men, he was not only in solidarity with them alone, but in a certain way is also with God Himself who has created him in His own image and likeness (Gen. 1:26). This primordial bond of solidarity with God, originating simultaneously from man's common destiny and his dignity in his possession of God's image (art. 12), and which has been disrupted by sin (art. 13), is restored and made even more conspicuous by the Incarnation of Christ. As GSp affirms in article 22:

He who is the 'image of the invisible God' (Col. 1: 15), is himself the perfect man. To the sons of Adam, he restores the divine likeness which had been disfigured from the first sin onward. Since human nature as he assumed it was not annulled, by that very fact it has been raised up to the divine dignity in our respect too. For, by His Incarnation the Son of God has united Himself in some fashion with every man.

Christ by His Incarnation has therefore become the center of unity, the center of that solidarity which saves. As the Constitution further explicates after stating how from the dawn of salvation God has chosen men in community and not as individuals, "this communitarian character is consummated in the work of Jesus Christ. For the Word made flesh willed to share in the human fellowship" (art. 32).

That salvation is therefore to be sought within a community of solidarity in which all share the responsibilities that form the network of human relationships and communion is neatly brought home to the modern man by the Constitution. For, in reading the "signs of the times" which is one of the most important, if not the most important theme of the Constitution,[14] the men of today cannot fail to discern in them and realise in them the reality and relevance of this value to his ultimate salvation in the world that surrounds him and testifies to its urgency and the deeper reality to which it points. It is this solidarity made most evident by the Incarnation of Christ that, GSp affirms "must be constantly increased until that day in which it will be brought to perfection," so that "saved by grace, man will offer flawless glory to God as a family of God and of Christ their Brother" (art. 32).

The pastoral activity of the Church, which therefore has as its end the salvation of every man, cannot ignore as purely profane and common, and therefore irrelevant any area of the human life in which solidarity plays a role. The truth of this reality is what has led PCCMW to assert how the human family is gradually recognising that it comprises a single world community, thanks to the increased opportunities for many kinds of interchange among nations.[15] Thus the Church, in bringing the salvation message of Christ to all men, Christ who is the center of that human solidarity which saves, recognises that she does not act outside the area of this message. For, "while helping the world and receiving many benefits from it, she has a single intention: that God's Kingdom may come, and that the salvation of the whole human race may come to pass" (art. 45).

Dagara Solidarity and the Salvation Proffered by Christ

In the light Pastoral Constitution on the Church in the Modern World, therefore, the Dagara cultural value of solidarity which we have discussed in its concrete practice, far from being a practice that is aberrant and incompatible with the quest for the salvation proffered by Christ, and even smacking of superstitious practices of ancestral worship and idolatry,[16] is a cultural value that cannot be ignored in any way in the presentation of the Christian message of salvation particularly in this given situation and generally in the modern existential circumstances in which solidarity as a value has become an unclouded sign of the times. Seen from within the Dagara context, solidarity is not only a cultural value which would "provide some preparation for the acceptance of the message of the Gospel,"[17] - the message of salvation – and be an enrichment to the Church's universal mission.[18] More than being the most suitable way through which the fullness of salvation – the salvation proffered by

Christ – could be presented and perceived, the Dagara cultural practice of solidarity which is considered as an essential dimension of salvation in their "Weltanschauung" must also be central to the presentation of the Christian message of salvation to them. It is within the bond of the group of solidarity that salvation exists, and can be found. It is under the protecting shadow of the ancestral congregation – that transcendent group of solidarity – that the individual member of the group of belonging finds security, and therefore, salvation.

Such a solidarity cannot be opposed to that brotherhood which is also an essential part of the Christian salvation, and which Christ Himself has made so evident through his Incarnation and the entire "Christ-event". It is through his solidarity with all men – having assumed their human condition – that Christ is able to make man's supreme calling to salvation, clear;[19] and through his Incarnation, he has demonstrated in human history the possibility of such solidarity, not only between God and man, but also among men. By the same token he has also manifested God's will which from the beginning of salvation history has been to save man as a community that will offer Him flawless glory.[20] Thus the Dagara solidarity which, in its practice, leads each member of the group to seek his own security – temporal as well as eschatological – in the security of every other member of the group of belonging, offers an irreplaceable category of values for the understanding and practice of the dimension of solidarity in the salvation that is offered by Christ.

Such an appreciation of the practice of the Dagara solidarity does not, however, have any pretentions whatsoever of being free from its ambiguities, shortcomings, and even apparent contradictions in some areas in the face of certain demands of the Christian message of salvation. As we pointed out in chapter three above,[21] the ties of solidarity binding the members of the group of belonging are sanctioned by the privilege place given to the ancestor. This makes the bond of solidarity among the members so powerful that, although within the system itself, it will be incorrect to say that there is little or no place for individual autonomy; against the background of Christian theological consideration, the initiative of the individual person, even in matters of salvation, will be perceived as being restricted in favour of that of the group. This could eventually stifle the personal initiative of the individual member. Such would surely be a valid critique.

But one important factor which cannot be left out in this consideration is how far the individual should be allowed in his initiatives in a matter which essentially pertains to the entire bond of solidarity. As Peter Rohner explains: "the type and degree of control, for example, the extent to which actions can be influenced, guided, attempted and avoided, is the direct coefficient of freedom, responsibility, accountability or otherwise, guilt and so on".[22]

Beside such ambiguity of the individual person of which the practice of the Dagara solidarity can be reproached, a number of shortcomings in it can also be recognised when examined against the background of the Christian message of salvation. From our discussion in chapter four for instance, it is clear that the group of solidarity within which the responsibility of each member for the other is effectively practised, is rather very limited. This falls short of that solidarity of brotherhood which is obvious in the Christian message of salvation. For, as the salvation that Christ proffers is for all men without distinction, the solidarity within the community that has accepted this salvation offered by him must also be universal. Whatever the Dagara solidarity, which in its effective practice is rather usually limited to within the clan and the tribe, is capable of going beyond these limits, is what has been discussed in section III of the same chapter.

The limits imposed on the group of solidarity within the society can create difficulties, making the practice of Christian charity, which is the expression of that common brotherhood of all men and which genuinely seeks the salvation of every member of the universal community of brotherhood, to be seen as an impossible demand to fulfill. For, in such a limited group of solidarity it is it is not possible and is even a contradiction to love effectively one who is outside one's group of solidarity and has shown himself a threat in one way or another, and therefore an enemy, to the interests of one's group of solidarity in which alone one can find his security – salvation. It is in this dimension that the commandment of Christ to love even one's enemy becomes an unprecedented novelty to the widening of the horizon of the practice of that responsibility which is the dynamism within the group of solidarity; a characteristic which belongs to the Christian message of salvation alone.

The "security" guaranteed by the Dagara value of solidarity can therefore not be equated with the fullness of "salvation" proclaimed by Christ and particularly in the event of his incarnation by which he entered into solidarity and brotherhood with all men and made all men solidary to one another in virtue of the same destiny to which he "re-calls" them. Drawing from a wealth of New Testament ideas in regards to salvation, Ingrid Maisch notes the temporal and eschatological character of the salvation proclaimed in the message of Christ: a) The call to the salvation in Christ is a call of man to share now in the glory of Christ the full realisation of which he awaits at the final coming of Jesus; b) It is both God and Jesus to whom belongs the initiative of this salvation, for man of himself cannot effect any salvation;

and c) This salvation is not the monopoly of particular groups, but extends to all men because of the universal nature of the efficacity of "the Christ-event".[23]

If therefore this is as representative description of the salvation that Christ offers, the shortcomings of the Dagara concept of salvation within a bond of solidarity that is too limited become visible. And though the quality of the solidarity practised within these rather limited spheres still has a fundamental value which needs to be perfected and enriched by Christ and the entire breath of his message of salvation. The attainment of this goal in the Dagara context, however, demands the development of a moral theology, and the pursuit of a pastoral programme of salvation, which not only takes into account the traditional and cultural values inherent in solidarity, but starts with these values as the 'Sitz-im-Leben" and the human rudimentary elements of salvation that have to be perfected by the salvation in Christ, which is the fullness of human security and the destiny of all men, and to which ALL ARE INDEED CALLED.

Chapter Six Endnotes

1 Juan Arias in his faith-stimulating and challenging book, *Give Christ Back to Us,* wonders if, for example, the dogma of the Trinity, which is considered too abstract, could not be interpreted and made understandable in terms of community; and the prayer of Christ for unity, also referred to by GSp (art. 32), be rendered more meaningful and more relevant. Cfr. Give Christ Back to Us, Mercier Press, Dublin, 1974, pp. 44 and 43 respectively.

2 Jacques-Marie Pohier, "One-Dimensional Christianity," Concilium, May (1971), p. 32.

3 Eugene Kennedy, "Religious Faith and Psychological Maturity," *Concilium,* 9(1973), pp. 119-127; also, Michael McEntee, "Maturity and Salvation," chapter IV, *Salvation: Perspectives for a Contemporary Formulation in Terms of Human Maturity,* Unpublished doctoral diss., Pontifical Urban University, Rome, 1975.

4 Ignace Berten, *Christologie,* Unpublished MS of course, Lumen Vitae, Brussels, 1971/72; Cfr also J.H. Walgrave, *Un Salut aux Dimensions du Monde,* Cogitatio Fidei, Editions du Cerf, Paris, 1970, pp. 57ff.

5 Peter Lippert, "Descrizione degli Sviluppi che marcano I nostril Tempi," Chapter 1, *La Fede Cristiana di Fronte al Mondo Moderno: Aspeti Pastorali,* Unpublished MS of Course, Academia Alfonsiana, Roma, 1973, pp. 8-10. In his preliminary observations to the chapter, Peter Lippert underscores the significance of GSp in relation to the Modern situation, cfr. p. 5.

6 GSp, arts. 9 and 10; 39.

7 Cfr. above, chapter three, section VI; especially chapter four, section IV: Dagara Solidarity as a 'Transcendent reality'".

8 In fact, Ingrid Maisch writes that the O.T. conception of salvation had its roots in the concrete experiences and situations, and that for the psalmist, salvation is deliverance from mortal danger, healing in sickness, liberation from captivity, etc.; but that it had also assumed an eschatological character, particularly in late Judaism and in the Qumran community within which alone

salvation was considered obtainable; cfr. "Salvation: Biblical Concepts," Sacramentum Mundi (SacMdi) vol. 5, pp. 409-10.

9 A.A. Kuuire, *The Christian Faith in the Dagaati Culture*, Unpublished Masters Thesis, 'Lumen Vitae': Catholic University of Louvain, Belgium, 1972, pp. 33ff. Callixtus Kalisa speaking about the cult to the dead as an expression of communitarian life, states the fact of the continual union between the living and the dead. As he writes: "Ces liens existent d'abord entre les vivants d'une meme lignee. Mais la mort ne reussit pas a romper cette union qui continue a s'exterioriser dans la culte des ancetres. Ceux qui meurent prolongent leur vie dans leur progeniture". Le culte et la Croyance aux Ancetres au Rwanda Confrontes avec le Message Chretien, Unpublished Doctoral Dissertation, Academia Alfonsiana, Rome, 1972, p. 406.

10 A.A. Kuuire, op. cit., pp. 86 ff.

11 If the N.T. conception of salvation is as Ingrid Maisch describes it, then the Dagara conception of the same reality is quite close to it. Despite the fact that it is used in the N.T. as a religious term with reference to spiritual life, it is also used even in reference to healing from illness, deliverance from mortal danger, although it always points to a more profound reality, being always connected with faith. See Ingrid Maisch, *op. cit.*, p. 410.

12 See Peter Sarpong, Ghana in Retrospect., pp. 14-9.

13 LGen., art 9.

14 Cfr. Chapter One above, Section III, subdivision D, number 2: "Signs of the Times". See also *GSp*, art. 32.

15 GSp, art. 33.

16 After tracing the notion of the term "superstition" in ancient Roman usage, in the Bible, then from the Fathers and St. Thomas Aquinas, C. Kalixa gives the different kinds and forms of superstitions, and subsequently rejects as always superstitious "The Cult of the Ancestors". He argues that some customary rites directed towards the ancestors are indifferent in themselves, and so he says: "Lorsqu'une coutume se montre en soi indifferente, c'est-a-dire, ne nuisant pas a la religion du Christ, il n'est pas du tout necessaire de la detruire. ... Certaines pratiques en apparence superstitieuses ne sont en realite que des observances vaines et

erronees ou encore des usages seculiers, des marques d'une civilization donnee," op. cit., pp. 319-20.

17 GSp, art. 57.

18 Ibid., art. 58.

19 Ibid., art. 22.

20 Ibid., art. 32.

21 See chapter three, section V: "Individual Morality and the Solidarity Tie".

22 Peter Rohner, "The Will," SacMdi, vol. 6, p. 358.

23 Ingrid Maish, op. cit., p. 410.

CONCLUSION

DAGARA SOLIDARITY AND CHRISTIAN SALVATION: A PASTORAL SYNTHESIS

Summary of Premises

The examination of the value of the Dagara solidarity, in the attempt to see how much it can be of value in the context of Christian salvation, and particularly in reference to the Constitution "Gaudium et Spes," the study has led to one apparently obvious conclusion. Salvation is fundamentally and basically a *communitarian endeavour* in which all the members of the community in quest for it are solidarily bound together. The salvation of the individual member lies in the salvation of every other member, and outside this bond of solidarity the individual cannot find any salvation. For the salvation that he longs for deep in himself is found in the midst of those who share the same aspiration with him. It is in their midst that he will find full security.

From our investigation on the value of solidarity among the Dagara People, it has become evident to us that the state of salvation, which is a life guaranteed against all evil and offers peace and happiness, is provided for by the group of solidarity to which one belongs, be it salvation in this life or salvation in the 'supernatural' world, salvation in the "After-this-Life" in the ancestral congregation. It is within this group of belonging, in which everyone is responsible for the other, that one can find this security, and it is this fact which influences the entire life of the Dagara. Positively, he sees all the other members of the group to which he belongs, the

289

group to which he is solidarily bound, as "brothers" to whom he owes a responsibility in his own actions. His actions affect them and can be the cause of their sufferings, or their happiness just as theirs can be the cause of his. Their destiny is the same, and it is through a life of co-responsibility that they can achieve salvation.

Perceived in this manner, such a solidarity which demands his co-responsibility in brotherhood, when practised in the light and under the influence of the salvation proclaimed by Christ, cannot be anything different from the true and genuine practice of that Christian charity which urges one to identify himself with the neighbour and so seek effectively his salvation.

That the salvation proclaimed by Christ is one that has as its premises the human community of brotherhood and solidarity is evident from the Pastoral Constitution on the Church in the Modern World. The common dignity and destiny of man (art.12) reaffirmed and made even more evident by the Incarnation and the entire "Christ-event" (arts. 22 and 32) demonstrates salvation as a communitarian task, and therefore one which has to be undertaken in solidarity. The entire community of mankind which looks for solidarity and brotherhood in the economic, political and social spheres of the modern world (art. 6) points to the deeper reality of *salvation in solidarity*, through this general movement which is indeed a true "sign of the Times". What seems a purely social movement that seeks to guarantee security for man in his actual existential society full of insecurities, and in a world of such great technological advances yet full of imbalances, is a sign (a sacramentum) of that supreme destiny of man for which Christ died and was raised.

The Christian charity which has all the potential of being dynamic remains, if presented in an abstract and prevalently individualistic way, static in practice when compared with the Dagara practice of solidarity. This is a real paradox, if one agrees that the most immediately perceivable law given by Christ in his message of salvation is that of charity, which identifies one with his neighbour to such an extent that it justifies even the giving of one's own life for the others (Jn, 15: 13). The Dagara solidarity as we have analysed it may seem only perhaps a human value, considering especially the narrow limits within which it is practised. Yet it does indeed in this practice contain what can be called a genuine element of that charity which Christ demands of those who accept the true and total salvation which he proclaims and proffers. Still unrefined? Certainly, yes. Nevertheless, it remains a value which is not contrary to the Christian Gospel, but rather, is a sound basis upon which that true Christian charity can be built.

The Pastoral Objective of the Church and the Value of Human Solidarity

Certainly, the mission of salvation entrusted to the Church is the basis for her missionary activity.⁵ As 'Ad Gentes' affirms: "Sent by God to the Gentiles to be 'the Universal sacrament of salvation' the Church ... strives to proclaim the Gospel to all men" (AdGen art. 1). Thus, the missionary activity of the Church "is nothing less than the manifestation of God's plan, its presence and realisation in the world and its history, in which God guides the whole history of salvation to its appointed end by means of the mission" (AdGen. Art. 9). In this basic pastoral activity of the Church – the salvation of every man – she has to use the values that exist in the given culture into which she comes to carry out her mission.⁶

It is however a well-known fact that the Church, in her solicitude to preach what has been often thought of as the "pure" Christian message of salvation, has indiscriminately condemned as "ancestral worship" and superstition in the so-called missions any mark of respect that the respective people may pay to their ancestors. This condemnation sweeps away practices which indeed fostered and maintained the ties between a People and its "*saints*" who though in another state of life nevertheless continue to be in communion with them.[2] In this way a cultural value, the value of solidarity which is indeed not contrary to the salvation message of Christ, but is rather an essential dimension of it, is purged of its value and salient force if not completely swept away.

If therefore solidarity, as a value, contains an important dimension of the salvation of Christ as our investigations have sufficiently demonstrated, the Dagara cultural value of solidarity should be seriously regarded as valid and really important element for consideration in a research for a genuine pastoral theology for the Dagara. Hence the value of solidarity, as it obtains among them, should be capitalized in such a theology. Because, if the pastoral objective of the Church's missionary activity is aimed at the salvation of the whole human race (GSp art. 45) and therefore of each people in their "Sitz-im-Leben," such a value which, in fact, aids the realisation of this objective cannot be considered lightly nor be relegated to the place of a footnote, much less be justifiably ignored or branded as irrelevant to the Christian Message. In fact, in virtue of her very mission, it becomes an obligation for the Church to identify and to promote such an already existing value which truly has the power to make the entire Good News of Christ to be at home in their midst and relevant to them in their situation of existence and not to be seen as something that is foreign; a coat that can be taken off at any time.

This is the objective which "Gaudium et Spes has made clear and achieved, even if only in principle. In its orientation and pastoral concern, the Pastoral Constitution of the Church in the Modern World has not only recognised the plurality of cultures (art. 53) but also the values inherent in them (art. 57). In reality, not only does it recognise the plurality of cultures and the values in them, but has even gone further to point out concretely and precisely, in particular the deeper reality that lies behind the values of human solidarity. The Dagara solidarity which permits such a practice of brotherly co-responsibility, though it may not he exclusive to them, is of particular importance in this dimension. For the Dagara, it can be seen in the light of the Christian message of salvation as the value which contains to a certain extent, and makes reasonable the attainment of the pastoral objective of the activity of the Church.

The Christian Message of Salvation does not exist in some 'pure' state, in some void, in some particular culture from where it will then only need to be imported and transplanted in any other culture, the tenants of which may have come to believe in the Gospel and so want to be baptized in order to be saved. This message of salvation comes into the situation of anyone who is willing to receive it; and it is this message itself which then will ***evangelize*** "the existing morals of the situation that it has come to encounter". It is precisely this characteristic of the ***saving message*** of Christ that gives it the capacity to penetrate all cultures in which it can then effectively *"re-call"* all men, without distinction, to their original destiny – now become SALVATION IN CHRIST.

Conclusion Endnotes

1 Cfr. chapter six above, Section II: "The Dagara Concept of Salvation"...

2 Cfr. Chapter three above, Section V, subdivision C: "Co-responsibility in Solidarity"

3 GSp, art. 4.

4 Ibid., art. 10.

5 LGen, art. 17; AdGen, art. 2.

6 Bernard Häring, "The Evangelisation of Morals," Chapter Two , *Evangelisation Today*, Fides Publishers, Inc., Notre Dame, Indiana, 1974.

7 Callixte Kalisa is right when in the third chapter of Part II of his study on Ancestral Cult and Belief in Rwanda, he describes the cult to the ancestors as a school of communion between men. After describing the cult to the dead as an expression of a communitarian life and a safeguard to the communion itself, he writes: "Ces liens existent d'abord entre les vivants d'une meme lignee. Mais la mort ne reussit pas a romper cette union qui continue a s'exterioriser dans le culte des ancetres". He came to the conclusion that the ancestral cult brings together the members of a family and establishes a relation between and their dead op. cit., p. 406.

BIBLIOGRAPHY

DOCUMENTS

Acts of Vatican Council II, *Acta Synodalia Sacrosancti Concilii Oecumenici Vaticani II, (ASSCO Vat)*, 3 vols (14 parts), Typis Polyglottis Vaticanis, 1971-1974.

FLANNERY, Austin (Editor), Vatican Council II: *The Conciliar and Post Conciliar Documents*, Dominican Publications, Dublin 1974.

JOHN XXIII, Pope, "Constitutio Apostolica 'Humanae Salutis' (25 December 1961)," *AAS*, 54(1962), pp. 5-13.

JOHN XXIII, Pope, "Homily in St. Paul's Outside the Walls, (25 December 1959)," *AAS*, 51(1959), pp. 70-74.

JOHN XXIII, Pope, "Mater et Magistra," (Encyclical), *AAS*, 53(1961), pp. 401-469.

JOHN XXIII, Pope, "Opening Speech to Vatican Council II, (11 October 1962)," *AAS*, 54(1962), pp. 786-795.

JOHN XXIII, Pope, "Pacem in Terris," (April 11 1963), *AAS*, 55(1963), pp. 257-304.

JOHN XXIII, Pope, "Princeps Pastorum," *AAS*, 51(1959), pp. 833-864.

JOHN XXIII, Pope, "Radio Broadcast," (11 September 1962), *AAS*, 54(1962), pp. 678-685.

JOHN XXIII, Pope, "Solemn Allocutio of 25 January 1959," *AAS*, 51(1959), pp. 65-69.

JOHN XXIII. Pope, "Whit-Sunday Sermon," (5 June 1960), *AAS*. 52(1960), pp. 517-526.

PAUL VI, Pope, "Address to the United Nations General Assembly," (4 October 1965), *AAS*, 57(1965), pp. 877-898.

PAUL VI, Pope, "Allocutio to the 'Unione Cristiana Impreditori e Dirigenti,'" AAS, 56(1964), pp. 547-579.

PAUL VI, Pope, "Discourse to the Artists of Rome," AAS, 56(1964), pp. 439-442.

PAUL VI, Pope, "Ecclesiam Suam," (Encyclical), AAS, 56(1964), pp. 609-659.

PAUL VI. Pope, "Populorum Progressio," (Encyclical), AAS, 59(1967), pp. 257-299.

PIUS XI, Pope, "Quadragessimo Anno," (Encyclical), AAS, 23(1931), pp. 177-228.

Sacra Congregatio de Propaganda Fide, "Instructio Circa Prudentiorem de Rebus Missionibus Tractandi Rationem," *AAS*, 6(1939), pp. 269-270.

Vatican Council II Draft Constitutions, *Schemata Constitutionum et Decretorum (SCD)*, Typis Polyglottis Vaticanis, 1962.

Vatican Council II Preparatory Documents, *Acta et Documenta Concilio Oecumenico Vaticano II Apparando (ADCO Vat II)*, Series I (Antepraeparatoria), 4 vols (15 parts), Typis Polyglottis Vaticanis, 1960-1961.

Vatican Council II Preparatory Documents, Acta et Documenta Concilio Oecumenico Vaticano II Apparando (ADCO Vat II), Series II (Praeparatoria), 3 vols (7 parts), Typis Polyglottis Vaticanis, 1964-1969.

Walter M. ABBOTT, (Editor), *The Documents of Vatican II*, American Press – Guild Press, New York, 1966.

COLLECTIONS

ABBOTT, Walter M., (Editor) *The Documents of Vatican II.*, American Press, Guild Press, New York, 1966.

BARAUNA, Guilherme (Editor) *La Chiesa Nel Mondo Di Oggi* (Second Edition), Vallecchi, Firenze, 1967.

BROWN, Raymond E., and others: *The Jerome Biblical Commentary.*, Geoffrey Chapman, London, Dublin, 1970.

CAPRILE, Giovanni (Editor), *Il Concilio Vaticano II*, 5 vols, Edizione "Civilta Cattolica," Roma, 1966-1969.

COMMISIONE MISSION ED EVANGELIZZAZIONE; "La Salvezza Oggi," *Atti della Commissione Missione ed Evangelizzazione,* (Bangkok 29 December 1972 – 12 January 1973, Bologna, 1974.

CONGAR, Yves, and M. Feuchmaurd; *L'Eglise dans le Monde de ce Temps. Constitution Pastorale "Gaudium et Spes*, 3 vols, Paris, 1967.

COUNCIL DEBATES; "De Cultus Humani Progressu Rite Promovenda," *La Civilta Cattolica,* pp. 169-176, Giovani Caprile, Editor, 1966-1969.

FLANNERY, Austin, (Editor); *Vatican Council II. The Conciliar and Post Conciliar Documents*, Dominican Publications, Dublin, 1975.

GIAMMANCHERI, Enzo, (Editore); *La Chiesa Nel Mondo Contemporaneo*, Second Edition), Queriniana, Brescia, 1967.

GUCHT, Robert Vandel and Herbert Vorgrimler; *Bilan de la Theologie du XXe Siècle*, 2 vols. Castermann, Tournai, 1970.

MAGILL, Frank N., (Editor); Masterpieces of Catholic Literature, Harper and Row, New York, 1965.

METZ, Rene and Jean Schick, (Compilers); *Ideologies de Liberations et Message du Salut*, Quatrieme Collogue du Cerdic, Strasbourg 10-12 Mai 1973, Strasbourg,1973.

RAHNER, Karl, Cornelius Ernst and Kevin Smyth, (Editors); *Sacramentum Mundi: An Encyclopedia of Theology* (*SacMdi*), 6 vols. Burns and Oates, London, 1970.

VORGRIMLER, Herbert, (Editor); *Das Zweite Vatikanische Konzil, Dokumente und Kommentare*, 3 vols, Herder, Freiburg, 1966-1968.

------, Commentary on the Documents of Vatican II, Burns and Oates/Herder and Herder, London/New York, 1969.

INDIVIDUAL AUTHORS

Theological

ALFARO, Juan, "Christian Hope and Hopes of Mankind," *Concilium* vol. 9, 6(1970), pp.59-69.

ANGEL, Alfred, "Liberation de l'Homme et Salut par la Foi en Jesu-Christ," *La Documentation Catholique*, 70(1973), pp. 532-536.

AQUINAS, Thomas, *Summa Theologiae*, Matriti, Madrid, 1962.

ARIAS, Juan, *Give Christ Back to Us*, The Mercier Press, Dublin, 1974.

ARRUPE, P., "Culture et Mission," Christus, 13(1966), pp. 395-405.

-----, "Pluralismo della Culture e Cristianesimo," Sapienza, 20(1967), pp. 7-16.

AUER, Alfons, Man's Activity throughout the World," in Commentary on the Documents of Vatican II, vol. V, pp. 182-201.

BALTHASAR, Hans Urs von, "Le Sacrament de Freres," in *Dieu et l'homme d'aujourd'hui*, Desclee de Brouwer, Paris, 1962, pp. 28-306.

BARON, Andre Barral, "Liberation en Jesus-Christ, *Christus*, 19(1972), pp. 393-405.

BERGER, Klaus, "Salvation, III. History of Salvation (Salvation History): A Theological Analysis, 1. Approach," in *SacMdi*, vol. V, pp.411-416.

BERTEN, Ignace, *Christologie* (MS of Course), 'Lumen Vitae,' Louvain University, Belgium, 1971/72.

BOFF, Leonardo, "Salvation in Jesus Christ and the Process of Liberation," *Concilium* vol. VI, 10(1974), pp. 78-91.

BONSIRVEN, j., *Le Regne de Dieu*, Edition Montaigne, Paris, 1957.

BROWN, Robert McAfee, "The Church: Response," in The Documents of Vatican II, pp. 309-316.

BUKENYA, Deogratias, Bantu Mukago and Christian Fraternal Solidarity, Unpublished Doctoral Diss., Academia Alfonsiana, Rome.

BUEHLMANN, Walbert, *La Terza Chiesa alle Porte*, Edizioni Paoline, Roma, 1975.

BULTMANN, Rudolf, Theology of the New Testament, 2 vols., SCM Press, London, 1974.

BURRIDGE, William, Destiny Africa, Geoffrey Chapman, London, 1966.

CAMPION, Donald R., "The Church Today: An Introductory Comment to the Church in the Modern World," in *The Documents of Vat. II,* pp. 181-198.

CAPRILE, G., "Die Chronik des Konzils," in Das Zweite Vatikanische Konzil, vol. III, pp. 624-664, H. Vorgrimler, Editor. Herder, Freiburg, 1966-1968.

CHENU, M.D., Peuple de Dieu dans le Monde, Foi Vivante. Editions du Cerf, Paris, 1966.

COMBLIN, Joseph, "Freedom and Liberation as Theological Concepts," in Concilium, Vol. VI, 10(1974), pp. 92-103.

CONGAR, Y,M,J., "L'Eglise, Sacrament Universel du Salut," *Eglise Vivante,* 17(1963), pp. 339-355.

-----, *Un Peuple Messianique: Salut et Liberation*, (Congregatio Fidei, 85), Les Editions du Cerf, Paris, 1975

-----, *The Wide World my Parish: Salvation and its Problems*, Donald Attwater, Translator, Darton Longman and Todd, London.

CROUZEL, Henri, "Patrologie et Renouveau Patristique," in *Bilan de la Theologie du XXe Siècle*, vol. II, pp. 661-683.

CULLMANN, O., *Christ et le Temps*, Neuchatel, Paris, 1957.

-----, Salvation in History, J.C.B. Mohr, Translator, SCM Press Ltd., London, 1962.

DARLAP, Adolf, "Salvation, III. History of Salvation (Salvation History), A. Theological Analysis, 2. Theological Explanation" *SacMdi*, vol. V., pp. 416-419.

DE LA POTTERIE, Ignace and Stanislaus Lyonnet: The Christian lives by the Spirit, John Morris, translator, Society of St. Paul, Staten Island, 1971.

DELHAYE, Philippe, "La Dignita della Persona Umana," in La Chiesa Nel Mondo di Oggi. Pp. 264-286.

DERY, Peter P., "Sermon," Enstoolment Ceremony 23 March, Tamale, 1975.

DHANIS, E., "Le Message Evangelique de l'Amour et l'Unite de la Communaute Humaine," *Nouvelle Revue Theologique (N.R.Th.)*, 2(1970).

DONDEYNE, A., *La Foi Ecoute le Monde*, Edition Universitaire, Paris, 1964.

Dorn, L.A., and G. Denzler, *Tagesbuch des Konzils II*, G.M. Sailer, Publisher, Nurnberg, 1965.

DULLES, Avery, "The Church: An Introductory Comment to LGen," *The Documents of Vat. II*, pp. 9-13.

DUQUOC, Ch., "Eschatologie et Realites Terrestres," *Lumiere et Vie*, 50(1960), pp. 4-22

DUSSEL, Enrique, "Liberation-Domination; A New Approach" *Concilium*, Vol. 10(1974), pp. 34-56.

FAGONE, V., "La Chiesa e l'Arta Contemporanea. Le Condizioni di un incontro," in *La Civilta Cattolica*, (1964), II, pp. 468-480.

FERET, H. M. "L'Amour fraternal vecu en Eglise et le Signe de la venue de Dieu," *Concilium*, 29(1967), pp. 19-36.

FESTORAZZI, Franco and Bruno Maggioni: *Introduzione alla Storia della Salvezza*. Elie di Ci, Torino-Leumann, 1973.

FUCHS, Joseph, *Human Values and Christian Morality*, Grill and Macmillan Ltd., Dublin, 1970.

-----, *Natural Law, A Theological Investigation*, Sheed and Ward, New York, 1965.

FULLAM, Raymond B. *Exploring Vatican II, Christian Living Today and Tomorrow*. Alba House, Staten Island, 1969.

GUILLOU, Marie-Joseph, "Church History of Ecclesiology," *SacMdi*, Vol. I, pp. 313-327.

GUTIERREZ, Gustave, "Liberation, Theology and Proclamation," *Concilium*, Vol. VI, 10(1974),

HAMER, J., "Il Pluralismo Culturale e la Chiesa," in *Sapienza*, 19(1966), pp. 24-33.

HÄRING, Bernard, "Bonne Nouvelle et Actualite du salut," *Eglise et Communaute Humaine; Etude sur 'Gaudium et Spes,'* Desclee, Paris, pp 6-8.

-----, Etica Cristiana, Edizione Paoline, Roma 1973.

-----, *Evangelization Today*. Fides Publication, Inc., Notre Dame, Indiana, 1974.

-----, *Faith and Morality in a Secular Age*. St. Paul Publications, Slough, England, 1973.

-----, "Fostering the Nobility of Marriage and the Family," *Commentary on the Documents of Vatican II*, Vol. V., pp. 225-246.

-----, *Hope is the Remedy*, St. Paul Publications Slough, England, 1971.

-----, *Morality is for Persons*. Farrar, Straus and Giroux, New York, 1971

-----, *Sin and the Secular Age*. Doubleday and Company, Inc., New York, 1974.

-----, *This Time of Salvation*. Herder and Herder, New York, 1966.

-----, *The Law of Christ*, 3 vols. The Mercier Press, Cork, 1963.

-----, "Viele prospettive nuove per il future," in *La Chiesa nel Mondo di Oggi*, pp. 605-613.

HEMMERLE, Klaus, "The Concept of Salvation; Some Considerations for Fundamental Theology," in *Communio*, 1972, pp. 210-230.

HOUTART, F., *Eglise et Monde*. Editions Universitaires, Brussels, 1964.

HOUTART, Francois and Jean Remy: *Eglise et Société en Mutation*, Mame, Paris, 1969.

HOUTART, Francois, *Sociologie et Pastorale*, Fleurus, Pari, 1963.

HUNERMANN, Peter, "Reign of God," *SacMdi*, Vol. V., pp. 233-240.

JOSSUA, J. P. "Christianisme horizontal ou Vertical," *Parole et Mission*, 41(1968), pp. 245-254.

KALISA, Callixte, *Le Culte et la Croyance aux Ancetres au Rwanda Confrontes avec le Message Chretien*, Unpublished doctoral diss., Academia Alfonsiana, Rome, 1972.

KENNEDY, Eugene, "Religious Faith and Psychological Maturity," Concilium, 9(1973), pp. 119-127.

KENNY, J. P., The Supernatural. Alba House, Staten Island, New York, 1972.

KOCH, Robert, Il Peccato nel Vecchio Testamento. Edizioni Paoline, Roma, 1973.

KOFON, Englebert N., "Socio-cultural Background of Pre-Christian Bafut," Chapter 2, section 1, in *Polygyny in Pre-Christian Bafut and New Moral Theological Perspectives*, Unpublished doctoral diss. Academia Alfonsiana, Rome, 1974.

KOHLER, L., Theologie des Altes Testament. Tübingen, 1936.

KPIEBAYA, Gregory E., *God in the Dagaaba Religion and in the Christian Faith*, Unpublished Masters Thesis in Theology, University of Louvain, 1973.

KUNG, Hans, *The Changing Church, Reflections on the Progress of the Second Vatican Council*, Sheed and Ward, London, 1965.

-----, *The Council and Reunion*. Sheed and Ward, London-New York, 1961.

-----, *Council, Reform and Reunion*. Sheed and Ward, New York, 1961.

-----, *The Living Church: Reflections on the Second Vatican Council*, Cecily Hastings and N.D. Smith, Translators, Sheed and Ward, London-New York, 1963.

KUUIRE, Albert A., *The Christian Faith in the Dagarti Culture*, Unpublished Masters Thesis, Institute of 'Lumen Vitae,' University of Louvain, Brussels, 1972.

LACROIX, J., *Le Sens de L'Atheisme Moderne*, Tournai, 1959.

LAKNER, Franz, "Salvation Theology: Satisfaction," *SacMdi*, Vol. V, pp. 433-435.

LATOURELLE, Rene, *Theology: Science of Salvation*, St. Paul Publications, Slough, England, 1969.

LAURENTIN, Rene, *Liberation, Development and Salvation*, Charles Underhill Quin, Translator, New York, 1972.

-----, *L'Eglise du Concile*, 4 vols, Seuil, Paris, 1962-65.

LEBRET, L.J., "La Vocation des peoples au development," in *46e Semaine Sociale de France, (1959)*.

LERCARO, G. "On Culture," *La Civilta Cattolica*, (1965) II, pp. 485-487.

-----, "Speech in the 35th General Congregation of Vat. II," *ASSCO Vat. II*, Vol. I, Part 4, pp. 327-330.

LESQUIVIT, Colomban, and Pierre Grelot: "Salut," VTB, pp. 1185-1192.

LIPPERT, Peter, *La Fede Cristiana di Fronte al Mondo Moderno*: Aspetti Pastorali, MS, Course given, Academia Alfonsiana, Roma, 1973/74.

LUZBETAK, L. J., "L'Eglise et les Culture," Lumen Vitae, 22(1967), pp. 29-42.

LYONNET, Stanislas, *La Storia della Salvezza nella Lettera di Romani*. Napoli, 1967.

MACKEY, J. P., "The Idea of Sin in the World," in *Sin and Repentance*, D. O'Callaghan, Editor, Dublin, 1967.

MACQUARRIE, John, *Christian Unity and Christian Diversity*. SCM Press Ltd., London, 1975.

-----, Principles of Christian Theology. SCM Ltd., London, 1966.

MAISCH, Ingrid, "Salvation: Biblical Concept," SacMdi Vol. V., pp. 409-410.

MAURIER, H., Essai d'une Theologie du Paganisme. Paris, 1965.

-----, Religion et Developpement, Tours-Paris, 1965.

MESSAGE of the Fathers of Vat. II: "Message of the Fathers to the World," ASSCO Vat. II, Vol. I, part I, pp. 230-232.

MOELLER, Charles, "History of the Constitution," *Commentary on the Documents of Vatican II*, Herbert Vorgrimler, Editor, Burns and Oates, London, 1969, Vil. V, pp. 1 76.

-----, "La Promozione della Cultura," in *La Chiesa nel Mondo di Oggi* (1967 Edition), G. Barauna, Editor, Vallecchi, Firenze, pp. 372-427.

-----, "Preface and Introductory Statement," *Commentary on the Documents of Vatican II,* Vol, V. pp. 77-114.

MOLINSKI, Waldemar, "Charity, II Love of Neighbour," *SacMdi*, Vol. I, pp. 292-294.

MOLTMANN, Jurgen, *Diskussion Uber die 'Theologie Hoffnung'* Munich., 1967.

-----, *Theology of Hope*, SCM Press, London, 1969.

MONTINI, Car. Giovanni Battista, "Speech in the 34th General Congregation of Vat. II," *ASSCO Vat. II*, Vol. I, Part 4, pp. 291-294.

MURPHY, John J., "Rerum Novarum," in *Master-pieces of Catholic Literature,* Frank N. Migill, Editor, pp. 699-702.

NELL-BREUNING, Oswald von, and Herbert Vorgrimler: "The Life of the Political Community" *Commentary on the Documents of Vat. II,* Vol. V, pp. 314-327.

NIEBUHR, H. R., *Christ and Culture.* New York, 1956.

O'RIORDAN, J., *La Teologia Morale Moderna del Sacramento del Matrimonio*, MS, Course notes, Academia Alfonsiana, Roma, 1972/73

-----, "Theologia Moralis Culturae Humanae," in *Theologia Moralis Systematica,* MS, Course given, Academia Alfonsiana, Roma, 1967/68.

ORTIGUES, Edmond, "Eglise Communaute de Charite," *Maison de Dieu,* 24(1950), pp. 63-78.

OUTKA, Gene, *Agape, An Ethical Analysis.* Yale University Press, New Haven and London, 1972.

PANNENBERG, Wolfhart, *Jesus – God and Man.* The Westminster Press, Philadelphia, 1974.

PELLEGRINO, M., "On Human Progress," in *Civilta Cattolica,* (1966), I, pp. 17 and ff.

POHIER, Jacques-Marie, "Liberation et Alienation, approache psychologique," in *Ideologie de Liberation et Message du Salut,* pp. 35-49.

-----, "One-Dimensional Christianity?," Concilium, 7(1971), pp. 27-38.

PROST, Andre, *Les Missions de Peres Blancs en Afrique Occidentale Avant 1939.* Paris, 1960.

RABUT, Olivier, "Repenser la Notion de Salut," *Esprit,* 39(1971), pp. 747-755.

RAHNER, Karl, *Christian at the Crossroads.* Burns and Oates, London, 1965.

-----, "Man, in the Church," in Theological Investigations, Vol. II, Darton and Todd, London,1963.

-----, "Salvation History: The New Testament Period," *Sacramentum Mundi*, Vol. V, pp. 423-425.

-----, "Salvation History: The Old Testament Period," *SacMdi*, Vol. V, pp. 419-423.

-----, "Salvation, IV. Theology: Soteriology," *SacMdi*, Vol. V. pp. 435-438.

-----, "Salvation, I. Universal Salvific Will," SacMdi, Vol. V, pp. 405-409.

RAHNER, Karl and Herbert Vorgrimler: Concise Theological Dictionary, Burns and Oates, London, 1965.

RATZINGER, Josef, Die Letzte Sitzungsperiode des Konzils. Koln, 1966.

-----, "Heil," in LTHK, J. Hofer and Karl Rahner, Editors. Vol. V, Freiburg-im-Breisgau, 1960.

-----, "The Dignity of the Human Person," Commentary on the Documents of Vat. II, Vol. V, pp. 115-163.

RAST, Thimotheus, "L'Eschatologie," in Bilan de la Theologie du XXe Siècle, Vol. II, pp. 501-519.

RIEDMATTEN, H. de, "Storia della Costituzione Pastorale," *La Chiesa nel Mondo Contemporaneo,* Enzo Giammancheri, Editor, Queriniana, Brescia, 1967, pp. 19-59.

ROBINSON, H, W., "The Hebrew Concept of Corporate Personality," *Zeitschrift fur die Alttestamentliche Wissenschaft*, 66(1936), pp. 49-62.

ROHNER, Peter, "Will,' SacMdi, Vol. VI, pp. 356-359.

RONDET, Henri, *Original Sin: The Patristic Theological Background*, Cajetan Finnegan, Translator. Staten Island, New York, 1972

ROQUEPLO, Philippe, "Salut et Liberation," *Esprit*, 39(1971), pp. 756-780.

ROUSTANG, Francois, "L'Amour universel dans le Christ et l'Espit," *Christus*, 18(1958).

-----, "La rencontre des Autres," Christus, 43(1964), pp. 314-328.

SCHABERT, I., "Solidaritat," in *Segen und Fluch im Alten Testament und seiner Umwelt*. Bonn, 1958.

SCHILLEBEECKX, E., *Christ the Encounter of the Sacrament with God*. Sheed and Ward, New York, 1963.

-----, *L'Eglise du Christ et l'Homme d'Aujourd'hui Selon Vat. II*. Mappus, Lyon, 1965.

-----, *Le Christ Sacrement de la Rencontre de Dieu, Etude Theologique du Salut par les Sacrements*. Cerf, Paris, 1960.

-----, *Le Sacrement Evenement de Salut, Bruxelles*, 1964.

SCHNACKENBURG, Rudolf, *Christian Existence in the New Testament*, 2 vols. University of Notre Dame Press, 1968.

-----, *God's Rule and Kingdom*. Herder and Herder, New York, 1963.

SCHOONENBERG, Piet, Man and Sin. Sheed and Ward, London, 1972.

SEMMELROTH, Otto, "The Community of Mankind," Commentary on the Documents of Vat. II, Vol. V, pp. 164-181.

SIGMAND, A. R. "Cultura e Culture alla luce della 'Gaudium et Spes,'" *Sapienza*, 20(1967), pp. 17-29.

SPIAZZI, R., "Salvezza," in *Enciclopedia Cattolica X*, Roma, 1953, p. 1722.

SPINETOLI, Ortensio, "Salvezza," Dizionario Teologico, Johaness Bauer and Carlo Molari, Editors, Assisi, 1974, pp. 655-665.

SUENENS, Card. Leon-Joseph, "Speech of 4 December 1962, in the 33rd General Congregation of Vat. II," *ASSCO Vat. II*, Vol. I, Part IV, pp. 222-227.

THOMAS Louis Vincent, *Les Religions d'Afrique Noire*, Fayard/Denoel, Paris, 1969.

THOMAS, M. "Benessere Materiale e Salvezza Spirituale," in *La Salvezza Oggi*, pp. 27-37.

THILS, Gustave, *"Non-Religious" Christianity*. The Society of Saint Paul, Staten Island, New York, 1970.

VEREECKE, Louis, *Storia della Teologia Morale in Spagna nel XVI Secolo e Origine della 'Institutiones Morales,'* MS. Course, Academia Alfonsiana, Roma, 1972/73.

VISCHER, Lukas, "L'Importanza della Costituzione per il Movimento Ecumenico," in *La Chiesa nel Mondo di Oggi*, pp. 558-562.

-----, "Uberlegungen Nach dem Vatikanischen Konzil" *Polis*, 26(1966), pp. 58-73.

WALGRAVE, J. H., *Un Salut aux Dimension du Monde*. Cogitation Fidei, (46), Les Editions du Cerf, Paris, 1970.

WEBER, Wilhelm, "La Communita degli Uomini," in *La Chiesa nel Mondo di Oggi*, pp. 287-307.

WENGER, A., *Vatican II, Chronique de la Premiere... Seconde... Troisieme...Quatrieme Sessions*, 4 vols, Centurion, Paris, 1963-1966.

WIESER, Thomas, "L'Eglise, Signe de Liberation et de Salut," in *Ideologies de Liberation et Message du Salut*, pp. 189-211.

ANTHROPOLOGICAL

BRIGHT, John, *A History of Israel*. SCM Press Ltd., London, (Second Edition), 1972.

DELAFOSSE, Maurice, *Haut-Senegal-Niger*, 3 vols, Emile Larose, Paris, 1912.

DIETERLEN, G., *Textes Sacres d'Afrique Noire*, Gallimard, Paris, 1965.

DURKHEIM, Emile, *Les Formes Elementaires de la Vie Religieuse*, Felix Alcan, Paris, 1912.

-----, *On Morality and Society*. Robert N. Bellah, Editor, University of Chicago Press, 1973.

-----, The Elementary Forms of Religious Life, Joseph Ward Swain, Translator, Free Press of Glencoe, Ill., 1947.

EYRE-SMITH, St. J., *Comments on the Interim Reports on the Peoples of the Nandom and Lambussie Division of the Lawra District*, Unpublished MS. Of a Study on the People of the Lawra District, 1933.

FORTES, Meyer, *African Political Systems*, London, 1940.

FORTES, MEYER, *African Systems of Thought*, Oxford University Press, London, 1949.

-----, *The Dynamics of Clanship Among the Tallinsi*, Oxford University Press, London, 1945.

FRAZER, James G., *Totemism*, 4 vols. and Supplement. Dawson Pall Mall, London, 1910.

GIRAULT, Louis, "Essai sur la Religion des Dagara," *IFAN*, Bulletin, 1959, Vol. XXI, Nos. 3-4, pp. 329-356, Dakar.

GOODY, Jack, *Death, Property and the Ancestors, a Study of the Mortuary Customs of the LoDagaa of West Africa*. Tavistock Publications, London, 1962.

-----, *Technology, Tradition and the State System in Africa*. Oxford University Press, London, Accra, 1971.

-----, *The Myth of the Bagre*. Clarendon Press, Oxford, 1972.

-----, *The Social Organisation of the LoWiili*. Oxford University Press, London, 1967.

-----, (Editor), "The Fission of Domestic Groups among the LoDagaa," in *Developmental Cycle of Domestic Groups*. Cambridge, 1958.

-----, "The Classification of Double Descent System," *Current Anthropology*, pp. 2-25, 1961.

GREENBERG, J. H., *Studies in African Linguistics Classification*. The (Compass Publication), New Haven, 1955.

LABOURET, H., Mariage et Polyandrie parmi les Dagari et les Oule," *Revue Ethnographie et Tradition Populaire*, 1920.

LESOURD, J., En Afrique occidentale francaise: Les Dagaris. Paris, 1939.

LEVI-STRAUSS, Claude, Anthropologie Structurale, Plon, Paris, 1958.

MAUS, Marcel, *The Gift*, Ian Gunnison, Translator. Cohen and West Ltd. , London, 1970.

NADEL, S. F., *Black Byzantium*. Oxford University Press, London, 1942.

RADCLIFFE-BROWN, A. R., *Structure and Function in Primitive Society*. Oxford University Press, London, 1945.

RATTERY, R. S., *The Tribes of the Ashanti Hinterland*. Oxford University Press, London, 1932.

ROOSENS, Eugene, Anthropologie Culturelle, MS. Lumen Vitae, University of Louvain, Brussels, 1970/71.

SARPONG, PETER, *Ghana in Retrospect: Some Aspects of Ghanaian Culture*, Ghana Publishing Corporation, Accra-Tema, 1974.

TOFFLER, Alvin, *Future Shock*. Pan Books Ltd., London, 1971.

WESTERMANN, D., *Die Sudansprache, eine Sprachvergleichende Studie*, Hamburg, 1913.

-----, *Die Westlichen Sudansprachen und ihre Beziehungen zum Bantu*, Berlin, 1927.

WESTERMANN, D., and M. A. Bryan: *Languages of West Africa*, London, 1952.

ABOUT THE AUTHOR

Msgr. Albert Kuuire served at Holy Apostles College & Seminary in Cromwell, CT, USA, as Vice-Rector, Director of Spiritual Formation, and Spiritual Director.

www.ingramcontent.com/pod-product-compliance
Lightning Source LLC
Chambersburg PA
CBHW031500270326
41930CB00006B/172